MORE HEROES
OF IRELAND'S GREAT HUNGER

For all refugees, past and present.

'The refugees cry and we cry'
(Report from Poland, NBC news, 11 April 2022)

MORE HEROES
OF IRELAND'S GREAT HUNGER

Edited by
CHRISTINE KINEALY,
JASON KING
and **GERARD MORAN**

QUINNIPIAC UNIVERSITY PRESS
CORK UNIVERSITY PRESS

Published by:
Quinnipiac University Press
275 Mount Carmel Ave
Hamden, CT 06518–1908
www.quinnipiac.edu
for

Ireland's Great Hunger Institute:
www.qu.edu/institutes-and-centers/irelands-great-hunger-institute/
Cork University Press:
www.corkuniversitypress.com

ISBN: 978-1-7361712-1-9

Cover design by the Office of Integrated Marketing Communications

Interior design and typesetting by Marsha Swan
Printed in Villatuerta, Spain, by GRAPHYCEMS

Contents

INTERNATIONAL INVOLVEMENT

INTRODUCTION

Christine Kinealy, Jason King and Gerard Moran

Naming somebody a hero is full of risks. The concept of what constitutes a hero is fluid, depending on multiple factors including context, time, place, gender, and social and cultural mores of the day. Nor is the concept static, as the recent removal of statues in multiple global locations has proved. Regardless of these shifting sands, and the subjective standards that accompany such a nomenclature, this volume identifies a number of men and women who can be considered famine heroes. As each author makes clear, however, these heroes come with their own flaws, failures and quirks. Perhaps, in part, it is their human failings that make their heroism even more remarkable. Whether responding to the Great Hunger of 1845 to 1852, the 'flu pandemic of 1918, or the COVID crisis of 2019 and beyond, it is clear that heroes come in all shapes and sizes, and their motivations fluctuate greatly. Perhaps, what matters most, is that their actions helped to give people hope and to save lives, sometimes at a risk to their own.

This publication follows on from *Heroes of Ireland's Great Hunger*, which was published in 2021. *More Heroes of Ireland's Great Hunger*, like its predecessor, is inspired by front-line workers who emerged as heroes during the COVID-19 pandemic. Both volumes had their inception in the Great Famine Voices 'Famine Heroes' project hosted by the National Famine Museum, Strokestown Park and Ireland's Great Hunger Institute at Quinnipiac University, funded by the Government of Ireland Emigrant Support Programme.[1] In 2022, the pandemic continued to dominate world news, but the focus had shifted to variants, anti-vaccers and vaccine inequalities. While COVID-19 continued to dominate international headlines and political decision making, the problems of food security, famine and refugee crises all continued to increase in magnitude. In the face of these inequalities and human rights abuses, new heroes continue to emerge, often to compensate for the inadequacies of national governments or foreign oppressors. The unwarranted invasion of Ukraine created many heroes, perhaps no-one more unexpected than President Volodymyr Zelensky.[2] It therefore seems timely to continue to recognize and honour the role of people whose actions can be considered heroic during Ireland's Great Hunger.

At a time when Ireland is commemorating the 175th anniversary of 'Black '47, the year when deaths, starvation and pestilence reached unprecedented levels, it is important to remember and acknowledge those who were prepared to sacrifice their time, their health and, in some cases, their lives, in their attempts to save their fellow human beings. Towards the close of that year, the British government publicly declared that the Famine had ended, yet over the following five years up to half a million tenants were evicted from their land as a result of the Quarter Acre Clause, more commonly called the Gregory Clause. It had been introduced by the Irish MP and County Galway landowner, William Gregory, and allowed landlords to evict families who were unable to pay their rents. For many, the only refuge was the workhouse where they faced death as a result of outbreaks of cholera and typhoid. There were those who continued to show compassion towards the poor, starving and dispossessed long after the limited government aid had ended and Ireland was expected to look after its destitute and homeless without any Treasury assistance. Their time and effort deserve to be acknowledged and not forgotten.

The role of the churches in providing relief and spiritual succour to Famine victims is complicated and not confined to Ireland. Members of religious orders of all persuasions, both male and female, came to the assistance of the poor, often at great risk to themselves. A number, including Bishop Edward Maginn of Derry, a hero of volume one, lost their lives.[3] In County Kerry, five Catholic clergymen perished from Famine fever while endeavouring to help their starving parishioners. The historian, Donal Kerr, writing in 1994, estimated that 40 priests died in Ireland administering to their parishioners.[4] In light of subsequent research, this is likely to be a gross under-estimate. Nor was this risk to religious personnel confined to Ireland. In the port city of Liverpool alone, at least 13 Catholic priests died of famine-related diseases. As the charitable work of James Hack Tuke, in his home city of York, has demonstrated, the reach of 'famine fever' extended far beyond the western towns of Britain.[5] The death from typhus fever of Roman Catholic Bishop Riddell, aged 40, in the Northern District of Newcastle-Upon-Tyne in November 1847 was part of a series of similar fatalities that year, which had wreaked 'havoc among the Catholic priesthood'.[6] Moreover, the works of Mark McGowan and Jason King have shown that the involvement of religious bodies, and the consequent risk, was evident thousands of miles away as the death of Bishop Michael Power, a number of sisters of the Grey Nuns, and others attest.[7] Death, however, was occasionally viewed as a release from earthly suffering. When Michael Slattery, the Archbishop of Cashel and Emly, heard of the condition of the people in his native Tipperary in the early 1847, he wrote, 'Oh that I could fly from this wretched country into some solitude where I might ... die in peace'.[8] Only weeks later, on hearing of the death of his friend, Bishop John Murphy of Cork, he admitted, 'I think those happy who are released from the calamities that have befallen our unhappy country'.[9] Nor, according to historian, Donal Kerr, was this feeling of despair and hopelessness unusual.[10] This volume features a chapter by Colum Kenny looking at the contribution of one Catholic priest in the south-west of Ireland, namely, Father John O'Sullivan of Kenmare in County Kerry. Individualist and wayward, O'Sullivan travelled to London to meet some of the most influential people involved in relief. This included the notorious Charles Trevelyan and leading members of the British Relief Association.

The suffering and mortality of the famine years was not confined to the Catholic clergy. According to Rev. John O Rourke, a Catholic priest who published one of the first histories of the tragedy, 'The clergy of every denomination came forward with a zeal and charity worthy of their sacred calling'.[11] Regardless of numerous examples of collaboration between Catholic and Protestant clergy, the aspersion of souperism cast a long shadow over the memory of private relief during the Famine, even if there was little evidence to substantiate such beliefs. Writing in 2002, however, local historian Patrick Hickey questioned the reality and myth of the existence of souperism in west Cork. He concluded, 'It is regrettable that the genuine and, indeed, heroic charity of men like the Trenches or Dr Traill should have been preserved in folk memory in this distorted fashion'.[12] The Rev. Robert Traill [also Trail] was the Church of Ireland minister in Skibbereen and Scull.[13] He represented the evangelical wing of the Established Church, which was often intolerant of Roman Catholicism. As food shortages began to devastate the poor of west Cork, Traill responded with a humanity that transcended religious differences, succumbing to fever in spring 1847.[14] Some years later, the reputation of Traill was redeemed, if not with full historical accuracy. In 2018, his great-great-great granddaughter, Daisy Goodwin, included Traill in an episode of the television drama, *Victoria,* in which a distraught Traill made a direct plea to a sympathetic British queen.[15] It was widely praised for its 'brutally honest' portrayal of the Famine.[16] Elsewhere, regardless of the rivalry that sometimes existed at a local level between the main religious congregations, there were many instances when clergymen were prepared to put aside their differences and establish relief committees to secure relief for the starving poor. This can be seen with the Lissadell Relief Committee in County Sligo whose members included two Catholic priests, Rev. Patrick O'Gara and Rev. M. Brennan, and the local Church of Ireland rector, Rev. William Jeffcott. The Ballymote Relief Committee had representatives of all denominations including the local rector, Rev. John Garrett.[17]

The role of the Catholic Church in relief operations during the Great Hunger has been highlighted by the late historian, Donal Kerr. His research indicated the international dimension of the Church in the collections taken up in parishes and dioceses in the United States, Europe and Canada.[18] Many of the sums of money thus collected were then forwarded to the Archbishop of Dublin, Daniel Murray, and distributed to parishioners throughout the country. Collections were taken up in places as far away as Boston and as near as Liverpool, where Catholics contributed £3,000, to be given to those most in need. Among those who donated directly was Pope Pius IX. As early as January 1847, he sent 1,000 Roman dollars to the Irish bishops. He also urged bishops throughout the world to hold collections in their dioceses for the famine victims and to 'vigorously assist the poor'.[19] This was the first time that the Catholic Church had coordinated a worldwide effort to provide relief to a starving nation. It happened at a time when the Irish were having an increasing influence in the Catholic Church, especially in Canada and the United States regardless of Protestant opposition, as can be seen in Mark McGowan's essay in the previous volume on Bishop Michael Power of Toronto. Other influential Irish prelates at this time included Bishop John Hughes of New York and Bishop Peter Kenrick of St Louis. Even in Rome, Irish influence was on the rise through the formidable Paul Cullen, Rector of the Irish College, who in 1850 was appointed Archbishop of Armagh. The role of Catholic parishes and dioceses in sending aid to the starving Irish can be seen in the Daniel Murray papers which are located at the Dublin Diocesan Archives, and a selection of which has been published in *Archivium Hibernicium*. These papers indicate where the donations were coming from and what parts of the country they were forwarded to, highlighting the important role that the Catholic clergy played during the Great Hunger.

The involvement of Jews in famine relief is a further example of the ecumenical, inclusive, and all-embracing nature of those who gave. When visiting New York in 2010, the then President of Ireland, Mary McAleese, made a point of visiting the congregation of Shearith Israel, to thank them for assisting Ireland 163 years earlier.[20] Nor was Jewish involvement confined to New York or America. In volume one, the role of the remarkable Count Paul de Strzelecki, who worked for no payment on behalf of the British Relief Association, was outlined. The Association was largely founded at the initiative of Jewish banker, Lionel de Rothschild, ably supported by other members of his community.[21] Peter Murphy broadens our understanding of the multiple and diverse contributions of Jews to Famine relief and asks why their involvement has been given so little attention by historians.

The scope and generosity of international assistance to Ireland was remarkable. The voyage of the *Jamestown* to Cork in the spring of 1847, captained by Robert Bennet Forbes, has been widely documented and praised.[22] While Forbes's role has been acknowledged, others who made this 'voyage of mercy' possible have been generally omitted from the narrative. William Rathbone, a philanthropist from Liverpool, was the man chosen by Forbes to oversee the disbursement of the *Jamestown's* cargo. As a result of his friendship with Father Mathew, his involvement would continue well beyond the arrival of this shipment. Rathbone's role is considered in the chapter by Christine Kinealy. In addition to Forbes, Rathbone and Father Mathew, several lesser-known figures are part of the story of the *Jamestown*. This includes Boston-born magnate, Joshua Bates, a key figure in the world-famous Barings' Brothers Company, who facilitated the arrival of the cargo. Although forgotten in the history of the Famine, Bates's death in 1864, in his ninetieth year, was reported in newspapers throughout the world, including Ireland. His role as a merchant prince, as a supporter of liberty, and a philanthropist who founded Boston Public Library was remembered, although his facilitation of famine relief was not.[23]

The media play a significant role in highlighting disasters through their coverage and reports. They alert us to crises which affect society at a national and local level, highlighting natural and manmade disasters, no less than with the Covid crisis and the invasion of Ukraine by Russia. Their importance was evident during the famines and subsistence crises in nineteenth-century Ireland. During the 'Forgotten Famine of 1879–1881', journalists like William O'Brien and James Redpath reported on the impending famine along the western seaboard.[24] During the Great Hunger one journalist and newspaper editor who stood out was the Irish-born Patrick Donahoe of the *Boston Pilot*, the subject of Catherine Shannon's essay. Using reports and letters from Ireland, Donahoe highlighted the famine conditions in Ireland and attacked the British government's inadequate response. He was to the forefront in organizing collections, serving on the relief committees in Boston, and forwarding money to Ireland. Throughout his later life he was prepared to work for Ireland during periods of crisis, as with the food shortages of 1861–1863 and the famine of 1879–1881. Donahoe's work shows the power of the media to provide an alternative view to the biased and objective statements of the government. Not only was he a hero, but also a consistent and valuable friend of Ireland.

In addition to being to the fore in providing aid and relief, the Irish clergy also highlighted the precarious position of their parishioners. Unfortunately, their pleas to officials in Dublin and London were largely ignored and regarded as exaggerated. However, in many instances, and especially along the western seaboard, the clergy were the only professional people who were able to give first-hand accounts of the death and starvation that existed. In these districts especially, many landowners were absentee, residing in Britain and sometimes on the continent, far away from the calamity that was devastating their estates. Not surprisingly, therefore, in both contemporary famine writings and in the early historiography, landlords are depicted as an uncaring, exploitive and selfish group. Absentee landlords, in particular, were regarded as villains who collected income or carried out long-desired large-scale evictions. More recently, research has shown the diversity of Irish landlords and how they changed as the Famine continued and intensified. In volume one, the complex role of the Sligo family of Westport House in County Mayo was explored, based on research in a previously unused collection of family letters, most written by Lady Sligo.[25] She, similar to a minority of members of the Protestant Ascendancy, completely defied being stereotyped.

Despite the exceptions, historians and collective memory has remained largely critical of the role which Irish landowners played during the Great Hunger. It is important to remember that they were not a homogenous group: some had very large estates, while the properties of others consisted of just a couple of hundred acres. Some depended solely on their estates to survive, others had additional income streams like the Wyndhams who owned the Castlecomer coalfield and Francis Spaight who, in addition to his estate in County Tipperary, was a successful shipping agent who sent many emigrants from Limerick to North America. While there was a small group of landed proprietors who were financially secure, others faced financial ruin before the Famine started. Cormac Ó Gráda estimates that one in eight Irish landlords were insolvent in 1845 and the failure of the potato brought others to a similar position as their tenants were unable to pay their rents. At the same time, landlords experienced additional financial burdens with the increase in the Poor Law rates that was needed to meet the rising number of paupers in the workhouses.[26] It was in these circumstances that Major Denis Mahon and his agent John Ross Mahon organized the assisted emigration scheme of 1,490 former tenants from the Strokestown Park estate in County Roscommon in May 1847. The emigrants were well provisioned, but chartered to cross the Atlantic on what became some of the most notorious coffin ships, such as the *Virginius* and *Naomi*, which lost hundreds of their passengers. Major Mahon achieved international notoriety when he became the first landlord to be assassinated during the Great Hunger.[27] After the harvest of 1847, when the tax burden increased, landowners—even previously benign ones—became more willing to evict tenants who were in debt and were unlikely to be able to pay the rent arrears that had accumulated. Some landowners looked upon this as a blessing as it allowed them to introduce changes that they otherwise would have been unable to carry out: the Earl of Lucan evicted 429 families starting in June 1848 and the largest group was cleared from the property in June 1849, facilitating the creation of large grazing farms.[28] The establishment of the Encumbered Estate Court by the government in 1849 allowed landlords who were in debt to sell their properties and, between 1849 and 1857, 3,000 properties, nearly one-third of the overall total, comprising five million acres, were sold to new owners. While the government had hoped that the new owners would be English and Scottish, the purchases were largely made by the Irish Catholic middle classes who often adopted the clearance practices of their predecessors. The contributions of individual landlords who were prepared to provide relief for their tenants becomes even more remarkable, and three are examined in this volume, namely Daniel O'Connell, Sir Robert Gore Booth and Lord George Hill.

The name of Daniel O'Connell is known to most people of Irish descent. In his life-time, O'Connell achieved the rare distinction of reaching heroic status both for his role in achieving Catholic Emancipation in 1829, and for his championing of international human rights, most notably in opposing the system of slavery.[29] His role as a Famine hero has received less attention. Laurent Colantonio examines the actions of O'Connell through two main prisms—as a politician who tried to influence policy-makers in both Dublin and London, and as a landlord who owned estates in County Kerry. Unfortunately, declining health and his death in May 1847 brought O'Connell's involvement to an end. The poor and oppressed people of Ireland and, indeed, of the world, had lost a peerless advocate.

Landlords, who were absentees and non-resident, tended to come in for the most criticism. Little of the rental that they collected was spent in those localities where they had their estates and they depended on agents to manage their properties who were more intent on carrying out their employers' instructions and looking after their economic interests than in the plight of the starving tenants. As Desmond Norton points out, the agents 'were subject to various kinds of policy lags' in relation to relief on the estates due to the hierarchal structures. It is estimated that the ten largest landowners in County Mayo, nine of whom were absentees, had a rental of over £100,000 annually, but very little of this was spent in the county.[30] The *Sligo Champion* estimated that the annual rental income in County Sligo to be nearly one-quarter of a million pounds, but landlords spent less than £2,000 in relief during 1847.[31] The importance of residency can be seen in two of the essays in this volume: Cathal Poírtéir's study of Lord George Hill in Gweedore and Gerard Moran's examination of Sir Robert Gore Booth's estate in County Sligo. Both landowners had carried out improvements on their estates in the years prior to the Great Famine which helped to mitigate some of its extreme aspects: in the case of the Hill estate, the population actually increased between 1841 and 1851. Old practices such as rundale and the subdivision of holdings were discouraged. More to the point, they spent much of the rentals they received in the localities where they lived and provided employment to the local population in Lissadell and Gweedore. The Gore Booths had accounts with local merchants in Sligo such as Leech and Sons, and Richard Smith, 10 Knox Street, where they purchased the food that was then prepared by their servants in the kitchen in Lissadell for their starving tenants.

For centuries, women—especially strong women who defied conventional categorization—were air-brushed out of the historical record. While the heroic role of the Grey Nuns of Montreal has received due recognition in recent years, the multiple contributions of the various female religious orders in Ireland still waits to be written. Eyewitness reports by Asenath Nicholson testify to their multiple and meaningful contributions. A particularly fruitful endeavour initiated by many female religious orders that provided immediate Famine relief and longer-term skills was lace-crochet. According to Melissa Fegan, 'Lacemaking provided an opportunity for the Irish poor not just to survive the Famine, but to improve in ways British and middle-class Irish observers very much approved of'.[32] In contrast, a woman who was herself a product of the middle-class Protestant Ascendancy challenged the response of the British government to the Famine, through the skillful use of her pen. Poetry of the Famine has also received relatively little attention given that the distress was so extensive and the tragedy coincided with an early phase of cultural revival associated with Young Ireland.[33] Christine Kinealy reexamines the role of the poet 'Speranza', but in the context of her contribution to the Great Hunger in providing a voice to the victims, most notably women and children. The chapter also explores the wider context of her family's multiple engagements with the history and culture of Ireland, particularly their role in keeping the memory of the Great Famine and other lesser-known famines alive.

The impact and legacy of the Great Hunger cannot be understood without reference to the global dimension. Donations to Ireland came from all parts of the world, while emigration, which continued well after 1852, took the Famine Irish to all corners of the world, either directly or through chain migration. Large numbers had left Ireland in the years before the potato failed, but in the decade 1845 to 1855,

2.1 million people emigrated, forced out by hunger, evictions and changing agricultural practices. Those with the resources, or who could rely on family and friends to provide the passage fare, often headed first for Britain, specifically the transatlantic port of Liverpool.[34] Others travelled with the intention of gaining employment to secure the money that would allow them to cross the Atlantic at some point in the future. Many arrived at ports such as Liverpool, Quebec, Montreal, St John, New Brunswick, New York and Boston infected with fever and in an emaciated state. Initially, the officials in these ports were prepared to look after and treat these refugees, but when the number arriving became a deluge, the attitude of many of the native population changed to that of anger and hostility. Nevertheless, there were individuals prepared to come to their aid, as seen in the previous volume, which examined heroes James Hack Tuke in York, Dr William Duncan in Liverpool and Bishop Michael Power in Toronto.[35] While the role of the local authorities and officials was to protect their populations from disease, crime and an influx of paupers, John McColgan's chapter shows that the Boston officials and medical personnel were prepared to provide as much help as they could. Consequently, Deer Island was established as a place for Famine emigrants. McColgan throws a fresh light on their reception in North America, especially in regard to the actions of city's authorities.

The death toll in British North America—now Canada—was much higher than in the United States.[36] The largest Famine Irish mass graves outside of Ireland can be found at Grosse Île and the Irish Memorial National Historic Site and the Black Rock site of Montreal's fever sheds in Quebec, both of which commemorate approximately 6,000 emigrants who lie buried there. Yet the Famine Irish continued to perish in large numbers as they travelled onwards from Canada East (Quebec) to Canada West (Ontario). Mark McGowan offers a wide-angle perspective as he traces their movements westward to destinations such as Bytown (Ottawa), Kingston, and Toronto. McGowan places particular emphasis on the role of female religious orders, such as Mother Élisabeth Bruyère, who founded the Soeurs de Charité d'Ottawa (Ottawa Grey Nuns), and Mother Amable Bourbonnière of the Religious Hospitallers of St Joseph in Kingston. They both played leading roles in caring for stricken migrants. Mary Cunningham was the first of many Irish emigrants to die in Bytown, despite the care of Mother Bruyère and her fellow Sisters. The death of 9-year-old Anastasia Brennan, whose body was 'black as coal' and 'emitted a foul odour', was one of the most harrowing scenes Bruyère recorded in a letter to her close friend, Mother Elizabeth McMullen of the Montreal Grey Nuns, on 13 July 1847.[37] The Annals of the Religious Hospitallers of St Joseph reveal the feelings of affection that the Sisters had for the Irish orphans in their care. They recount that 'it was very painful to witness such a scene' when the children were separated from the Sisters to be placed in surrounding households:

> When any of them heard their name mentioned, they knew they were going, they began to cry and could not be consoled at seeing themselves separated from their companions in misfortune and from their Mistresses, who had also done their share of weeping.[38]

McGowan also pays tribute to Toronto Emigration Agent Edward McElderry whose pregnant widow and seven children were left destitute when he perished on 29 October 1847. He notes the irony of McElderry's superior, Chief Emigration Agent for Upper Canada Anthony Bowden Hawke, acknowledging that he has 'fallen a victim to his duty' and 'persisted in working beyond his strength, and the dysentery set in fatally', with no pension to provide for his family.

Jason King's chapter also follows in the footsteps of Famine Irish emigrants from Canada East to Canada West, as witnessed in the unpublished journals and letters of Stephen De Vere. Perhaps no member of the Irish Protestant upper classes could match his bravery in personally escorting his former tenants from his estate at Curragh Chase in County Limerick to help them resettle in Canada West in 1847. De Vere was uniquely positioned amongst Famine Irish emigrants not only in risking his life—travelling below deck to document the suffering of steerage passengers—but also attesting to the heroic acts of Canadian caregivers such as the clergy on Grosse Île, the Grey Nuns in Montreal's fever sheds, Bishop Michael Power, and Emigration Agent Edward McElderry in Toronto. No Irish Famine emigrant was more influential or travelled further physically or socially than De Vere, who keenly observed and kept copious notes of migrants in peril and the compassion they received. He provided a conduit and a voice for suffering emigrants from the steerage and the fever sheds to the British parliament because of his class, long before he succeeded his brother to become the landlord in Curragh Chase in 1880. Yet, King notes, De Vere was oblivious to other peoples' peril, as in his final encounter in Canada West in 1848 with the Anishinaabe (Ojibwa) Methodist preacher and chief Peter Jones, or Kahkewaquonaby (Sacred Feathers), in 'Munsee Town Indian village'.[39] As chief of the Mississaugas of the Credit River mission, Kahkewaquonaby had contributed to the United Irish and Scotch Relief Fund on behalf of his people only weeks before they were deprived of their land. De Vere also inadvertently beheld the foundation and Kahkewaquonaby's repudiation of Canada's residential school system. In paying tribute to Canadian caregivers for relieving migrant misery, he witnessed the origins of an enduring national tragedy.

The final chapter is a tribute to a modern hero, Jim Callery, founder of the National Famine Museum at Strokestown Park, written appropriately by his daughter, Caroilin. Jim was awarded a prestigious European Prize for Cultural Heritage/Europa Nostra Award in 2017, the Jury acknowledging that:

> Through his small business, Mr. Callery has saved a vital historic country estate for Ireland and has created an important museum and archive dealing with this pivotal moment in the country's history. He has ensured an expert restoration of the house, opened it to the Irish public and preserved the legacy of this important memorial.[40]

In the Afterword, Caroilin explores this legacy in depth. The publication of *More Heroes of Ireland's Great Hunger* coincided with the reopening of the National Famine Museum, Strokestown Park after a €5.1 million investment that enhanced it as a state-of-the-art facility on the 175th anniversary of Black '47. It is a fitting moment to pay tribute to its founder.

The men and women featured in this collection, similar to those recalled in volume one, reinforce the message that heroes are not perfect, or monolithic, or even necessarily altruistic, but that they come in many guises. This volume pays tribute to a small number of them.

NOTES

1. All of the Great Famine Voices Roadshow 'Famine Heroes' short films and post-show discussions can be viewed at http://greatfaminevoices.ie/famine-heroes/.
2. 'Zelensky: The TV president turned war hero', *Washington Post*, 4 Mar. 2022; '*An Unlikely Hero.* We look at Volodymyr Zelensky's rise', *New York Times*, 14 Mar. 2022.
3. See chapter by Turlough McConnell on Bishop Magee in Christine Kinealy, Jason King and Gerard Moran (eds), *Heroes of Ireland's Great Hunger* (Hamden and Cork: Quinnipiac University and Cork University Press, 2021), vol. 1.
4. Donal Kerr, *A Nation of Beggars: Priests, People and Politics in Famine Ireland, 1846–1852* (Oxford: Clarendon Press, 1994).
5. Chapter by Gerard Moran in volume one.
6. 'Death Of Roman Catholic Bishop from Famine Fever', *Kerry Examiner and Munster General Observer*, 12 Nov. 1847.
7. Chapters by Mark G. McGowan and Jason King in volume one.
8. Slattery to Murray, 5 Feb. 1847, Murray papers, quoted in Kerr, *Nation of Beggars*, p. 40.
9. Ibid., Slattery to Renehan, 3 Apr. 1847, Renehan papers.
10. Ibid.
11. Rev. John O'Rourke, *The History of the Great Irish Famine of 1847* (Dublin: James Duff and Co, 1902), p. 64.

12. Patrick Hickey, *Famine in West Cork: The Mizen Peninsula Land and People 1800–1852* (Cork: Mercier Press, 2002), p. 263.
13. Rev. Dr. Robert Traill (1793–1847).
14. *Tipperary Free Press*, 1 May 1847.
15. The Famine was the subject of series two, episode six of *Victoria*, first produced by ITV in 2016.
16. 'Viewers were shocked by Victoria's "brutally honest" depiction of the potato famine', *Radio Times,* at: www.radiotimes.com/tv/drama/viewers-were-shocked-by-victorias-brutally-honest-depiction-of-the-potato-famine/
17. See chapter by Gerard Moran on Sir Robert Gore Booth.
18. Kerr, *A Nation of Beggars*.
19. Donal Kerr, *The Catholic Church and Famine in Ireland* (Dublin: Columba Press, 1996), pp 34–35.
20. '163 Years Later, a President Visits to Say Thank You', *New York Times,* 21 May 2010; Speaker Quinn, President of Ireland Mary McAleese, Mayor Bloomberg, and Congregation Shearith Israel Commemorate Jewish Relief During The Great Famine, 23 Dec. 2010 at https://council.nyc.gov/press/2010/12/23/1024/; 'New York Jews Rescued Irish in Great Famine', *Jewish Press,* 5 July 2013, at: /www.jewishpress.com/news/breaking-news/new-york-jews-rescued-irish-in-great-famine/2013/07/05/.
21. Christine Kinealy, *Charity and the Great Hunger in Ireland. The Kindness of Strangers* (London: Bloomsbury, 2013).
22. Chapter by Catherine Shannon in volume one.
23. 'The late Mr Bates', *Morning Advertiser*, 4 Nov. 1864; A Merchant Prince, *Bombay Gazette*, 4 Nov.1864; *The Evening Freeman* (Dublin), 26 Sept. 1864; 'The Death of Joshua Bates, of the firm of Baring & Bros., London', *New York Times*, 22 Oct. 1864.
24. See Gerard Moran, '"Giving a helping hand": international charity during the Forgotten Famine of 1879–81' in *New Hibernia Review*, 24:2 (Summer, 2020).
25. The Sligo Letters are part of the Irish collection at Quinnipiac University.
26. Cormac Ó Gráda, *'Black 47: The Irish Famine: History, Economy and Memory* (Princeton University Press, 1999), pp 128–129.
27. See Mark G. McGowan, 'When Famine "Victims" Challenge Historians: The Case of the Strokestown "1,490" and the Assisted Migration of 1847', and Jason King, 'In the Footsteps of Strokestown's Famine Emigrants to Niagara: Transatlantic Press Coverage and Retribution for Major Denis Mahon's Coffin Ships', in Christine Kinealy & Gerard Moran (eds), *Irish Famines before and after the Great Hunger* (Quinnipiac and Cork University press, 2020), pp 101–118, pp 119–134.
28. Donald E. Jordan, *Land and Popular Politics in Ireland: County Mayo from the Plantation to the Land War* (Cambridge University Press, 1994), pp 112–113.
29. Christine Kinealy, *Daniel O'Connell and Anti-Slavery. The Saddest People the Sun Sees* (London: Routledge, 2011).
30. Jordan, *Land and Popular Politics*, pp 146–157.
31. Chapter by Gerard Moran on Sir Robert Gore Booth in volume one.

32. Melissa Fegan, '"This most humane commerce": Lace-making during the Famine', in Marguerite Corporaal, Oona Frawley, and Emily Mark-Fitzgerald (eds) *The Great Irish Famine: Visual and Material Culture* (Liverpool: Liverpool University Press, 2018), pp 110–127.
33. An exception is Christopher Morash. For Young Ireland and their cultural legacy see Christine Kinealy, *Repeal and Revolution. 1848 in Ireland* (Manchester University Press, 2012).
34. Chapter on Dr William Duncan on Liverpool in volume one.
35. See *Heroes of Ireland Great Hunger*, volume one.
36. Jason King, *Irish Famine Migration Narratives: Eyewitness Testimonies* in Christine Kinealy, Jason King, Gerard Moran (eds), *The History of the Irish Famine*, vol. 2 (New York: Routledge, 2019), p. 3.
37. The letters of Élisabeth Bruyère to Elizabeth McMullen have been partially digitized and translated in Canada Ireland Foundation's 'Irish Famine Migrant Stories in Ontario' virtual exhibit, funded by Digital Museums Canada, Canadian Museum of History: https://irishfaminestories.ca/en/compassion_and_struggle (Jason King, 2021).
38. The Annals of the Religious Hospitallers of St Joseph have been partially digitized and translated in Canada Ireland Foundation's 'Irish Famine Migrant Stories in Ontario' virtual exhibit, funded by Digital Museums Canada, Canadian Museum of History: https://irishfaminestories.ca/en/kingstons_famine_orphans (Jason King, 2021).
39. Stephen De Vere, Trinity College Dublin Manuscripts, MS 5062, p. 55.
40. www.europeanheritageawards.eu/winners/mr-jim-callery/.

Irish Involvement

CHAPTER ONE

'FAMINE AND PESTILENCE ARE AT OUR DOOR'

Daniel O'Connell (1775–1847)

Laurent Colantonio

You cannot adjourn the eating of food from day to day,
as you would adjourn the meeting of an assembly.
(Daniel O'Connell, *Freeman's Journal*, 29 October 1845)

When the blight first struck Ireland, Daniel O'Connell had long since acquired the status of political leader, voice of the downtrodden, and folk hero. He had been dubbed 'The Liberator' by his countrymen since Catholic Emancipation had been enacted in 1829, following a long campaign under his leadership. Until his death, he stood at the forefront of the fight for national sovereignty and the Repeal of the Act of Union, whose culmination in the summer of 1843 saw some 40 'monster meetings' gathering tens of thousands of people drawn largely from those often excluded from politics.

Although he did not directly risk or sacrifice his life to help the victims of the Famine—unlike other protagonists in this and the previous volume—O'Connell was one of the first political figures, from the autumn of 1845, to draw attention to the approaching crisis and to take action against it. He went on to issue a barrage of proposals to combat the disaster, repeatedly appealing to the authorities to convince them that Ireland was facing not a regular subsistence crisis, but a major catastrophe: a 'death-dealing famine' of such scale that its resolution would require immediate contributions from all sides, and above all the British state.[1] Both in Dublin and the House of Commons in London he kept up the fight to the end, never ceasing to use his last remaining strength to attempt to influence the decisions of the government and parliament.

O'Connell incarnated political heroism, in the sense that he displayed 'exceptional moral strength' and 'exemplary behaviour' characterised by extreme courage in the face of danger and total devotion to the cause for which he fought.[2] This chapter outlines the main forms this determination took, the methods for action involved, and the radical solutions he proposed to overcome the Famine. It will also highlight the limits of his strategy and the gradual disillusionment that set in, in the face of the obstacles that blocked his path. O'Connell fought this final struggle against the Famine at the highest political levels in the United Kingdom and Ireland, but equally at the local level, as a landlord struggling with the consequences of the tragedy on his own lands. This role will be discussed in the final part of this essay.

In the autumn of 1845, blight reduced one-third of the potato crop to inedible rot. The arrival of this previously unknown disease raised the spectre of famine in Ireland, where more than 30 per cent of the population was affected by extreme poverty, according to the *Third Report of the Commissioners on the Condition of the Poorer Classes in Ireland* (1836). As the first plants were being destroyed, O'Connell was engaged in a mass campaign aimed at injecting new momentum into the movement for the Repeal of the Union. To this end, four major meetings were held in succession between 26 September and 15 October in Thurles, Killarney, Castlebar and Sligo. Although the speaker received a warm welcome each time, the crowds were below expectations, the mobilisation was much weaker than in 1843, and revenue from the Repeal Rent was low.[3]

During his travels, O'Connell seemed to have realised early on the potentially devastating effects of the spoiled harvest. The energy he displayed in alerting the authorities and seeking solutions foreshadowed his course of action subsequently. On 21 October 1845, he joined a Dublin Corporation committee formed on his initiative, with the aim of investigating the causes and spread of the blight.[4] One week later, on the basis of the alarming information that had been gathered, he presented the city council with an action plan to address what he already regarded as a 'national calamity'. He proposed that 'a deputation should be appointed from the committee to wait on the Lord Lieutenant, and request that the government would turn its immediate attention to the adoption of measures tending to mitigate the calamitous state of the country'.[5] This speech was also the first time O'Connell listed the emergency measures he sought: the opening of Irish ports to duty-free food imports; a ban on exporting foodstuffs and on distilling or brewing grain; the construction of granaries for food storage, facilitating access for the population;

providing a loan of £1,000,000 to £1,500,000 to facilitate the purchase of food at low cost; the establishment of useful public works (railway, drainage) in order to give work to the indigent. The latter would be partly financed by a tax of 20 per cent to 50 per cent on the income of absentee landlords, and 10 per cent on that of resident landlords.[6]

Three days later, a mass meeting open to all the 'Citizens of Dublin' adopted the measures proposed by O'Connell and extended the committee to include influential Liberal figures, such as the Earl of Leinster and Lord Cloncurry.[7] On 3 November the two men accompanied O'Connell and the Lord Mayor to a meeting scheduled with Lord Lieutenant Heytesbury. The latter, sticking to instructions issued by the government, would not commit himself to any of the delegation's requests, regarding them as too rash and too radical. In soliciting robust state intervention the committee had deviated from certain principles of political economy.[8] Yet at this stage, these requests still fell within the framework of Liberal doctrine, since the proposed assistance did not involve distributing food but offering work to the indigent to enable them to buy food at reasonable prices.

Lord Heytesbury's rebuff led O'Connell and a few others to transform the 'special committee' into a more permanent organization of around 30 members, 'to sit daily at the Mansion House, Dawson Street, and be called "The Mansion House Committee"', in order to continue the work of research and reflection.[9] Created on 4 November, it served as a platform for Repealers and Irish Whigs. On 7 November, Lord Cloncurry sent a letter to the Prime Minister on its behalf, again detailing the main measures to be adopted to save 'the lives of the people of Ireland'. Meanwhile, the committee became a hub for information available on the crisis. Based on responses to two questionnaires sent to the four corners of the island in November and December 1845, it offered summaries, as useful as they were alarming, on the spread of the disease and the ineffectiveness of the attempts to remedy it.[10] They recorded in their minutes, 'Famine and pestilence are at our door'.[11] O'Connell summarised to William Smith O'Brien, a fellow Repeal MP and Irish landlord, in December 1845:

> My attendance on the Mansion House Committee has made me acquainted with the frightful certainty of an approaching famine ... If the Government does not act promptly and most bountifully in affording ample means of employment and placing within the reach of the labouring classes a sufficient quantity of food, to be paid for out of the money they received as wages ... it is impossible to calculate the number of people that will perish in Ireland within the next twelve months of famine and pestilence.[12]

The struggle against the Famine became the Irish leader's priority, shattering the usual political rules: 'If I had only the alternative of keeping the people alive or giving up the repeal', he declared in one meeting, 'I would give up the repeal'.[13]

From January 1846, O'Connell continued his activities from London, in the very House of Commons that he had avoided attending since 1842. Between 28 January and the resignation of Prime Minister Robert Peel five months later, he spoke in 39 sessions on various themes, but almost all associated with the situation in Ireland. He spoke on ten occasions about the Famine, and eight times, from the end of March, to oppose the severe Protection of Life (Ireland) Bill presented by the government—in reality, yet another coercion bill. His speeches varied in length from a few minutes to nearly two hours. A first long tirade, on 17 February, was given over to the subsistence crisis. The main thrust of his argument was to demonstrate, in great detail, 'from documents ... the increasing misery of the Irish nation' since the 1820s. He then presented the main recommendations for emergency measures, similar to those of the Mansion House Committee, and appealed to the responsibility of parliament and the government 'to stop the impending calamity':

> You are not to be guided in such a case as this by ordinary rules. It is a case beyond every rules. The people are not to blame ... It is your business to mitigate that calamity as much as possible ... Famine is coming on—fever is coming on—this House ought to place in the Queen's Government powers adequate to such an exigency.[14]

During the first months of the Famine, the Tory government did not sit idle. Peel had secretly purchased Indian Corn in the United States, stored in 76 depots in Ireland and sold at cost. He set up public works, employing over 100,000 people by the start of the summer. While they may not have met all of O'Connell's demands—namely, there was no ban on food exports, no tax on absentee landlords—these measures were enough to prevent loss of life. The Irish leader's criticisms in the House of Commons focused less on the nature of the government's initiatives than on its limited generosity—'a great deal more money will be necessary'—and its cumbersome administrative machinery—'the inactivity of the persons employed in Ireland to superintend the distribution of food ... the wanton delay in some localities'.[15] There was, however, one proposal that O'Connell spoke against forcefully in Parliament: the Protection of Life (Ireland) Bill. On 3 April, during a nearly two-hour diatribe against this coercion bill which he considered unfair and inappropriate, O'Connell's bite and intellectual vitality seemed intact, but signs of physical decline weakened the impact.[16] His voice was so faint that he could only be heard by the members seated on the nearest benches. The young Tory MP, Benjamin Disraeli, who was present, described:

> a strange and touching spectacle to those who remembered the force of colossal energy and the clear and thrilling tones which had once startled, disturbed and controlled senates. To the house generally it was a performance in dumb show, a feeble old man muttering before a table.[17]

Moreover, Peel made use of the Irish crisis to accelerate his campaign in favour of repealing the Corn Laws. This bill had O'Connell's support, his motivations as much moral as economic. In his view, 'the Corn Laws are unchristian and uncatholic, because they are unjust and oppressive'; quite simply, they enabled landlords to get rich on the backs of the farmers.[18] O'Connell believed that this reform could prove an effective means to lower food prices, increase wages and thus alleviate his countrymen's suffering.[19] The question, however, divided the nationalists. A number of Repealers, Smith O'Brien chief among them, did not support completely abolishing the Corn Laws, which risked weakening Irish agriculture.[20] In the name of the higher interest of the nation, therefore, O'Connell voted in favour of the bill, bringing with him 34 Irish MPs.[21] He then quickly returned to his position among the most determined opponents of the Protection of Life (Ireland) Bill and contributed, with 47 other Irish MPs, to the bill's defeat, leading to the resignation of the Peel Cabinet at the end of June 1846.

The political alliance that O'Connell sought with the Whig ministry began a few days later, in a troubled context very different from that of the years 1835–1841. This time, the Repeal Association's activities were not suspended, and their leader promised his followers that the ultimate goal remained the repeal of the Union. For the time being, the Liberator prepared a list of eleven 'sweeping measures' addressed to Lord John Russell's hastily-formed government.[22] Several of these—strengthening tenants' rights, and a specific tax for absentee landlords—had clear echoes of the recent subsistence crisis, for while the potato blight had not yet reappeared, the spectre of famine was on everyone's mind. Other noteworthy, and more conventional, measures sought to widen the franchise in Ireland and to reform local government. 'I will place confidence in [the government]', O'Connell promised in a meeting on 6 July, 'when I see performances, but not a day sooner'.[23]

In mid-July, O'Connell learnt that the blight had returned. In the House of Commons on the 23 July he raised the matter with the new Chief Secretary, Henry Labouchere, who agreed: 'The disease had unfortunately made its appearance; and [I] feared that there was every prospect of its spreading to a serious extent'.[24] At the same time, the national movement was weakened by the split with Young Ireland, one of its most dynamic elements. This group of young intellectuals, founding members of *The Nation* newspaper, imagined the Irish nation through an exaltation of its historical and cultural roots. The Catholic Church's privileged relationship with nationalism within the Repeal Association catalysed the first tensions, the Young Irelanders particularly criticising O'Connell for locking himself into the role of defending Catholic interests alone. A split was narrowly avoided in 1844–1845. Rapprochement with the Whigs, sought by O'Connell, was the second bone of contention. For Smith O'Brien and Young Ireland, such an alliance would distort the movement, limit its independence and risk sacrificing Repeal on the altar of hypothetical reforms for Ireland. The tension, already palpable by late 1845, was at its height when the political pact was concluded early in the summer of 1846.[25] In July, to reassert his authority and forestall any disputes, O'Connell imposed the Peace Resolutions, a series of declarations signed by members categorically condemning the use of violence. This issue was, in fact, the third point of tension between O'Connell and the Young Irelanders, even if the latter never seriously considered resorting to force. Faced with the ultimatum, Smith O'Brien, Thomas Francis Meagher, John Mitchel and several others left the assembly after a stormy final debate.[26] This schism weakened the already sluggish momentum within the movement to repeal the Union. It created an unprecedented and embarrassing situation where the same measures were now demanded by two rival groups, unequal in strength given that the masses remained loyal to O'Connell, all within the dramatic context of the potato blight's return.

Back in Dublin in August, O'Connell 'cannonaded Russell, directly or indirectly, with requests, demands and pleas', in the words of historian Oliver MacDonagh.[27] He sought for the Prime Minister to persuade parliament to grant the government 'the extraordinary powers of directing, without any delay, the execution of works of public utility and of supplying the immediate means of paying the wages of the labourers employed at such works'.[28] He received assurances from Russell that the Treasury would indeed advance funds, with a view to quickly setting up 'works of public utility', the Whig ministry's main famine relief scheme in 1846.[29] This year, however, almost the entire crop was destroyed, and over the next weeks the measures proved to be insufficient to tackle the crisis. The first famine deaths were reported in late October.

Bitterness and disillusionment set in on the island.[30] O'Connell and his inner circle were not spared criticism. A 'Remonstrance' letter, signed by 80 Repeal Wardens and 400 members of the Association, was particularly critical of the attacks on free speech within the movement, the intransigence towards Young Ireland, and the mistakes of partnering with the Whigs.[31] For his part, O'Connell expressed some doubts over the public relief policies, but for now only to deplore their slow implementation and inflexible bureaucracy rather than the government's choices. 'I, who on the spot see the working of starvation, cannot express sufficiently my agony and anxiety until the people are set to work', he wrote to Labouchere from his residence in Derrynane in County Kerry, on 4 October.[32] Early that autumn the deteriorating situation also led him to decline income from the national subscription, which he had received every year since 1830: 'It would be the absurdest of all absurd things to think of a Tribute in such times as these'.[33]

In spite of his deteriorating health, noticed by several of those close to him, O'Connell continued his campaign against the Famine, stating: 'This, in truth, is so all-absorbing a subject as to banish all politics unconnected with the distress'.[34] He even intensified his action in the closing weeks of 1846. With mass mobilisation becoming increasingly difficult, he began focussing his efforts into forming a common front of the gentry and the Irish middle classes, in order to finally assess and obtain the long-requested measures. He elaborated on this goal during the Repeal Association's weekly meeting on 7 December, this time holding nothing back in stressing the failure of the 'miserable small schemes' currently in place: 'I am bound to announce that the means of the government are totally inadequate to meet the emergency ... It would require twice, or probably five times the means at their disposal to meet the calamity'.[35] In an attempt to restore some unity, a meeting with a delegation from Young Ireland was held on 15 December in Dublin, but each side stuck to its precepts and no common ground was found.[36] This confirmed the political cost of the summer's divide. Having previously sought to exclude the 'rebels', O'Connell failed to mend the rift. For historian Patrick Geoghegan, 'The decision to break from the Young Irelanders proved to be a costly final mistake'.[37] The failure of reconciliation was sealed on 13 January 1847 with the creation of the Irish Confederation, an offshoot of Young Ireland that pursued the same sovereignty objectives as the Repeal Association. Amidst the worst moments of the Famine, the national movement was acting in piecemeal fashion.

On the other hand, an idea was gaining ground for greater elite involvement through a 'national convention'.[38] A ready ear was found among landlords angry at government measures falling short, and at the tax burden imposed on them. The large gathering was eventually held in Dublin on 14 January 1847, attended by more than 600 gentlemen—landlords, lawyers, journalists, etc.—of all religious and political persuasions, including 35 MPs and 20 peers. The message to London was clear, as were the 38 resolutions adopted by the assembly. The Famine was not a regional subsistence crisis but an 'imperial calamity', Ireland could not overcome it alone, and private enterprise and charity were not enough to meet the needs of a starving population. Costs associated with emergency employment programmes, therefore, should be borne by the Imperial Exchequer. Relief funds should be spent primarily on productive works such as land drainage and remediation, port development and improving rural housing. Lastly, the issue resurfaced of taxing absentee landlords and granting appropriate compensation to any evicted tenant, in light of improvements made while renting the land.[39]

In the wake of this initiative by O'Connell, 83 parliamentarians—Nationalists, Liberals, and Conservatives—decided to join forces and overcome their differences to form an independent group in Westminster, serving Irish interests.[40] O'Connell arrived to join them in London on 28 January 1847. A few days later, the Tory MP Lord Bentinck presented a fairly ambitious Railways (Ireland) Bill which provided for massive public investment, in the form of a loan of £16 million to develop railways in Ireland and provide work for the needy. During the debate, however, party instincts regained the upper hand. Most of the Irish Liberal MPs followed government instructions to oppose the bill. O'Connell opted to support the proposal—attesting to the distance between him and the Whigs—while the Repealers were split.[41] Meanwhile, divisions within the 'Irish Party' were further exacerbated by the debate around the Poor Relief (Ireland) Bill. This government proposal was widely criticised by Irish lawmakers, as it made the Famine a local issue, rather than the responsibility of the imperial state. Only the O'Connellites gave it their half-hearted support, on the basis that it contained a clause authorising outdoor assistance for the able-bodied poor and the use of temporary soup kitchens.[42]

The unprecedented and fragile 'party truce' between Irish parliamentarians lasted mere weeks. It failed to dissuade British decision makers from placing the bulk of the tax burden for the Famine onto Irish shoulders. This failure reflected the great challenges faced by the nationalists in general, and O'Connell in particular, in attempting to influence the course of events during the Famine despite constant campaigning. When he spoke in Westminster on 8 February 1847, the Liberator was a shadow of his former self. His speech was short and inaudible, his voice weak. The transcript of his speech begins: 'Mr. O'Connell was understood to say'.[43] Running out of arguments, he said he was:

> ... ready to support any Bill which would afford any additional means of relief in the present calamity ... He did not think they [the MPs] understood the miseries—the accumulation of miseries—under which the people were at present suffering ... 25 per cent of the whole population would perish ... of famine and disease unless the

> House did something speedy and efficacious—not doled out in small sums—not in private and individual subscriptions, but by some great act of national generosity ... She [Ireland] was in their hands—in their power. If they did not save her, she could not save herself. He solemnly called on them to recollect that he predicted with the sincerest conviction, that one-fourth of her population would perish unless Parliament came to their relief.[44]

These are the closing words of O'Connell's final political speech. That same morning, he confided to his friend P.V. Fitzpatrick: 'The prospects are dismal. At a period when the Parliament could not do half enough for Ireland it is not disposed to do half as much as it can. There's every reason to despond of anything like efficient succour'.[45] O'Connell left public life a few days later to undertake a pilgrimage to Rome, cut short by his death in Genoa on 15 May 1847.

'The feeding of the people must be provided for by the government no matter at what cost and without delay'.[46] O'Connell's demands, summed up in this sentence, stood in stark contrast to the general attitude of British authorities between the summer of 1846 and winter 1847, famously preoccupied with limiting state intervention and expenditure in the Irish crisis. Yet, even in spite of his growing disillusionment, O'Connell did not formally break with the Whig ministry, clearly convinced that the return of the Tories would open an even darker chapter in his country's history. 'This stance', historian Sean Connolly points out, 'shared by most other Repealers, left the movement pathetically tied to the Liberal government even as it presided over policies that sacrificed growing numbers of Irish lives to the doctrines of free market economics'.[47]

O'Connell challenged, occasionally scolded, and ultimately implored the British people and their political representatives during the Famine, but how did he himself behave, as an individual and as an Irish landlord confronted by disaster? Did he act to relieve the distress of his tenants with the same determination and generosity that marked him in public life? How far did he go in his efforts to help Famine victims on his own lands? One of the first to ask these questions was the Englishman Thomas Campbell Foster. In the summer of 1845, this young barrister was commissioned by the London *Times* to investigate the social situation in Ireland. He travelled across the island for five months, reporting his observations and impressions in some 40 'Letters on the Condition of the People of Ireland', written at regular three-to-five-day intervals between 14 August 1845 (before the Famine began) and 6 January 1846.[48] Foster described the plight of the population in detail. In an analysis not unlike that of the *Times*' editorials, he blamed the Irish and their national character for all their misery: the landlords were careless and selfish, the peasants indolent and unproductive.[49] These letters, twice reissued in 1846 and 1847, presented Ireland as an inverted mirror of Great Britain. They helped shape British opinion about the neighbouring island at the start of the Famine. They also reflected the prejudice against the Irish that was prevalent in British society, and particularly in the circles of power, at the start of Victoria's reign.[50]

These articles did not fail to trigger a reaction in Ireland. They angered O'Connell in particular, who singled out Foster for ridicule during the Repeal Association's weekly meetings, calling him the 'gutter commissioner of the Times', a 'liar', and a 'scoundrel'.[51] November 1845 saw Foster travel to O'Connell's holdings in Kerry. He wrote:

> The distress of the population was horrible. There is not a pane of glass in the parish [of Derrynane Beg], not a window of any kind in half the cottages ... In not one in a dozen is there a chair to sit upon ... In many of them the smoke is coming out of the doorway, for they have no chimneys ... The poor creatures are in the lowest degree of squalid poverty I have yet seen.[52]

This image of tenant misery led him to depict O'Connell as the archetypal 'bad landlord', scarcely concerned about the fate of the poor, interested only in extracting rents for profit, and ultimately at fault for the inhabitants' hardship:

> It will be remembered that amongst the most neglectful landlords who are a curse to Ireland, Daniel O'Connell ranks first—that on the estate of Daniel O'Connell are to be found the most wretched tenants that are to be seen in all Ireland.[53]

Faced with such accusations, O'Connell and his son Maurice, to whom he entrusted the administration of the family estate, responded vigorously to denounce the slander. The controversy engulfing Ireland's most famous figure soon grew, with speeches, letters, testimonies for or against, and extensive press coverage.[54] In a meeting on 24 November 1845, O'Connell drew up a long inventory of everything that made him an 'improving landlord': in Cahirciveen, he was the main patron of the parsonage, schools, convent, fever hospital, dispensary, new quays and bridges, and provided struggling residents with work in construction. Yet, he added, 'All of that is suppressed in [Foster's] report'.[55] In a letter published in the *Times* on 20 December, Maurice O'Connell highlighted the longstanding and solid ties that united his family and their tenants. He asked: 'Is it for not evicting these people ... that [my father] is censured? ... Most of these people formed the seventh generation of their families who had held those farms under ours. Was no feeling of pity to be entertained toward them?'[56]

The allegations in the *Times* were picked up in major illustrated weeklies such as *Punch*, *The Pictorial Times* and *The Illustrated London News*. The latter, which was not always hostile to O'Connell, nonetheless portrayed him as Ireland's worst landlord in a report entitled 'Views of the O'Connell Property in Ireland', published on 10 January 1846. The article accompanying the engravings quoted many passages from Foster's 'Letters', and inferred O'Connell's inability to govern Ireland from the mismanagement of his estate.[57] Conversely, O'Connell received unexpected support from several English conservative newspapers, such as *The Morning Herald*, which deplored the claims as unfair defamation.[58] The press also published numerous letters from public figures, including Lord Cloncurry, John Gray, and testimonies from residents, both Catholic and Protestant, Liberal and Conservative, often approached directly by O'Connell, who described him as a landlord attentive to the needs of his tenants, especially in difficult times.[59]

The controversy waned by late winter without causing too much damage to O'Connell, but he had been forced to dedicate much time and energy to defending his name. Over the course of several months this short-lived polemic generated a considerable number of documents which essentially tell us more about contemporary political and ideological issues than about O'Connell's real actions as a landlord during the Famine. Further detail can be drawn from his correspondence with his son, Maurice. The frequency and content of the letters exchanged between 1845 and 1847 confirm that he was hardly present in Kerry (a few weeks each year, in summer or autumn), but that this did not make him an absentee landlord, in the sense that he always cared about his estates. He managed his land from afar, proving attentive, keeping informed of food stocks and other developments, was highly directive (constantly sending instructions to Maurice), and, at times, autocratic.

In March 1846, faced with the prevailing uncertainty, O'Connell wrote to his son: 'The dogs must not be fed to the detriment of the poor. We must, at all events, secure our own tenants from destitution. You will of course let them know that any money they necessarily lay out for provisions will be allowed as part of their rent'.[60] This appears to have been his approach in previous decades, whenever the situation became critical and scarcity set in. At that time, he would request his local agent, John Primrose, to show patience or take active measures to help the tenants—providing money, meat, or fishing boats.[61] Faced with the cholera epidemic in 1832–34, O'Connell had taken charge of the relief efforts, giving precise instructions for how they should be organised: 'Above and before all things, be prodigal with relief out of my means—beef, bread, mutton, medicines, physician, everything you can think of'.[62]

In late August 1846, when the situation became critical again, O'Connell issued two firm recommendations to Maurice, 'to meet the coming emergencies'. He encouraged him, on the one hand, to 'get ... in the rents as far as [he] can' and, on the other, to stock up on Indian corn and 'American saved beef' to feed farm workers as required.[63] The rest of their correspondence testifies to his efforts to both protect family interests, and to live up to his role as landlord, regarding it as his responsibility to alleviate, even prevent, the tenant-farmers' misery during the crisis.[64] Again, he emphasized, 'I wish you to be as abundant to the people as you possibly can, recollecting, however, that we have dreadful times before us'.[65]

From Dublin, at the height of the crisis, O'Connell oversaw the purchase and delivery of sufficient quantities of cereals to Cahirciveen, promising Maurice, 'I will arrange to have at least ten tons of Indian meal sent to you from Kilrush as speedily as possible'.[66] The movement of food was often achieved under difficult conditions.[67] O'Connell was also very careful about how local public works were organised and planned. He made several notable approaches to the Board of Works to reduce administrative delays, secure additional resources to hire more workers, and ensure that those eligible for jobs on construction sites were not penalised by illegal local arrangements.[68] In December 1846 he also sent £100 to the Tralee District Relief Committee and became a founding member of the General Central Relief Committee, which received donations from all over the world.[69] More importantly, during the Famine O'Connell was not a 'clearing landlord'.[70] He evicted no tenants, and seems to have reduced or adjusted payments owed by tenants who were in difficulty.[71] These initiatives and choices were not unique to him, but they were far from the norm among landlords during the Famine; historian James S. Donnelly estimates the number of tenant-farmers expelled during this period to be half a million at least.[72]

Clearly, O'Connell was not the 'bad landlord' portrayed by Foster and other political opponents. In line with the image of the Gaelic chief watching over his 'clan', his rather dutiful and paternalistic management played a role in strengthening his reputation as a 'good landlord', as evidenced in the folk tradition.[73] His approach to his own lands was more about continuity than innovation and rupture. Although not quite the exemplary 'improving landlord', he took action and made courageous decisions to help the most disadvantaged. Despite being at heart a social conservative, he showed, particularly in the exceptional conditions of 1845–1847, that he could act differently and make bold proposals, particularly in overseeing the expansion of tenants' rights.[74] He repeatedly supported the principle of providing compensation for land improvements made under tenancy to evicted or emigrating farmers. Moreover, O'Connell 'talked at different times of repealing post-Union legislation that had made evictions easier to arrange, and of restricting the right to recover unpaid rents by legal process to those landlords who had granted their tenants twenty-one year leases'.[75] He generally advocated for the 'tenant-right' system that was prevalent in Ulster and provided greater security of tenure, to be extended to the whole island.[76] These proposals, seeking to rebalance landlord-tenant relations without modifying the underlying property structures, were considered radical; they were often poorly received within the Nationalist movement, whose executives and elected officials were, like their Liberal and Conservative peers, drawn mainly from the landowning class. Even those who were the most daring on the question of political reform were reluctant to consider an overhaul of social relations that would erode their privileges.

From the moment the potato blight was announced, Daniel O'Connell made use of his influential position to alert political leaders and the public in Ireland and England as to both the extent of the threat, and the drastic measures urgently needed to address it. As a member of the Dublin Corporation and the Mansion House Committee, as leader of the Repeal Association and as Member of Parliament for Cork in the House of Commons, he devoted himself tirelessly to the fight against the Famine. He gathered extensive information and issued a multitude of proposals, frequently departing from liberal orthodoxy, or breaking with it altogether: from banning cereal exports, to imposing a tax on landlords' income; from public funding for productive works, to strengthening tenants' rights. He also encouraged and supported collective initiatives to maintain pressure on government and parliament, such as the national convention of January 1847. As a landlord, he showed concern for the wellbeing of the tenants living on his land: again, drawing upon his influential position, he intervened to secure food and to expedite matters when relief measures proved too slow.

However, despite his resolve and status, the hero of 1829 struggled to make himself heard in London and influence government decisions. This relative weakness, for which we have seen he bore some responsibility, stemmed from a range of factors. When the Famine struck, the flurry of mass meetings of the summer of 1843 seemed long passed, the national movement now weakened by internal quarrels. On top of this division, the alliance with the Whigs, in which O'Connell had placed great hope, proved counterproductive and crippling, as the government refused to depart from its principles of political economy. Moreover, the Irish leader's main solution, namely, robust intervention by the state in the name of the Union and humanity, hit against the fact that, for the Repealers, the true remedy for Ireland's ills was the dissolution of the very same Union. Finally, he found himself confronted by the difficulties of mobilising a heterogeneous and desperate population in a period of crisis.

During the last two years of his life O'Connell focused his energy and deployed most of his activity towards fighting the disaster of the Famine. Less exuberant than he had once been, he continued to exemplify political heroism, until his strength at last left him. His death in Genoa on 15 May 1847 left the Irish people without their greatest champion.

NOTES

1. Maurice R. O'Connell (ed.), *The Correspondence of Daniel O'Connell. Volume VIII, 1846–1847* (Tallaght: The Blackwater Press, 1980), letter 3264, to Lord John Russell, 12 Aug. 1846. The term is reused by Christine Kinealy, *A Death-Dealing Famine: The Great Hunger in Ireland* (London: Pluto Press, 1997).
2. 'Héroïsme', in *Centre national de ressources textuelles et lexicales (CNRTL)*: www.cnrtl.fr/definition/h%C3%A9ro%C3%AFsme
3. Oliver MacDonagh, *The Life of Daniel O'Connell 1775–1847* (Dublin: Weidenfeld & Nicolson, 1991), pp 555–556; Michael Keyes, *Funding the Nation: Money and nationalist politics in nineteenth-century Ireland* (Dublin: Gill & Macmillan, 2011), pp 104–6.
4. 'Meeting of the Corporation', 21 Oct. 1845, *Freeman's Journal*, 22 Oct. 1845.
5. 'The Potato Disease-Meeting of the Corporation', 28 Oct. 1845, *Freeman's Journal*, 29 Oct. 1845.
6. Ibid.
7. 'The Potato Disease-Public Meeting of the Citizens', 31 Oct. 1845, *Freeman's Journal*, 1 Nov. 1845.
8. 'Deputation to His Excellency the Lord Lieutenant', 3 Nov. 1845, *Freeman's Journal*, 4 Nov. 1845.
9. 'The Potato Disease. Adjourned Meeting of Citizens', 4 Nov. 1845, *Freeman's Journal*, 5 Nov. 1845; *Report of the Mansion House Committee*, p. 2.
10. *Report of the Mansion House Committee on the Potato Disease* (Dublin: J. Browne, 1846), pp 3–11.
11. Ibid., p. 5.
12. Maurice R. O'Connell (ed.), *The Correspondence of Daniel O'Connell. Volume VII, 1841–1845* (Tallaght: The Blackwater Press, 1978), letter 3181, to William Smith O'Brien, 20 Dec. 1845.
13. *The Nation*, 8 Nov. 1845, cited by Kevin B. Nowlan, *The Politics of Repeal: A study in the relations between Great Britain and Ireland, 1841–1850* (London: Routledge & Kegan Paul, 1965), p. 97.
14. *Hansard,* The Parliamentary Debates, Third Series, vol. 83, House of Commons, 17 Feb. 1846, cc. 1050–68.
15. Ibid., vol. 85, 24 Apr. 1846, cc. 1006.
16. Ibid., vol. 85, 3 Apr. 1846, cc. 493–527.

17. Disraeli cited by Angus D. Macintyre, *The Liberator: Daniel O'Connell and the Irish party, 1830–47* (London: Hamilton, 1965), p. 290.
18. Daniel O'Connell, *Observations on Corn Laws* (Dublin: S.J. Machen, 1842), p. 15.
19. O'Connell (ed.), *The Correspondence. Volume VII,* letter 3181, to William Smith O'Brien, 20 Dec. 1845; ibid., letter 3189, 7 Feb. 1846: 'I am a free trader in provision of every kind ... from the most thorough conviction'; *Hansard,* The Parliamentary Debates, vol. 84, 6 Mar. 1846, c. 760 and vol. 85, 25 Apr. 1846, c. 1007.
20. O'Connell (ed.), *The Correspondence. Volume VII,* letter 3180, from William Smith O'Brien, 18 Dec. 1845; Robert Sloan, *William Smith O'Brien and the Young Ireland Rebellion of 1848* (Dublin: Four Courts Press, 2000), pp 142–148.
21. *Hansard*, The Parliamentary Debates, vol. 86, 15 May 1846, c. 727.
22. O'Connell (ed.), *The Correspondence. Volume VIII*, letter 3240, to William Smith O'Brien, 30 June 1846.
23. 'The Liberator's Letter', read at the Repeal Association Meeting, 29 June 1846, *Freeman's Journal*, 30 June 1846; 'Weekly meeting of the Loyal National Repeal Association', 6 July 1846, *The Freeman's Journal*, 7 July 1846.
24. *Hansard*, The Parliamentary Debates, vol. 87, 23 July 1846, c. 1383; see also O'Connell (ed.), *The Correspondence. Volume VIII*, letter 3253, from Rev. N. McEvoy, 23 July 1846.
25. O'Connell (ed.), *The Correspondence. Volume VII*, letter 3227, from William Smith O'Brien, 18 Dec. 1845; ibid., *Volume VIII*, letter 3180, from Martin Crean, 15 June 1846; debate at the Repeal Association, Conciliation Hall, 15 June 1846, *Freeman's Journal*, 16 June 1846.
26. 'Meeting of the Repeal Association', 27 July 1846, *Freeman's Journal*, 28 July 1846, and 'Adjourned meeting', 28 July 1846, *Freeman's Journal*, 29 July 1846; Charles Gavan Duffy, *Four Years of Irish History, 1845–1849* (London: Cassell, Petter & Galpin, 1883), chap.VI, 'The secession', pp 217–239.
27. MacDonagh, *The Life of Daniel O'Connell*, p. 579.
28. O'Connell (ed.), *The Correspondence. Volume VIII*, letter 3264, to Lord John Russell, 12 Aug. 1846.
29. Ibid., letter 3267, from Lord John Russell, 14 Aug. 1846.
30. See the editorials in *The Nation* during the autumn of 1846, particularly 'Letter from Smith O'Brien, MP, to the Right Honourable Lord John Russell', 9 Sept. 1846, *The Nation*, 12 Sept. 1846: 'The measures hitherto adopted are not only wholly inadequate to the crisis, but also, in many respects, unjust in their nature' for landlords and tenants.
31. 'Meeting of the Friends of Freedom of Opinion', 27 Sept. 1846, *The Nation,* 3 Oct. 1846; Christine Kinealy, *Repeal and Revolution: 1848 in Ireland* (Manchester University Press, 2009), p. 76.
32. O'Connell (ed.), *The Correspondence. Volume VIII*, letter 3297, to Henry Labouchere, 4 Oct. 1846; letter 3290, to Henry Labouchere, 29 Sept. 1846.
33. Ibid., letter 3299, to P.V. Fitzpatrick, 5 Oct. 1846.
34. 'O'Connell's Letter', dated 2 Oct. 1846, read at the weekly meeting of the Repeal association, 5 Oct. 1846, *Freeman's Journal*, 6 Oct. 1846.

35. 'Weekly meeting of the Repeal Association', 7 Dec. 1846, *The Freeman's Journal*, 8 Dec. 1846.
36. O'Connell (ed.), *The Correspondence. Volume VIII*, letter 3365, from James Haughton, 15 Dec. 1846; Gavan Duffy, *Four Years of Irish History,* pp 339–349; Sloan, *William Smith O'Brien*, pp 170–174.
37. Patrick Geoghegan, *Liberator: The life and death of Daniel O'Connell, 1830–1847* (Dublin: Gill & Macmillan, 2010), p. 226.
38. O'Connell (ed.), *The Correspondence. Volume VIII*, letter 3361, to Frederick W. Conway, 10 Dec. 1846.
39. 'Important meeting of the Peers, Representatives, and Gentry of Ireland', 14 Jan. 1847, *Freeman's Journal*, 15 Jan. 1847; Gavan Duffy, *Four Years of Irish History,* pp 366–70.
40. Nowlan, *The Politics of Repeal*, p. 127.
41. Hansard (ed.), *The Parliamentary Debates*, vol. 90, 16 Feb. 1847, cc. 123–6; Gavan Duffy, *Four Years of Irish History,* p. 373.
42. James S. Donnelly, Jr, *The Great Irish Potato Famine* (Stroud: Sutton Publishing, 2001), pp 194–196.
43. *Hansard*, The Parliamentary Debates, vol. 89, 8 Feb. 1847, c. 942.
44. Ibid., cc. *943*–945.
45. O'Connell (ed.), *The Correspondence. Volume VIII*, letter 3373, to P.V. Fitzpatrick, 8 Feb. 1847.
46. Ibid., letter 3265, to David R. Pigot, 13 Aug. 1846.
47. Sean J. Connolly. 'The Great Famine and Irish Politics', in Cathal Póirtéir (ed.), *The Great Irish Famine* (Dublin: Mercier Press, 1995), p. 41.
48. These have been collected in the work: Thomas Campbell Foster*, Letters on the Condition of the People of Ireland* (London: Chapman & Hall, 1846).
49. Ibid., preface, pp viii–x.
50. Leslie A. Williams, *Daniel O'Connell, the British Press and the Irish Famine: killing remarks* (Aldershot: Ashgate, 2003), chap. 4, pp 101–24; Peter Gray, *Famine, Land and Politics: British government and Irish society 1843–1850* (Dublin: Irish Academic Press, 1999).
51. 'Meeting of the Repeal Association', 27 Oct. 1845, *Freeman's Journal*, 28 Oct. 1845; 'Meeting of the Repeal Association', 3 Nov. 1845, *Freeman's Journal*, 4 Nov. 1845.
52. Foster, *Letters on the Condition of the People of Ireland*, 'Letter XXVI, Kenmare, Kerry, 10 Nov. 1845, 'Mr. O'Connell and his wretched Tenantry', pp 394–398.
53. Ibid.
54. For instance: 'O'Connell and his calumniators', *Freeman's Journal*, 25 Nov. 1845; Foster, *Letters on the Condition of the People of Ireland*, 'Letter XXXI, Waterford, 29 Nov. 1845, 'Mr. O'Connell to prove the condition of his estate', pp 457–63, 'Appendix XI–XIV', pp 660–727; O'Connell (ed.), *The Correspondence. Volume VIII*, letters 3183 and 3184, from his son Maurice, 4 Jan. 1846.
55. 'Weekly meeting of the Repeal Association', 24 Nov. 1845, *Freeman's Journal*, 25 Nov. 1845.
56. Maurice O'Connell, 'Letter to the Editor', *The Times*, 20 Dec. 1845, cited by Williams, *Daniel O'Connell, the British Press and the Irish Famine*, p. 145.

57. 'Views of the O'Connell Property in Ireland', *Illustrated London News*, 10 Jan. 1846, cited by Williams, *Daniel O'Connell, the British Press and the Irish Famine*, p. 145.
58. W.J. Fitzpatrick (ed.), *Correspondence of Daniel O'Connell, the Liberator. Volume II* (New York: Longmans & Green, 1888), pp 366–367.
59. O'Connell (ed.), *The Correspondence. Volume VII*, letter 3182, to Lord Cloncurry, 27 Dec. 1845; ibid., *vol. VIII*, letter 3184, from his son Maurice, 4 Jan. 1846, note 1; John Gray, *The Pilot*, 19 Jan. 1846.
60. O'Connell (ed.), *The Correspondence. Volume VIII*, letter 3196, to his son Maurice, 26 Mar. 1846.
61. Maurice R. O'Connell (ed.), *The Correspondence of Daniel O'Connell. Volume II, 1815–1823* (Dublin: Irish University Press, 1973), letter 985, to John Primrose, 31 Dec. 1822; *Volume IV, 1829–1832* (Tallagh: The Blackwater Press, 1977), letter 1691, to John Primrose, 7 July 1830.
62. Ibid., *Volume IV*, letter 1892, to John Primrose, 3 May 1832; Maurice R. O'Connell (ed.), *The Correspondence of Daniel O'Connell. Volume V, 1833–1836* (Dublin: Irish University Press, 1977), letter 2047, to John Primrose, 1 March 1834; letter 2048, to John Primrose, 3 Mar. 1834.
63. Ibid., *Volume VIII*, letter 3271, to his son Maurice, 27 Aug. 1846.
64. Ibid., letter 3334, to his son Maurice, 5 Nov. 1846; letter 3341, to his son Maurice, 21 Nov. 1846.
65. Ibid., letter 3353, to his son Maurice, 5 Dec. 1846.
66. Ibid., letter 3354, to his son Maurice, 5 Dec. 1846.
67. For instance: Ibid., letter 3355, from Sir Randolph Routh, 7 Dec. 1846; letter 3356, from Sir Randolph Routh, 8 Dec. 1846; letter 3370, to his son Maurice, 13 Jan. 1847.
68. Ibid., letter 3334, to his son Maurice, 5 Nov. 1846; letter 3337, to his son Maurice, 11 Nov. 1846; letter 3339, from his son Maurice, 18 Nov. 1846; letter 3341, to his son Maurice, 21 Oct. 1846; letter 3362, to his son Maurice, 10 Dec. 1846.
69. Ibid., letter 3353, to his son Maurice, 5 Dec. 1846; Christine Kinealy, *Private Charity to Ireland during the Great Hunger: The kindness of strangers* (London: Bloomsbury Press, 2013).
70. To use his term: *Hansard*, The Parliamentary Debates, vol. 85, 24 Apr. 1846, c. 1007.
71. O'Connell (ed.), *The Correspondence. Volume VIII*, letter 3370, to his son Maurice, 13 Jan. 1847.
72. James S. Donnelly, Jr, 'Mass Eviction and the Great Famine: the Clearances Revisited', in Póirtéir (ed.), *The Great Irish Famine*, p. 156.
73. Maurice R. O'Connell, 'O'Connell: Lawyer and Landlord', in Kevin B. Nowlan and Maurice R. O'Connell (eds), *Daniel O'Connell: portrait of a radical* (Belfast: Appletree Press, 1984), p. 115; Ríonach Uí Ógáin, *Immortal Dan: Daniel O'Connell in Irish folk tradition* (Dublin: Geography Publications, 1995).
74. Laurent Colantonio, 'Exploring Daniel O'Connell's Political Ideology', in Olivier Coquelin, Patrick Galliou and Thierry Robin (eds), *Political Ideology in Ireland: From the Enlightenment to the present* (Cambridge: Cambridge Scholars Publishing, 2009), pp 68–81.
75. Connolly, 'The Great Famine and Irish Politics', p. 47; O'Connell (ed.), *The Correspondence. Volume VII*, letter 3047, to Charles Buller, 9 Jan. 1844; letter 3141, to Pierce Mahony, 25 Apr. 1845; letter 3142, to Pierce Mahony, 26 Apr. 1845.

76. See for instance: 'Weekly meeting of the Repeal Association', 8 Dec. 1845, *The Freeman's Journal*, 9 Dec. 1845; O'Connell (ed.), *The Correspondence. Volume VIII*, letter 3209, to P.V. Fitzpatrick, 12 May 1846.

CHAPTER TWO

'JOHN OF KENMARE'

Father John O'Sullivan (1807–1874)

Colum Kenny

He was certainly not feeling heroic. During the summer of 1847 the weather grew 'dreadfully hot' in Kerry, wrote Father John O'Sullivan. There was a constant wind from the north. Even gooseberries and flowers turned black. He hastened out to a potato field after dinner and found it all 'blasted, blighted, withered'. He thought, 'Good God, what a store of misery awaits us for twelve, fifteen months more. Will His anger be ever appeased?' By the riverside one day, he lay on his back and wished God would let him die.[1]

Fever raged through O'Sullivan's combined parishes of Kenmare and Templenoe, and he was constantly called on to visit the dying. 'May God Almighty speedily take me to Himself; the ordeal we will again have to go through is truly terrific, but God's will be done', he recorded.[2] His worst fears were soon confirmed: 'The potatoes gone again, the people starving and no likelihood of public works being resumed'.[3] Yet O'Sullivan rose to the occasion. He organized food imports, demanded poor relief as 'an established right' of the people and lobbied parliament at Westminster. While in London, he befriended the key civil servant, Charles Trevelyan, and on two successive days lobbied in person at a meeting of high-level bankers who agreed to send aid to Kenmare. He continued to build up a local educational infrastructure too.

O'Sullivan also fiercely resisted proselytisers who he felt were exploiting the misery by enticing families with promises of food and clothing if they sent their children to Protestant schools. He claimed to have been 'the first that ever baptized them soupers', a contemptuous term for proselytisers that came to be used nationally.[4] Among those who have supported his claim was the historian Canon John O'Rourke

(1809–1887).[5] O'Sullivan's bitter relations with a Templenoe landlord and clergyman, Denis Mahony, which led to a violent clash that was thought to have contributed to the latter's untimely death, has largely if not entirely gone unnoticed by historians of proselytism in Ireland, although religious tensions in his parish received some national attention at the time.[6] He wrote in 1854, 'I defy a man to meet souperism without carrying agitation to its acme'.[7]

O'Sullivan's initial response to the failure of potato crops was entrepreneurial. Rather than seek immediate state relief, he sought to bring down the price of food in his parish, as he had earlier done when a curate elsewhere. In 1849, and at Westminster, he explained to a parliamentary select committee on poor laws in Ireland:

> I saw the potatoes had gone, horse and foot, and I saw there was a great deal of speaking and nothing doing, and I found that it was necessary for some person to take very active measures. Accordingly, [in October 1846] I went to Mr. [James] Hickson, Lord Lansdowne's agent, a particular friend of mine, about seven years before, when I was curate in the town of Dingle. There was a considerable pressure, and I collected a subscription of 50*l*. [£50] in the town of Dingle, and it was nominally supposed to be collected for the purpose of distributing in charity. I insisted upon its not being so distributed, and I got hold of it myself, and I sent to Skibbereen and imported a cargo of potatoes. As soon as I imported them I sold them out to the people and sent for more; and by means of the 50*l*. which I got hold of in that way, I imported about 1,000*l*. worth of potatoes, and all parties acknowledged in the end that more good was done by that management than would have been done if the 50*l*. had been distributed at once.[8]

So too in Kenmare, in 1846, he had gone again to Hickson—who lived locally on Lord Lansdowne's extensive estate in the area—and persuaded the agent to advance him £200 for the same purpose: 'In this manner I imported about 4,000*l*. worth of food on my own account'.[9] Yet, such was the extent of the crisis then unfolding that the most imaginative efforts to respond by managing the market or massaging the distribution of existing food were inadequate.

John O'Sullivan had been born in Tralee, County Kerry, in 1807, the eldest son of a painter also named John, and Elizabeth Walsh. He had one brother, Stephen, and one sister, Ann. He claimed that his family was related to Daniel O'Connell, the Kerry-born champion of Catholic Emancipation and member of the British parliament. When John was 6 years old, his father died. The future priest was educated by Bob Slattery, who ran a small school in Tralee attended by both Catholics and Protestants. The Kerry historian Mary Hickson was to write in the 1870s that O'Sullivan was fond of recalling those days spent 'with many of the sons of the Protestant gentry of Kerry, some of them his relatives', and that he believed he had derived benefits 'from a free intercourse with young companions of another creed who in after life continued as his friends'.[10] Encouraged by Bishop Cornelius Egan of Kerry, John attended Maynooth College where he trained to become a priest, and was ordained in Killarney on 10 July 1830.[11] O'Sullivan had hoped to continue in Maynooth, believing that its president had promised him a place 'on the Dunboyne' (a scholarship for further study), but Bishop Egan decided that his services were needed in Kerry as soon as possible. In 1827 Egan had been 'grieved' to inform Daniel O'Connell, 'I am unable, from a scarcity of priests, to supply the wants of some parishes in my diocese'.[12]

O'Sullivan's posting as a young curate in Dingle in 1830 was something of a baptism of fire, with an international cholera epidemic soon bringing him face to face with desperate and needy people. He recounted that:

> Dingle was the Hacelddoma [Aceldama, or 'field of blood'] of Kerry that year. The cholera raged there with greater fury than in any other part of the diocese. It was not an unusual thing for one of us to go out at night and not return till nine or ten the following morning, moving from house to house preparing the dying. I was myself taken out of bed thirteen successive nights to prepare cholera patients.[13]

The establishment of an active Protestant 'colony' at Ventry, on the Dingle peninsula, also kept O'Sullivan busy. He later wrote: 'When souperism began first to spread in Dingle the whole burden of its opposition fell upon me. I was continually pelting and pounding them', including by severe, public excommunication.[14] In an open letter published in 1839, a few months after O'Sullivan left Tralee to become parish priest in Kenmare, a local evangelical Protestant wrote: 'The priest who most violently opposed the work at Ventry, and who by his harangues stirred up the people to insult and ill-treat the converts, has been removed, and our enemies are comparatively at peace with us'.[15]

As parish priest in Kenmare, a town which had been founded and laid out in the late eighteenth century, O'Sullivan set about improving the physical and spiritual welfare of his parishioners, building up chapels and schools in the district while formulating opinions on the best use of land. He shared some of his opinions with the Devon Commission when it visited Kenmare in 1844.[16] By then, unfortunately, it was already too late to make changes in the use of land that could significantly alter the impact of the approaching famine. The extent of that catastrophe was still unforeseen when, in November 1845, the Kenmare workhouse opened as a resource for the destitute. Reporting to the Poor Law Commissioners in January 1846, its newly appointed guardians noted that the potato crop was 'above an average one'. This should have been good news but, ominously, half of the crop had been lost to disease.[17]

By early 1847 the *Kerry Evening Post* was reporting that Kenmare was almost drained of provisions, with no prospect of immediate relief except that afforded by the local relief committee–which was said to have just £230 left. A local family of five persons reportedly lived two days on one hen, and another family made four meals of a starving goose.[18] The poor law guardians appointed Dr Thomas Taylor of Dunkerron, Templenoe, as medical officer of Kenmare workhouse. He was a Unitarian who as a botanist and physician has merited entries in both the *Dictionary of Irish Biography* and the *Dictionary of National Biography*. He had acquired great experience at Sir Patrick Dun's Hospital in Dublin during the fever epidemic of 1817–1818.[19] In January 1847, Taylor reported that:

> Two, three and even four fever patients are put into one bed for want of straw. The convalescent from fever in the House cannot rise for want of fire. Sometimes they cannot rise for want of clothes. Coffee continues to be substituted for milk.[20]

Shockingly, 'Florence Sullivan born in the house on the 9th inst., the mother having no suck, received coffee instead of milk and perished in seven days'.[21] Taylor and dozens of other doctors who quietly worked to help fever victims are among forgotten heroes of the Famine. He himself, like many of his patients, fell victim to 'famine fever' and died of it just as he had feared he might when he wrote that more than 40 workhouse medical doctors had already perished of fever caught in the discharge of their duties. Sadly, his surviving family felt it necessary to threaten to sue for outstanding fees due to him.[22]

In January 1847, 'when famine was staring us in the face', as O'Sullivan wrote, the Kenmare Relief Committee deputed both O'Sullivan and Rev. James Going of the neighbouring Church of Ireland parish of Kilgarvan to go to London on their behalf and lay the state of the Kenmare Union before the government.[23] It was then that O'Sullivan first met Charles Trevelyan, the most influential civil servant in respect to Irish famine policy. During their visit, O'Sullivan and Going also succeeded in being received in person by the committee of the recently formed British Association for the Relief of Distress in Ireland and the Highlands of Scotland. The association was to play a central role in helping to co-ordinate the government's response to famine that year. It had been established by a group of rich private individuals, including in particular very powerful and busy bankers such as Samuel Jones-Loyd, Moses Montefiore, Baron Lionel de Rothschild and his brother Meyer, Thomas Baring and Samuel Gurney. A letter from Nicholas Cummins of Cork to the London *Times* in December had been the catalyst for the formation of the association. His uncle, James John Cummins, a London banker, was one of two members of the association's committee who came from Ireland. Nicholas's letter followed a visit by him to Skibbereen and was partly why that town became a byword for famine.[24] Nevertheless, there is no reason to believe that the effects of the Famine were not felt equally or worse in a number of other districts. Indeed, by the end of the year Deputy Commissary-General Dobree reported to Trevelyan that Kenmare was the most miserable and destitute poor law union in Ireland.[25]

The British Association first met on 1 January 1847 and moved quickly to organize ships to bring meal, potatoes and peas to Ireland, together with clothing and blankets. David Salomons, a future Lord Mayor of London with whom O'Sullivan established a rapport, joined the committee on 6 January. It was already receiving many petitions for aid from Ireland but permitted only two witnesses related to these appeals to attend in person. These were Marshal Cummins of Glanmire, who spoke particularly to 'the condition of the peasantry' around Skibbereen, and Rev. George Hazelwood, who wished the association to direct some of its aid through an evangelical group in Ireland. However, the bankers were anxious to avoid accusations of religious bias.[26]

The British Association worked closely with transport companies on the logistics of the relief operation, and Queen Victoria donated £2,000 to its efforts. It met on no fewer than 25 days during its first month in existence. Notably, O'Sullivan and Going were permitted to appear before the association at the beginning of February; that meeting was held at South Sea House in Threadneedle Street. The fact that they met the committee once was an achievement, and that O'Sullivan himself was brought back on a second day was remarkable, not least given that just two other petitioners had been heard in person since its foundation. The first meeting at which O'Sullivan was present was attended by the Lord Mayor of London, John Kinnersley Hooper, who was a member of 'The Honorable Irish Society', established in the seventeenth century to assist in the plantation of Ulster. Before responding to the case of Kenmare, the committee decided they should first consult the powerful local landlord, Lord Lansdowne, with whom O'Sullivan diplomatically maintained good relations.[27] Having seen him, the association resolved that 100 tons of meal be 'dispatched to Kenmare to the Rev. John O'Sullivan–the said one hundred tons of meal to be sold by him at such price as he may deem advisable and a further five tons sent for gratuitous [free] distribution by him'. Rothschild personally put an additional vessel at the association's disposal.[28] O'Sullivan wrote:

> There they were, sitting every night–men with millions of money–to whom every moment was of the greatest importance–there they were night after night, listening

> to our details of the state of our unfortunate country. If a prince of the blood came there, he could not be treated with more deference or courtesy than we, the humble representatives of our suffering poor.[29]

O'Sullivan believed that what had been achieved in London for Kenmare that week ultimately saved thousands of lives.[30] After returning to Kenmare, he wrote to Trevelyan:

> Bad as matters were when we left home, they were immeasurably worse on our return. The mortality, the havoc, that death is making among the poor creatures is more than the most hardened can endure; it is calculated to unman, to unnerve, the most obdurate. The cries of starving hundreds that besiege me from morning until night actually ring in my ears during the night, and if God Almighty, in his wisdom, be pleased to continue so heavy a hand on us, the whole face of the land must needs be desolate.
>
> A few days since my curate prepared an unfortunate man, whose wife died of starvation, and at either side of him lay two children–one dead two days, the other some nine or ten hours. I attended myself a poor woman, whose infant, dead two days, lay at the foot of the bed, and four others nearly dead in the same bed; and, horrible to relate, a famished cat got up on the corpse of the poor infant and was about to gnaw it, but for my interference. I could tell you such tales of woe without end; such is not my object. Our common duty is to try and mitigate the evil, to try and propitiate the offended Deity by our exertions for our fellow men.[31]

There was some good news that same month when a steamship, *Blazer*, finally reached Kenmare with 40 tons of meal on board. The authorities worried that this government assistance might induce O'Sullivan and others to relax their own efforts to feed the local people—efforts 'worthy of imitation by other localities'.[32] Surviving correspondence from Trevelyan to O'Sullivan in 1847 shows that the priest kept up the pressure to ensure that aid continued to reached Kenmare.[33]

O'Sullivan supported calls for a meeting of diocesan priests in order to, as he put it privately in his journal, 'try and raise a cry against the landlords', amongst other objectives.[34] He also met with two Quakers who were in Kerry gathering information so that their society could distribute relief appropriately. They thought that O'Sullivan 'appears to be very actively engaged in mitigating the suffering of those around him' and that 'the clergymen of both persuasions, generally speaking, are humanely engaged in this arduous undertaking'.[35] The medical officer of the Kenmare workhouse described the institution as 'an engine for producing disease and death'.[36] Nor was disease confined to the workhouse. In May 1847, O'Sullivan wrote in his journal that 'fever and dysentery are ravaging every quarter of the parish. One hundred and twenty-four persons were buried in Old Kenmare between the first and the fourteenth of this month and it seems in no wise [sic] to be on the wane'. The fever had taken, among other people that week, two Kerry priests. Five curates were ill with it.[37]

As the potato harvest again approached, O'Sullivan inspected his own crop in a field beside his house. He thought that the only plants that might still be healthy were 'the few I got from London from the eminent Jew, David Salomons, and the four sacks I got from Cork from John Mahony–being Jersey potatoes. These are still doubtful'.[38] It appears that Salomons of the British Association had sent him potatoes that the former thought might grow well locally. Some people in Kenmare today think the motif of the Star of David that O'Sullivan later included in the church that he constructed in their town was a tribute to the London Jews who responded to his parishioners' needs during the Famine.

By April 1847 the Kenmare guardians were already noticing that a large portion of property in the Kenmare Union 'has changed hands or is altogether waste by the numbers of emigrants during the present season'.[39] In November, O'Sullivan reflected on the continuing decline around Kenmare. He noted that the failure of the potato crop in 1845 had been 'alarming enough', but that the abundance of the crop that year had compensated to a great extent for any loss. As he wrote:

> A more fatal blight destroyed it in the July of 1846 and so completely blighted them that the like misery and destitution was never before witnessed since the days of Titus before Jerusalem.
>
> The entire food of the population destroyed, the destitution that one can conceive ensued; nothing more usual than to find four or five dead bodies on the street every morning. They would remain dead in their home unburied until putrefaction would ensue, had we not employed three men to go about and convey them to the graveyard. Theft and plunder and robbery became so universal that every man's hand seemed to be lifted up against his neighbour.[40]

He found 'the frightful condition of the people ... more than flesh and blood can bear up against', admitting:

> I often bethink of taking myself to some other country rather than see with my eyes and hear with my ears the melancholy spectacles and the direful wailing of the gaunt spectres that persecute and crowd about me from morning until night imploring for some assistance. Through my English acquaintances I have been able to collect £80 for their relief–and my having afforded assistance to a good many thereby it has brought such hordes of distressed people around me that I know not what to do or how to manage.[41]

The deteriorating situation meant that O'Sullivan returned to England in late 1847. This time, he met not only with Trevelyan, but also Lord Lansdowne–who chose not to visit his vast Kerry estates during the Famine years. Trevelyan invited O'Sullivan into his own home to dine with Trevelyan's wife Hannah and her sister. O'Sullivan afterwards sent a message to the women, whose brother was the politician and historian Thomas Babington Macaulay. Trevelyan replied, 'The next time you come to London I hope you will again give us the pleasure of your company'.[42]

It was 1849 before O'Sullivan again made the long journey to London. In March of that year, he gave evidence to a select committee of the House of Commons appointed to report to parliament on the Irish poor laws. When O'Sullivan sailed for Britain from Dublin, he had not known if he would be called before the committee. Trevelyan had made it clear to O'Sullivan that 'I have nothing whatsoever to do with the summoning of the witnesses for the Committee on the Poor Law, and could not with any propriety interfere'.[43] During O'Sullivan's visit, John O'Connell MP invited him to dinner, along with 'a good many Irish', and songs were sung on that occasion.[44] This was a big moment for an Irish country priest, and he acquitted himself well. He vividly evoked the plight of the poor while proposing long-term solutions to poverty.[45] Moreover, O'Sullivan believed:

> Even though I fail, my journey to England will frighten the bigots here and I possibly may yet get summoned [to parliament] and thus come by my expenses. I will go then in God's name. My two other trips thereto [in 1847] were of infinite use to me and who can tell what good may come out of the present.[46]

Appearing before the select committee on 16 and 19 March 1849, O'Sullivan gave evidence that was both detailed and poignant. He estimated that in addition to more than 2,000 paupers within the precincts of the workhouse, a further 7,000 impoverished people were by now in receipt of outdoor relief in the Kenmare Union. He did not think that the food given in the workhouse was sufficient in quality or quantity; by now he had visited English workhouses in Stafford and London where the diet appeared to be better than in Ireland. 'I take it that Irish paupers ought to be fed as well as English every day in the year', he remarked. Work was only found for a very small proportion of those in the workhouse and O'Sullivan described those who resorted to it as being 'in great distress, emaciated, and filthy and dirty ... I do not think any pauper would go into the poorhouse till all resources failed; but of course exceptions to that will arise'. He noted that some people died rather than accepting workhouse relief. 'I know that a protracted existence has frequently occurred from their reluctance to enter the workhouse', O'Sullivan recounted, 'and thus they have wasted away by degree, till they have been like a candle that has blown out'. He was aware of instances where the very poor had died sooner than accepting relief and giving up their land. Indeed, 'I have within the last four or five weeks, known four or five persons in great destitution who hold land, and who cling to it to the very last, rather than give it up', he attested.[47]

No paupers gave evidence at Westminster. However, O'Sullivan defended them, and the Irish poor generally, against common prejudices:

> My opinion of the lower orders in Ireland is such, that they will not throw themselves upon the rates, even for out-door relief, if they can at all earn a livelihood otherwise ... With regard to some who were supposed not to need relief, I found afterwards that I had wronged those people, and that if I had administered relief to them when I was in a condition to do so, I would have kept them in their status, and they would now have been in a condition to support themselves, instead of being paupers in the workhouse ... My opinion is that no pauper will enter into the workhouse until he has been driven to it by the direst destitution ... The readiness to submit to workhouse confinement is a sufficient test of the destitution of an Irish pauper, generally speaking ... I take it to be a grievous calumny on the Irish people, to say that they prefer idleness in the workhouse to subsisting by labour outside; I am satisfied that it is, morally speaking, a positive test of a man's destitution to find him ready to submit to an Irish workhouse.[48]

O'Sullivan stressed that it was not just paupers within the workhouses but also men on outdoor relief work who were desperate. He observed that 'the families of some of them are lying down, even to my own knowledge, in fever, and they are themselves very emaciated, wretched, squalid-looking creatures.'[49] He was prepared to give credit where it was due for measures to relieve famine:

> There would have been a great many more corpses in the streets in Kenmare than we had in 1846 and 1847, if it had not been for the poor law; I am convinced of that. It was an ordinary thing in February and March 1847 to find five or six dead bodies in the streets of Kenmare every day. We had three men employed regularly, at 10*s.* 6*d.* a week each [more than twice the standard labourer's wage], and a horse and cart along with them, in conveying those dead bodies to the grave-yard [at old Kenmare]; and we had another man in the grave-yard engaged in digging a pit of a sufficient depth to receive those bodies, and all those bodies were huddled together into that pit, and that man was employed to cover them with a sufficient quantity of earth, to prevent the dead bodies being scratched up by the dogs, and to prevent effluvia escaping from those bodies. I am satisfied that we should have had the same thing occur again if it had not been for the introduction of the poor law ... As soon as it was ascertained that the potatoes had failed at once the workhouse was crowded from that time, and the people began to fall in the streets.[50]

According to O'Sullivan, whenever the Vagrancy Act had been invoked as a threat against beggars, it far from upset them, for 'we had hundreds of people imploring the police to put them in the Bridewell, in order that they might get a night's lodging and something to eat'. Some people were even committing crimes in order to be locked up.[51] More contentiously, O'Sullivan told the select committee that he personally went to great lengths, when rates were being collected under the poor law, to impress on people how important this was, 'upon the principle of its being the first law that was ever made for the poor'.[52] He sounded a radical note, calling for the reclamation and better use of land by the landlords of Ireland:

> My view is that a workhouse ought to be made as expensive as possible to the landlords, and I do not think the landlords will ever move to support the people outside the workhouse till the support of the paupers inside the house shall be made so heavy that they must, in their own defence, cultivate the land ... I would not spend beyond that which was necessary for the support of the paupers; I would not put silk stockings upon them, which would make them more expensive, but I would not go out of my way to take a burthen off the landlords which I conceive ought to be put on them, in order to induce them to cultivate the land, and employ the people.

O'Sullivan claimed that there was no priest 'who stands better with the landlords of the district than myself, no one who has given less annoyance to the landlords', but this had not stopped him pointing an accusing finger at them as a class.[53]

He was more concerned with the plight of their tenants. Regarding those able-bodied men in the workhouse who were given contrived tasks to keep them busy, but who would prefer to be working productively, he told the committee: 'I never see them in that way, rolling their wheel-barrows along, while thousands of acres which might be cultivated are at their doors, without feeling that it is enough to drive the people to desperation'. When Joseph Napier, the Conservative MP for Dublin University (Trinity College), asked him if he thought the legislature should take the unfarmed estate of one man for the purpose of supporting the pauperism on the estate of another, he answered simply 'yes'. O'Sullivan elaborated:

> If parties want land for a railroad, the legislature empowers them to take it away from the owner on paying him for it, and I propose to take the land for the purpose of supporting the people, which is of more importance than merely giving an easy drive by the construction of a railroad.

He thought that the landlords should be paid full value for the land so taken.[54]

O'Sullivan further explained how, in October 1846, he had tried to feed people by importing food and selling it at cost. 'I felt myself that it was an unusual business for a person in my sphere of life to turn flour merchant', he recalled, 'but still somebody must have done it at the time'. Asked by William Trant Fagan, Repeal MP for

Cork,[55] if the purchase and sale of provisions such as he had organised was a better mode of relieving destitution than the operation of the poor law, O'Sullivan replied firmly in the negative:

> Certainly not, because that was a thing that was entirely dependent upon the exertions of individuals. It gave the poor no established right to relief; it was a transient thing; a person may take it up today, and another may be unwilling to do it tomorrow.[56]

O'Sullivan suggested that 'if the landlords could be induced to sell part of their waste lands, and to cut them up into lots (at £500 to £1,000 each), hundreds of persons in towns, who are possessed of some capital, would be delighted to make investments in such lands'. At times, he sounded like a reforming economist, pressing the possibility of permitting the compulsory purchase of land at a fair valuation. He insisted:

> Looking to the quantity of wasteland in our union and the want of employment, one cannot understand how it is that people should be forced to go and cultivate the prairies of America when there is so much land at their doors upon which they might be profitably employed.

O'Sullivan added that he would not object to the consolidation of farms so long as it did not result in evictions, for 'that which causes such an outcry is the heart-rending scenes upon witnessing those poor creatures being cleared out in the manner they are'.[57]

O'Sullivan was troubled when the *Dublin Evening Mail* published a 'version of what I did not say' at the select committee. He informed Charles Trevelyan that he had written to another newspaper, the *Dublin Evening Post*, to correct the *Mail*. He also told Trevelyan that due to reports of the select committee appearing in the papers, 'I am lauded and abused by my friends and my foes with as much zeal on one side and acrimony on the other as if on my humble testimony was depending the entire Poor Law'. He bared his heart to the Treasury official:

> If I could go on my knees to you or to anyone and by doing so procure the discharge of the immense crowds by which the workhouse is thronged I would not hesitate in doing so ... There they are, 1,800 inmates in a house built for 500, without shoes, without clothes, in filthy rags and misery, the women squatted on the ground on the bare, cold, clay floor ... unfortunate poor women on the naked clay floor, without as much as a stool to sit on ... When you add to this the almost certainty of the cholera now in Ennis and Limerick it is frightful to reflect on the consequences.[58]

O'Sullivan told the committee that 'the wretches have not the "animus" to combine', but if they had, 'they would have long since sacked or burned the town, or done something that would of necessity have caused them to be better cared and provided for than they are at present'. During that same year, he noted that 'seven poor people who were put out of the workhouse a few days ago on outdoor relief were found dead on the road to the west of Sneem on their way home to Bordoneen'.[59]

O'Sullivan became increasingly indignant at the harrowing scenes in the Kenmare workhouse. He informed George Poulett Scrope MP, whom he also encountered in London and who was a fierce critic of the government's relief policies: 'If I am asked the question how the expense of keeping all these people alive is to be met, I would say that wherever it comes from, the thing ought to be met'.[60] As he further explained to Scrope, the workhouse was in a dreadful condition:

> In a corner you might be disgusted with the nakedness of some unfortunate wretch covered over with vermin and his unhappy comrades helping him to clean himself of some portion of it. Three and four of them sleep in a bed to which I believe they have no objection as they help to keep each other warm and the quantity of covering allowed them is no more than a mockery. They are wasting away by degrees; you could well imagine that a single breath would blow them into eternity.
>
> The most pitiful sight you could possibly witness is those poor children on the backs of others as sick and as emaciated as themselves, seeking to crawl from the auxiliary [workhouse dormitory] to the parent workhouse, to be prescribed for by the doctor. The auxiliary workshop stands a fair chance of being a pest house to the town; with 500 children in it without sewerage, the stench from it is such—and the same in the case of the workhouse—that one is obliged to hold their breath when passing by them. The poor children have no one to look after them from nightfall till the following morning but a few of the grown paupers; and such was the abuse that one of them got that the poor child died of the beating. Five paupers were put out on outdoor relief the week before last and they were found dead on the road on their return to their cabins.[61]

O'Sullivan proved to be an advocate for his parishioners in other ways. When, at Tralee Assizes, Baron Richards sentenced Patrick O'Shea, a labourer, to 12 months' imprisonment for receiving a stolen workhouse shirt, O'Sullivan appealed to Richards and Sir William Somerville for clemency. He attested to O'Shea's character, his partial disability and his industry at building dry walls ('such that even in the great dearth of employment he was never without it'). More practically, he pointed out that O'Shea's family, six in number, 'must now go into an already crowded workhouse–and the jail of Tralee at present has three times the number of prisoners for which it was built'. The prisoner was released early. O'Sullivan wrote: 'This is a satisfaction for me and will give no small annoyance to the Tories. It is a novel thing in their eyes for a priest to have as much influence'. However, his perceived influence resulted in great pressure on him by way of incessant applications for help.[62]

Privately, O'Sullivan came under increasing strain from the terrible scenes he had witnessed. He contemplated that if the potatoes would fail yet again, at least the continued calamity might 'bring about a radical change in the relations of society ... a thing that in my opinion will never be effected if the potatoes return—and can be only secured while the landed proprietors are so frightened and while the pressure on them is great'.[63] His wish was granted. In May 1849, walking out to let 'my honest dog Rover' swim in a little river nearby, O'Sullivan discovered symptoms of potato blight. He even sent some diseased stalks to Trevelyan in London, telling him of the reappearance of 'the destroying angel'. He warned that 'you can have no idea of the panic among all classes in consequence of its early appearance.'[64] That year, O'Sullivan also published a controversial letter to the people of Templenoe suggesting that, for their own sake, they should emigrate. He would prefer if they could stay at home but considered emigration necessary in the absence of radical reform. His critics regarded his proposal as a mean attempt to depopulate the lands of his foe, Rev. Denis Mahony.[65] Later in 1849, William Steuart Trench replaced the older and gentler Hickson as Lansdowne's estate agent. Trench found on his arrival around 10,0000 people were receiving government relief in the Kenmare union, inside and outside the workhouse. [66] O'Sullivan would gain notoriety for strongly encouraging and assisting the mass emigration of Lansdowne's tenants to North America.[67]

As chaplain of the Kenmare workhouse, O'Sullivan worried about the spiritual needs of its inmates. The dangerously ill were lying in beds so close to one another that 'it is very difficult for the priest to take the confession of one of these without it being overheard by those in the beds convenient'.[68] Twenty years later, J.A. Froude, the English historian who sometimes visited Kenmare and who was unsympathetic to Catholicism, was to write that 'religion down here means right and wrong, and materially, perhaps, not much besides'.[69] O'Sullivan's papers show that even during the Famine, he wanted children to learn the fundamentals of orthodox Christian faith and adults to have the sacraments made available to them with dignity. Saving souls remained as important to him as saving lives. Despite all that he had gone through, O'Sullivan experienced a sense of guilt for surviving the Great Famine in relative comfort. 'How it saddens me', he confessed, 'and makes me fear that God's judgments are in store for me to find so many of my fellow creatures so shipwrecked and myself still comparatively safe'.[70]

In the post-Famine years, O'Sullivan continued to work to improve his district, bringing in nuns to found a convent in the town and to provide education. He had a fine church erected in Kenmare, at no expense to the parishioners, financing it through donations and the diocesan trust fund. To furnish the building he had local craftsmen make copies of designs that he selected from a book of church architecture, rather than commissioning more expensive fitments from abroad.[71] Within his own church, he was a controversial figure. In 1850, O'Sullivan attended the national Synod of Thurles when Bishop Egan was ill, but neither Cardinal Paul Cullen nor the Archbishop of Tuam, John MacHale, had found his manner to their liking. There was a certain irony in this because a local Protestant, Tory newspaper had previously dubbed O'Sullivan 'John of Kenmare', a reference to the energetic and combative 'John of Tuam'–as MacHale himself was widely known.[72] In contrast, such was the impression that O'Sullivan had on his peers in Kerry that in 1853 the priests of the diocese chose him as their nominee to replace the retiring Bishop Egan. The bishops of Munster agreed with that choice. Cullen, however, thought that O'Sullivan was 'most unfit to be a bishop, a boisterous, rough man'. Instead, he ensured that David Moriarty, whom he considered 'fond of order, a disciplinarian', was appointed.[73] In 1857, Bishop Moriarty conferred the honorary title of 'Archdeacon' on O'Sullivan.[74]

Politically, O'Sullivan proved to be just as divisive. He described himself as 'a bare Repealer', being satisfied to see Ireland remain within the United Kingdom if treated fairly.[75] He strongly opposed organisations that he considered to be violent and likely to incite trouble that might rebound on young people. On one occasion, this led to his giving information to Dublin Castle that he appears to have received from a man who came to him to confess, albeit perhaps imparted outside the confessional. That incident, highlighted critically by the Fenian veteran, Jeremiah O'Donovan Rossa, was not O'Sullivan's finest moment.[76] Considering it today, it is a reminder that heroes have feet of clay, and that whatever good deeds people do, they do them despite their faults. They remain fallible, imperfect human beings.

Father John O'Sullivan of Kenmare was a complex figure whose attitudes to poverty, politics and the poor laws were complicated and, at times, controversial. Nonetheless, he embodied the spirit and sacrifice of a select group of men and women who not only devoted their lives to God, but also to the parishioners that they served. This devotion was most evident in the years after 1845 when his determination to save the lives of the poor of Kenmare brought him into contact with some of the most influential people in London society. O'Sullivan's actions during the Great Famine make him one of the many unsung heroes of these dark years.

NOTES

1. John O'Sullivan Papers (Kerry Diocesan Archives MSS), 'Random Recollections and Effusions', 1843–49 (hereafter Recollections, unpaginated but with dates, in box 1), 1–4 June 1847. Also cited from these papers below are his 'Notes of a Visitation in Kerry by a Queer Fellow', 1850–55 (hereafter Notes, 2 vols, in box 2) and "*Praxis parochi*", 1849–52 (hereafter *Praxis,* two hardback volumes numbered sequentially, in boxes 2a and 3). The O'Sullivan Papers are not simply 'diaries'–as sometimes referenced–but a mixture of notes, occasional dated entries that are not all made on the date given, drafts etc.
2. Recollections, 12 July 1847.
3. Ibid., 29 Oct. 1847.
4. See O'Sullivan's note on page 47 of his copy of (Mrs) D.P. Thompson, *A Brief Account of the Rise and Progress of the Change in Religious Opinion Now Taking Place in Dingle* (London: Seeley, Burnside and Seeley, 1846), in Kerry Library Local History Department, Tralee.
5. O'Rourke, *The Battle of the Faith in Ireland* (Dublin: Duffy, 1887), p. 532n; National Folklore Collection (UCD), Schools' Collection, vol. 0461, pp 443–4 (from Jeremiah O'Connor, aged 67, of Rock Lane Kenmare on 16 Jan. 1935).
6. Colum Kenny, *Kenmare: History and Society–Fr John O'Sullivan and the Famine Poor* (Dublin: Eastwood, 2021), pp 174–99; *Belfast Newsletter*, 21 Aug. 1849; *Freeman's Journal*, 16 Aug. 1849; *Cork Examiner*, 13, 15–16 and 24 Aug. 1849.
7. *Praxis*, pp 860–922, 938.
8. *Third Report from the Select Committees on Poor Laws (Ireland)*, with evidence, HC 1849, xxxiii, pp 133–4 (16 Mar. 1849).
9. *Ibid.*, p. 134.
10. Mary Agnes Hickson, *Selections from Old Kerry Records* (London: Watson and Hazell, 1st series 1872, 2nd series 1874), 2nd series, p. 322.
11. P. J. Hamell, *Maynooth Students and Ordinations Index 1795–1893* (Birr, Co. Offaly, 1982), p. 147 gives O'Sullivan's matriculation date as 25 Aug. 1824.
12. Egan to O'Connell, 20 Jan. 1827, cited in Pádraig de Brún, 'A Census of the Parish of Ferriter, January 1835', *Jn. Kerry Arch. and Hist. Soc.*, 7 (1974): 37–70, at p. 42.
13. Recollections, 14 Apr. 1849; Notes, pp 304–6 (3 Aug. 1851). At his copy of Thompson, *A Brief Account of ... Dingle*, p. 7 he notes this work over 13 nights, but does not deny a claim published there that 'Popish priests, terrified by the idea of contagion, actually fled the scene'.
14. Notes, pp 239–40 (28 July 1851); See O'Sullivan's copy of Thompson, *A Brief Account of ... Dingle*, pp 21–2 for his notes on this.
15. Reports of Dingle Colony: Charles Gayer, 'My Dear Christian Friends', Dingle, 26 Sept. 1839 (National Library of Ireland (NLI), MS 24,445), p. 1. For O'Sullivan in Dingle see also Bryan MacMahon, *Faith and Fury; The Evangelical Campaign in Dingle and West Kerry 1825–45* (Dublin: Eastwood, 2021), p. 345.
16. *Evidence Taken Before Her Majesty's Commissioners... on the Law and Practice in Respect to the Occupation of Land in Ireland* (Devon Commission), Part 2 (Dublin: HMSO, 1845), pp 910–23 (7 Sept. 1844) and 942–3 (7 Sept. 1844).

17. Kenmare Union Board of Guardians Records: Minute Books (Kenmare BGMB), Kerry Library Tralee MSS, 3 Jan. 1846.
18. *Kerry Evening Post*, 30 Jan. 1847.
19. Kenmare BGMB, 7 Nov. 1846 and 2 Jan. and 27 Feb. 1847; Gerard Lyne, 'An enterprising Cromwellian family: the Taylors of Dunkerron', *Jn. Kerry Arch. and Hist. Soc.*, 17 (1984), pp 61–76; G. Sayre, 'Biographical sketch of Thomas Taylor', *Journal of Bryology*, 14 (1987), pp 415–27; Burke, *Landed Gentry* (1879 ed.), 2, p. 993 suggests Taylor's grandmother was 'the daughter of an Indian Rajah'.
20. Kenmare BGMB, 9 and 30 Jan. 1847. See also 2 and 23 Jan., 6, 13 and 20 Feb., 6, 13 and 20 Mar. 1847.
21. Ibid., 12, 19 Dec. 1846.
22. Ibid., 3 July 1847, 17 Jan., 5 Feb., 17 June and 29 July 1848; *Kerry Examiner*, 18 Feb. 1848; Lyne, 'Taylors of Dunkerron', p. 72.
23. Recollections, 18 May 1847; Notes, p. 430 (21 Aug. 1851); *Praxis*, p. 905; *Select Committee 1849*, p. 134.
24. Christine Kinealy, *Charity and the Great Hunger in Ireland: The Kindness of Strangers* (London: Bloomsbury, 2013), p. 171; Christine Kinealy, 'The British Relief Association and the Great Famine in Ireland', *Revue Française de Civilisation Britannique: French Journal of British Studies*, 19, no. 2 (2014), pp 49–65; *Cork Examiner*, 31 Dec. 1849.
25. Dobree to CET, 12 Dec. 1847 (Trevelyan Papers, Irish Relief, National Archives, PRO, T64/369A/2), cited at Robin Haines, *Charles Trevelyan and the Great Irish Famine* (Dublin: Four Courts Press, 2014), p. 384.
26. British Association Minute Book 1847–48 (NLI, MS 2022), 4, 9 and 18 Jan. 1847.
27. Ibid., 2 Feb. 1847.
28. Ibid., 4 Feb. 1847.
29. *Tralee Chronicle*, 29 Dec. 1849.
30. *Praxis*, p. 905.
31. *Parliamentary Papers 52 (1847): Relief of Distress Ireland*, pp 166–7 (John O'Sullivan, vicar-general, to Trevelyan, Feb. 1847).
32. *Parliamentary Papers 52 (1847): Relief of Distress Ireland*, p. 196 (Rear-Admiral Sir Hugh Pigot to the Secretary of the Admiralty, 27 Feb. 1847, and Commodore H.E. Wingrove to Pigot, 25 Feb. and to Captain Hamilton, 27 Feb. 1847).
33. CET Archive (Newcastle University MSS), CET/1/12 pp 209–211 (CET to O'Sullivan, 25 Feb. 1847); CET/1/14 pp 164–165 (CET to O'Sullivan, 30 Apr.1847); CET/1/18 p. 153 (CET to O'Sullivan, 7 Dec. 1847); CET/1/18 pp 186–7 (13 Dec. 1847).
34. Recollections, 15 Nov. 1847, 21 May 1847.
35. Report of Richards and Fitt, 5–6 May 1847, transcribed by Kay Caball from Quaker archives (https://mykerryancestors.com/great-famine-kerry-1847/).
36. Kenmare BGMB, 22 May 1847.
37. Recollections, 15 Nov. 1847.
38. Recollections, 1 June 1847.
39. Kenmare BGMB, 10 Apr. 1847.

40. Recollections, 15 Nov. 1847.
41. Ibid., 15 Nov. 1847.
42. CET Archive, CET/1/18 p.153 (CET to O'Sullivan, 7 Dec. 1847). Kenny, *Kenmare*, pp 15–24 for a critique of Macauley's account of Kenmare's past in his four-volume *History of England*.
43. *H.L. Deb.*, 30 May 1848; CET Archive, CET/1/21 p. 264 (CET to O'Sullivan, 15 June 1848).
44. Recollections, 26 Apr. 1849.
45. *Select Committee 1849*, pp 131–64.
46. Recollections, 1 Mar. 1848.
47. *Select Committee 1849*, pp 139, 148.
48. Ibid., pp 148, 150, 155.
49. Ibid., p. 156.
50. Ibid., p. 152.
51. Ibid., p. 152.
52. Ibid., p. 140.
53. Ibid., pp 153–4, 158.
54. Ibid., pp 163–4.
55. For more on Fagan, also see chapter on William Rathbone.
56. *Select Committee 1849*, pp 134, 144.
57. Ibid., pp 144–5, 157–62.
58. Recollections, 2 Apr. 1849.
59. Ibid., 17, 21, 26 Apr. 1849.
60. George Poulett Scrope (1797–1876) was an English political economist who had a long-standing interest in Ireland. In 1835, he had used the phrase 'human encumbrances' to describe the treatment of the Irish poor by their landlords.
61. Recollections, 30 Apr. 1849.
62. Ibid., 9 Apr., 13 May 1849. Also, O'Sullivan to Somerville, at Recollections, 30 Apr. 1849.
63. Ibid., 26, 30 Apr. 1849.
64. Recollections, 8 and 9 June 1849.
65. *Select Committee 1849*, pp 157–8; *Kerry Evening Post*, 14 Mar. 1849; Kenny, *Kenmare*, pp 144–6.
66. Trench, *Realities of Irish Life*, 3rd ed. (London: Longmans, Green, 1869), p. 116.
67. C. Ó Gráda, T. Anbinder and S. Wegge, 'Assisted emigration as famine relief: lessons from the Lansdowne Estate', in *Kerry: History and Society*, M.J. Bric (ed.) (Dublin: Geography Publications, 2020), pp 367–90; Gerard Lyne, *The Lansdowne Estate in Kerry under the Agency of William Steuart Trench 1849–72* (Dublin: Geography Publications, 2001), pp 3–119.
68. *Praxis*, pp 659–60.
69. James A. Froude, 'A fortnight in Kerry', no. 1 (1869) and no. 2 (1870), in Froude, *Short Studies on Great Subjects* (New York: Scribner, 1872), pp 178–201, 344–8 at p. 200; Kenny, *Kenmare*, pp 239–40, where Oscar Wilde's mockery of a novel about the area by Froude is also considered.
70. *Holy Cross Church Kenmare 150 (1864–2014): A Social and Local History*, Holy Cross 150 History Group (eds) (Kerry: Holy Cross 150 History Group, 2014), pp 129–30.
71. Kenny, *Kenmare*, pp 235–8; *Holy Cross Church Kenmare 150*, *passim*.

72. *Kerry Evening Post*, 18 Aug. 1848, 14 Mar.1849, 5 and 12 Oct. 1850; Kenny, *Kenmare*, pp 219–21, 225–8.
73. Notes, pp 737–42 (26 Oct. 1853–3 Feb. 1854); The Papers of Tobias Kirby (Archives of the Irish College Rome), cited at Emmet Larkin, *The Making of the Roman Catholic Church in Ireland 1850–1860* (Chapel Hill: University of North Carolina Press, 1960), pp 210–11.
74. *Kerry Evening Post*, 21 Feb. 1857; *Cork Examiner*, 22 Feb. 1858.
75. *Praxis*, pp 941–3.
76. Kenny, *Kenmare*, pp 171–3.

CHAPTER THREE

LORD GEORGE HILL (1801–1879)

An Improving Landlord in Gweedore

Cathal Poírtéir

Lord George Hill bought half of the parish of Gaoth Dobhair in north-west Donegal several years before the Great Famine. By the time the potato blight first arrived in 1845, he had carried out an extensive building programme and improved the infrastructure on his 23,000-acre estate, including a quay capable of receiving large vessels, an efficient mill to grind meal, a large grain store, a dispensary and several business premises. During the Famine years, these developments were central to sustaining relief efforts in the area, as was Hill's active participation on relief committees, setting up soup kitchens and successfully lobbying government and charitable agencies for aid. One result was that the census figures for 1841 and 1851 show an increase of population in Gaoth Dobhair (Tullaghobegley West), an exceptional outcome for a parish on the impoverished Atlantic seaboard and in contrast with a devastating national population decline due to death and emigration. For that achievement alone, Lord George Hill may be regarded as a 'Famine Hero'.

Lord George Augusta Hill was born into one of the most powerful families of the Anglo-Irish nobility. They owned an estate of over 100,000 acres of good farming land in Ireland and had for generations held influential positions in Irish and British politics and society. Having arrived in Ulster with Elizabethan forces, just before the Plantation of Ulster, they had been granted and purchased extensive lands, mostly in County Down. They married well for 200 years, increasing their wealth and connections with leading families on both islands, the head of the family being raised to the rank of Marquis of Downshire. To be a Hill of Hillsborough Castle had a social cachet and was an entrée into high society in Ireland and England and royal courts in London and other European cities.

Hill was born the posthumous son of the second Marquis of Downshire who had died, perhaps by his own hand, a few months earlier. He was named after his godparents, King George III and his sister Princess Augusta. The Hill family's political fortunes had gone into decline as the second Marquis was punished for his opposition to the Act of Union of 1801, the year Lord George was born. An added misfortune was that his posthumous son was not named in his father's will and so failed to inherit a share of the family wealth in his own name. To make matters worse, relatively speaking, he had four older brothers and was most unlikely to inherit either the title of Marquis of Downshire, on his father's side, or Baron Sandys on his mother's. That left him financially dependent on his formidable mother, Mary Hill (1764–1836), Marchioness of Downshire and 1st Baroness Sandys, and on his oldest brother, the third Marquis of Downshire, Arthur Blundell Sandys Trumbull Hill (1788–1845), who took over the management of the family's estate on coming of age.

As the son of a Marquis, Hill was accorded the honorary title of Lord but was not entitled to sit in the House of Lords or pass on his title. While he enjoyed the comforts and respect accorded to the son of a wealthy and titled family, he would have to find his own way in adult life with whatever wealth family settlements, marriage or his own efforts might bring him. He received the education and upbringing that a young gentleman of his class could expect in the early nineteenth century, including private tutors at home and public school in England where he learnt languages, music and dancing, as well as becoming competent in horsemanship and fencing. Following the end of the Napoleonic Wars, he went on a grand tour of continental Europe, with his slightly older brother, Arthur Augustus (1800–1831) and a tutor, which rounded off his education before he was bought a commission in the army. His family relationship to the victorious Duke of Wellington would have added an extra bit a glamour to his arrival at the grand balls and dinners he attended.

By all accounts, Hill, the dashing young Dragoon, was popular with both men and women who found him pleasant, spirited and intelligent. While on leave from his Irish regiment in London in the summer of 1827, he met an attractive young woman, Cassandra Knight. On his return to duty in Ireland, he wrote to her with a marriage proposal, which she accepted with the blessings of her family. However, when he asked his own mother for her approval, she refused to allow the engagement, declaring famously that Cassandra was 'all charms, no money'. In his dependent financial state, Hill could not marry without his mother's consent or support. To her way of thinking, Cassandra was far from wealthy enough to be considered a good catch for her youngest son, as she would not add to his wealth or progress in society. The fact that Cassandra was a niece and godchild of the celebrated novelist Jane Austen did not sway the Marchioness of Downshire. The size of a prospective wife's dowry was her prime concern. After all, Mary Sandys was regarded as 'one of the richest of her sex in the empire'.[1] She had brought a large fortune of £60,000 into the Hill family, as well as 25,000 acres in Ireland and England and £3,000 a year. Her upbringing demanded that her youngest son must make a good match to secure his future.

Hill had to abandon hope of marrying Cassandra. He concentrated on making his way in life, occasionally benefitting from his family's wealth and enviable connections with the top echelons of society. He gradually rose through the army ranks, spent a year or so representing the family's interests as Member of Parliament for Carrickfergus (1831–1832), and served as aide-de-camp to Lieutenant General Sir John Byng, Commander of Forces in Ireland, and later as Comptroller of the Lord Lieutenant's Household in Dublin. His family's long-standing networks stood him in good stead as he moved with ease among the elite of Dublin Castle and the social life that went with that. His attendance at balls and official functions in Dublin, London, Brighton and Hillsborough was often noted with other 'fashionables' in the press, and he frequented royal occasions in the Brighton Pavilion and other favoured venues. For all that, as far as was reported, he carried on no other courtships and his mother's hopes for a good match were left unfulfilled. Several years after her refusal to allow him to marry Cassandra, Hill was informed that his first love was on the brink of an undesirable marriage. He rushed to England and proposed to her a second time. She again accepted, to her family's delight. On this occasion, his mother gave her blessing to the engagement. It is not known why she changed her mind, but she was there, in 1834, to celebrate the marriage of Hill and Cassandra at the fashionable St George's Church in Hanover Square, London, with members of the Irish and British nobility in attendance.

When Mary Hill, Marquess of Downshire and Baroness Ombersley, died in 1836, Hill was left about £25,000. It was part of a family settlement, somewhat more than he would have inherited but for the sad fact that his two sisters, Charlotte (1794–1821) and Mary (1796–1830), and his brother, Arthur Augustus Edwin Hill (1800–1831), had already died. His oldest brother, Arthur Blundell Sandys Hill, had inherited the Downshire title, and second oldest Lt.-Gen. Arthur Moyses William Hill inherited the Sandys title, leaving George and Arthur Marcus Cecil Hill to share £50,000. Hill's inheritance following his mother's death gave him the venture capital he needed to decide on his own future. He might reasonably have been expected to put money into the prospering industrial sector in Belfast or into agriculture in his native County Down but, instead, he decided to invest in the underdeveloped and inaccessible Gaeltacht parish of Gaoth Dobhair in north-west Donegal.

Hill had visited the area only once before he bought the bulk of the land that would make up his estate from 1837/1838. While on the Lord Lieutenant's staff in Dublin Castle, Hill had met Sir James Dombrain, Inspector General of the Coastguard, and had accompanied him when he was inspecting conditions in the most poverty-stricken areas on the Atlantic coast in 1834.[2] In 1829, Dombrain had bought a property in Dún Lúiche, a picturesque lake valley at the foot of Mount Errigal which dominates the skyline of Gaoth Dobhair. Hill stayed as his guest and that visit was to change the course of his life and the lives of all who lived in Gaoth Dobhair for generations to come. He was greatly affected by the dreadful conditions he witnessed. The crops had again failed that year in an area where people led a precarious existence with regular food shortages and other deprivations.

Between Hill's first visit to Gaoth Dobhair and his buying land there, Patrick McKye, a local schoolteacher, captured the dire conditions the people were living in when he presented a memorial to the Lord Lieutenant in 1836. Hill's position in Dublin and friendship with Dombrain would have given him access to the memorial, reminding him of conditions in the area where he had stayed briefly a couple of years before. It is worth quoting a stark passage from that memorial that Hill later reprinted as part of a pamphlet which he displayed in the foyer of the hotel he built there in 1842. It stated that:

> There are about 4,000 persons in this parish, and all Catholics, and as poor as I shall describe, having among them no more than-
>
> One cart, No wheel car, No coach, or any other vehicle, One plow, Sixteen harrows, Eight saddles, Two pillions, Eleven bridles, Twenty shovels, Thirty-two rakes, Seven table-forks, Ninety-three chairs, Two hundred and forty-three stools, Ten iron grapes, No swine, hogs or pigs, Twenty-seven geese, Three turkeys, Two feather beds, Eight chaff beds, Two stables, Six cow-houses, One national school, No other school, One priest, No other resident gentleman, No bonnet, No clock, Three watches, Eight brass candlesticks, No looking glasses above 3*d.* in price, No boots, no spurs, No fruit trees, No turnips, No parsnips, No carrots, No clover or any other garden vegetables, but potatoes and cabbage, and not more than ten square feet of glass in windows in the whole, with the exception of the chapel, the school house, the priest's house, Mr Dombrain's house and the constabulary barrack.
>
> None of the either married or unmarried women can afford more than one shift, and the fewest number cannot afford any, and more than one half of both men and women cannot afford shoes on their feet, nor can many of them afford a second bed, but whole families of sons and daughters of mature age are indiscriminately lying [sic] together with their parents, and all in the bare buff.

> They have no means of harrowing their land but with meadow rakes. Their farms are so small that from four to ten farms can be harrowed in one day with a rake, Their beds are straw, green and dried rushes, or mountain bent; their bedclothes are either course sheets or no sheets, and raggy, filthy blankets.
>
> And worse than all I have mentioned, there is a general prospect of starvation at the present prevailing on them, and that originating from various causes, but the principal cause is a rot or failure of seed in the last year's crop, together with a scarcity of winter forrage, in consequence of a long continuation of storms since October last in this part of the country. So that they, the people, were under the necessity of cutting down their potatoes, and give [sic] them to their cattle to keep them alive. All these circumstances connected together, have brought hunger to reign among them to that degree, that the generality of the peasantry are on the small allowance of one meal a day, and sometimes one meal in three days. Their children are crying and fainting with hunger, and their parents weeping, being full of grief, hunger, debility and dejection, with glooming aspect, looking at their children likely to expire in the jaws of starvation.
>
> Also, in addition to all, their cattle and sheep are dying with hunger, and the owners forced by hunger to eat the flesh of such. 'Tis reasonable to suppose that the use of such flesh will raise some infectious diseases among the people, and it may very reasonably be supposed, that the people will die even faster than the cattle and sheep, if some immediate relief be not sent to alleviate their hunger.[3]

The writer offers support for the accuracy of the memorial by referencing the Parish Priest, Father Hugh O'Friel, the local head constable, and Capt. Penfold, chief officer of the Coastguard in the area. O'Friel had written the previous year to the *Ballyshannon Herald* complaining of widespread distress in the area with nine-tenths of the people starving. He castigated those landlords who had failed to contribute to relief measures and thanked those who did.[4] Having witnessed similar dire circumstances, Hill decided over the following few years to invest his legacy in Gaoth Dobhair. He spent the rest of his life involved in the uphill task of developing his Gaoth Dobhair estate to support its population while making enough profit from it to sustain himself and his growing family. For the first time, the tenants of Gaoth Dobhair had an improving and, more or less, resident landlord. He visited each family on his estate and the tenants were reported to have found it difficult to believe that this young man who spoke Irish to them could be a landlord.[5]

Hill's interest in the Irish language and literature predated his arrival in Donegal and he already had an impressive collection of Irish language manuscripts. Owen Conellan, first Professor of Celtic in Queen's College Cork, described Hill as 'a zealous investigator of Irish literature'[6] and dedicated a translation of St John's Gospel to him, 'grown under your lordship's fostering influence'.[7] When he published

A Practical Grammar for the Irish Language in 1844, he also dedicated that to Hill, citing 'respect for your Lordships acquirements as an Irish scholar'.[8] Hill's brother, the third Marquess of Downshire, was the first president of the Ulster Gaelic Society, Cuideacht Gaedhilge Uladh, in 1830.[9] Enthusiasm for Gaelic culture was not entirely unusual among the gentry, but Hill's commitment is notable for his sustained effort to increase his knowledge of the language and in trying to inspire a similar interest in his children, as witnessed in a letter from Connellan to the antiquarian John Windele.[10]

As the owner of an estate, Hill took his cue from his mother and brother in aiming to be an efficient and progressive landlord. He immediately began modernising his estate, setting up businesses and services, transforming traditional farming practices and settlement patterns, improving communications and building the area's first hotel, all within seven years of becoming the main landlord in Gaoth Dobhair. He saw the traditional rundale system of agriculture as archaic and inefficient and prioritised putting an end to it. In Ireland, this co-operative system still operated in a few less developed areas where it was seen as a way to share limited resources in a fair way. Under population pressure and continued sub-division, the system was already under threat before Hill arrived with his ideas of more modern agricultural practices.

As his brother, the Marquis of Downshire, had recently done in County Down, Hill employed surveyors to draw up a detailed plan of the entire estate during 1841–1843, asking them to design a more efficient method of land division. The proposed 'squaring' of the traditional open, scattered patchwork of family holdings was revolutionary in pre-famine Gaoth Dobhair. It ignored the accepted logic that had produced a co-operative system for generations and aimed at transforming where and how those families lived and farmed. People would have to demolish their old homes in the traditional house clusters (referred to as *clachans* by many geographers, but known as *baile* and *bailte* by Irish speakers) and rebuild them as stand-alone houses in a regularly shaped and enclosed family holding. The disruption would be on such a large scale and of such long-term consequence that it was unlikely to be accepted without protest from a community that had previously been left to live by its own lights.

A tenants' committee, led by the local priest, objected. They impressed on Hill and his surveyors that their proposals would mean that one squared farm would be in a place with good land and another in a place with poor land and that such inequality was not acceptable. Under the old system, people held unfenced patches in various places that ensured that everyone had an equitable mixture of good, middling and poor land and access to water. The parish committee proposed that each holding be in two strips of varying quality with access to natural resources. Hill eventually compromised by allowing farms in one long narrow strip, an arrangement not ideal for either side; but the tenants accepted the revised plan although there was still some opposition to it. As Thomas Campbell Foster observed:

> They suspected everything that was attempted and opposed it, thinking it was intended for their injury and the landlord's benefit, and by harassing and vexatious opposition hoped, as they expected it, in the end to tire out Lord George Hill, prevent the divisions from being occupied and thus defeat the new plans altogether.[11]

The landlord's willingness to accommodate the tenants' committee helped him accomplish most of his intended revolutionary transformation reasonably peacefully. Perhaps this was helped by his knowledge of the Irish language, personal visits to each household and the fact that most tenants would have recognised that as landlord he had the upper hand in how his estate was managed. The people may also have realised that a growing population was overstretching the traditional rundale system. The devastation caused to many coastal holdings by the Night of the Big Wind in January 1839 added to land pressure as salt water and sand encroached and put some land beyond agricultural use. It would also have helped that the new landlord offered to write off long standing arrears if tenants paid just two years of outstanding rents. The possibility of starting with a clean slate would have been an attractive proposition for those in serious arrears. Hill also announced that all rents would in future be collected regularly and arrears would not be tolerated. He would allow tenants to pay their old rents on the new farms for several years while they rebuilt their houses and improved their new holdings at their own expense. While he later portrayed his transformation of Gaoth Dobhair as having gone off almost without a hitch, the truth is that there were some who opposed him from the beginning: 'bad advisers, and would-be agitators'.[12] Despite his early willingness to compromise, Hill left tenants in no doubt about what he found acceptable. He was not averse to placing tenants under notice to quit to enforce his policies.

Hill also offered the enticement of living rent-free for several years to young couples who agreed to build houses and farm 'new cuts' of six to nine acres on previously rough pasture. These 'cuts' were on terrain that tenants regarded as common land which they grazed or occasionally cultivated on the fringes of the settlement area. Hill made this land available for new farms to prevent parents sub-dividing their holdings and to create new tenancies that would eventually earn him increased rental income. His thinking was that a family would make a greater effort to improve a clearly defined holding that would not be subject to redistribution under rundale. Hill announced the outlawing of any return to sub-division of farms and the new cuts were quickly taken up by young married couples from the community, some worried that they might otherwise be allotted to outsiders. In his own words:

> The old plan of dividing the Land among the Children of a Family has made many Beggars; this will, therefore, no longer be allowed.
>
> No Land can now be Divided, nor Bought, nor Sold, whether by Will, or under any pretence: nor can any House be built or Enlarged without permission being first given for the same by Mr. Forster, through the District Bailiff. [...] Any Tenant breaking through these rules will be Ejected from his Farm, and be put out of the Estate.
>
> The Bailiffs have strict orders to see that these regulations are enforced: and it is hoped that the Tenants will see that these Rules are made, like the new division of the Land, for their good.
>
> By their sincere Friend and Landlord,
> GEORGE A. HILL
> Gweedore, 1844.[13]

Hill was not as wealthy as the people and priests of Gaoth Dobhair might have imagined from what they knew of his prestigious family background. He had already spent much of his inheritance buying and developing his Gaoth Dobhair estate and in purchasing and renovating Ballyare House where he and his family lived near Ramelton, about 17 miles from Gaoth Dobhair. From Lord George Hill's memorandum book, it appears that he spent £19,000 on purchasing lands in Gaoth Dobhair[14] and a further £9,000 on building developments there, as well as £8,000 he spent on Ballyare.[15] His early expenditure on his major investments, particularly on the quay, buildings and infrastructure around An Bun Beag, and later on the hotel and model farm in Mín an Chuing, limited what further developments he could afford until rental income allowed him to do so. His notebook shows that he was dependent on loans from family and friends on several occasions for personal and estate expenditure.

From the early 1840s, Hill promoted annual premiums to encourage improvements in agricultural practices, animal husbandry and living conditions. He expressed his thanks to charitable bodies which helped fund cash prizes for the winning tenants. While not a single tenant entered the first year of the competition in 1839, 36 took part the following year and by 1844, 239 competed for a prize fund of £60. In 1843, the judges, including the parish priest of Gaoth Dobhair, Father Hugh McFadden, recorded the improvements made by some of Hill's tenants, contrasting greatly with the picture given in Patrick McKye's memorial to the Lord Lieutenant just a few years before in 1836. Hill himself observed that:

> Now we behold in all directions neat and comfortable cottages, attracting the eye by their well-thatched roofs and white-washed walls, giving an aspect of life, health

> and cheerfulness: nor were we disappointed on a closer inspection; we found that the interior of the houses fully realised the expectations raised by their exterior appearance, clean, orderly, and well ventilated rooms, comfortable and suitable beds and bedsteads, with a supply of bed clothing and furniture equal at least to the wants of the inmates, and in many instances showing a taste in the arrangement for which we were quite unprepared.[16]

The rules of the competitions included disqualification for anyone found guilty of a crime, including the making or drinking of poteen, and a few tenants were disqualified who would otherwise have been winners, causing understandable resentment. Illegal whiskey distillation and poteen drinking was widespread in the area and although Hill was happy to sell alcohol in his hotel, he was determined to stamp out illegal distillation and alcohol abuse among the tenants. One of his reasons for building the large grain store in Bun Beag was to encourage local people to sell their grain to the store at market price rather than supply or barter it with poteen makers as many had been doing. He had some limited success in reducing illicit distillation, but eventually had to admit that the poteen trade continued no matter what he did.

Hill's name and position in society carried weight when he brought pressure to bear on the authorities. His efforts helped Gaoth Dobhair not only receive emergency aid when needed, but also saw improved bridges and roads that made travel and commerce easier for landlord, tenant and tourist alike.

Commerce was central to Hill's vision for Gaoth Dobhair. One of the first tasks he set himself was to improve the well-sheltered harbour at An Bun Beag by constructing a new quay that could take larger ships and facilitate the import and export of goods. He invested in buildings to encourage business and improve services in the area. In his first five or six years, he built a large grain store and a cash-only general store, a corn-mill, a saw-mill, a flax-mill, an ice-house, a lime kiln, houses for the coast-guard, a barracks, a dispensary, a bakery, a school and a church for the new Protestant community he had enticed to come to the area to rent business premises from him and to provide skilled labour. The grain mill cost him £750 to build and was crucial in the area during the Famine as it was the only one for miles that could grind Indian corn.[17] The presence of a local doctor and dispensary were also important and Dr Brady worked with Hill to distribute aid. He recounted that:

> I have frequently been made the almoner of Lord George Hill. He has repeatedly given me money to distribute to the people there, not only during the famine but many times since and he has always been most particular, whenever he came to the country, in enquiring of me as to the state of the parties, or if I thought that any of them wanted relief in any way, particularly when I lived at the Gweedore Hotel.[18]

The hotel was the showpiece of Hill's estate. He opened it in 1842 to attract tourists to north-west Donegal. He hoped the Gweedore Hotel would become a popular destination, providing locals with employment and himself with another income stream. Hunting, shooting and fishing were among the attractions, along with boat trips on the lake, hill walking and pony trekking. The hotel quickly developed a reputation for high quality accommodation, excellent food and drink and a warm welcome, often from 'the noble proprietor' himself. The two volumes of the Gweedore Hotel visitors' book give ample evidence of customer satisfaction and the highest praise for Hill's hotel and his efforts to improve the conditions of his tenants.[19]

In 1845, Hill published a pamphlet called *Facts From Gweedore*. It was a celebration of what he had achieved in the area in his first seven or eight years as landlord. It was entirely uncritical of Hill and was written to publicise the improvements that an enterprising and reforming landlord could achieve, even in such a challenging environment. Another pamphlet, *Useful Hints for Donegal Tourists*, was published the following year and the two were later combined in future editions in 1846, 1854, 1868 and 1887. Hill became one of the best-known landlords in Ireland, partly due to *Facts*, which put the area on the map for politicians and administrators, as well as for many writers and journalists who visited Gaoth Dobhair as part of their fact-finding tours. They included Asenath Nicholson, an American philanthropist,[20] James Hack Tuke, an influential Quaker,[21] Campbell Foster, 'The *Times*' Commissioner',[22] and Thomas Carlyle, a social commentator,[23] to name but a few.[24] Gaoth Dobhair, almost totally unknown outside the north-west before the arrival of Lord George Hill, was now mentioned in the British parliament and international press, a factor likely to encourage more attention from the authorities than before.

The Hills had rented Gortlee House near Letterkenny while renovations were being carried out to Ballyare House, outside Ramelton, which was to become their family home. It was there that Cassandra gave birth to their fourth child in March 1842, the first of their children to be born in Ireland. Unfortunately, and unexpectedly, Cassandra died of puerperal fever a few days after the birth, leaving her grieving husband to look after four children under seven years of age.[25] Cassandra was just 36. Her unmarried sister, Louisa Knight, undertook to look after her nieces and nephews in a house that Hill rented for them in Uptown, Kent. As he came to terms with his loss and made arrangements for his family's future, Lord George asked his oldest brother Downshire to oversee the completion and staffing of the Gweedore Hotel which was due to open that summer. He soon returned to Donegal to oversee the finishing touches to Ballyare House and to greet the first guests to the hotel in August 1842. He travelled every week from Ballyare to Gaoth Dobhair to welcome guests and consult with his estate staff. He made regular trips to England to see his children and Louisa later consented to move to Ireland to look after her nieces and nephews in the house which was originally to have been her deceased sister's Irish home.

Hill had appointed a minor landlord from the Rosses as his agent. Francis Forester ensured that Hill's plans were put into action. Another appointment Hill made was of William Robinson, a Scottish agriculturalist who helped him make more efficient use of his land and served as an advisor to the tenants, encouraging them to adopt modern efficient practices on their farms. Hill reclaimed land around his hotel and turned it into a model farm, providing vegetables for hotel guests, hay for their horses and, he hoped, a good example for his tenants on how to improve their own holdings. Hill, of course, had the financial resources to carry out his improvements quickly, whereas few of his tenants had the means to do the same. Nevertheless, many visitors remarked on what could be achieved by investing time and money, even on unpromising land. They often referred to the hotel and farm as Hill's 'oasis in the wilderness'.

The details of any long-term business plans that Hill may have had for his Gaoth Dobhair estate are not known. It is reasonable to assume that he was hoping that his initial investment in buying and developing the estate would later begin to pay off, perhaps from the late 1840s or early 1850s when the grace period of old rents on new farms and no rents on 'new cuts' would have come to an end, giving him increased and regular rental income. Whatever projections or hopes he may have had, the arrival of the potato blight in 1845 and the famine that followed for several years would have forced him to abandon any original strategy and to concentrate instead on saving his tenants from the worst ravages of what was to become known as the Great Famine.

Hill's actions contrasted starkly with the general perception of how Irish landlords responded to the crisis. He became chairman of the local relief committee and helped set up soup kitchens in Sraith na Corcra, Dún Lúche and an Bun Beag.[26] When it quickly became obvious that the scale of the disaster was beyond what Hill could provide from his own resources, he appealed to government and to charities for funds to help his tenants and he involved his in-laws in fund raising in England.[27] He lobbied the Central Relief Committee in Dublin and warned them of the perilous situation of the impoverished population in west Donegal, requesting shipments of seed and emergency food supplies.[28] Hill's social standing also allowed him to ignore official policy when he saw dire need and he openly sold corn below market price—something that government relief committees were unable to do.[29] As Christine Kinealy notes:

> It is significant that in the crucial winter of 1846–7, the committees in this area flouted the strict guidelines of the government and sold corn to the population at below the market price and before the designated time. In areas where the local

> relief committees had neither the capital, the foresight, nor the motivation to initiate an effective remedy, the local population bore the fatal consequences of the government's short-sighted policy.[30]

There is no doubt that there was extreme hardship and widespread hunger in the area, but it appears that few if any tenants on Hill's estate died of starvation. He claimed that none of them died of hunger but did admit that some were lost due to their age and weakened condition:

> The people are all of them in a starving condition, few having more than one scanty meal in the twenty-four hours. On this account, together with the very unwholesome nature of the food, severe Dysentery has broken out, and is daily hurrying numbers into eternity.[31]

In addition to attending to the needs of his tenants, Hill served on one of the national committees established in the wake of the second crop failure. The Irish Relief Association had been formed on 2 September 1846, with an office in Sackville Street in Dublin. Hill was one of its honorary secretaries.[32] One of the first actions of the committee was to charter a steamship in Liverpool and load her with provisions for counties Donegal and Mayo, at a cost of £1,796.[33] During the spring of 1847, the Association provided hundreds of boilers throughout the west of Ireland to facilitate the opening of private soup kitchens.[34] Hill's reputation and connections also meant that he received grants from the British Relief Association to support the work of the local relief committees in Gweedore.[35]

During 'Black '47', one of the worst years of famine, Hill did not collect any rent from his tenants who were struggling to buy food with what little money they had. In 1854, another year where the crops largely failed, they appealed to him to forgive another year's rent and he reduced it by one third, with a commitment from the tenants that they would pay the full amount the following year, which they did. He was the only local landlord who allowed a rent reduction that year. The people of Gaoth Dobhair managed to survive the Great Famine with little loss of life. The census figures even recorded a slight growth in the population from 1841–1851, although shortcomings in the general 1841 census figures might have accounted for this number. Nonetheless, it was in marked contrast to the experience of many districts in County Donegal.

The opening of the Gweedore Hotel in the summer of 1842 and the warm reception of the publication of *Facts from Gweedore* in 1845 saw almost universal praise for Lord George Hill and his achievements as an improving landlord on the eve of the Great Famine. He was lauded in the press and in parliament and was held up as an example to other Irish landlords by Prime Minister Sir Robert Peel and by many other politicians and journalists. As a consequence, Hill became the best-known and most highly praised Irish landlord of the period. As a result of the publicity engendered by *Facts from Gweedore*, tourists, officials and writers of various types came to stay at the hotel. The vast majority of them lavished praise on what Hill was doing there, although some did question whether he could turn a profit from such a challenging undertaking.[36] That had always been a difficult proposition given the unpromising environment, but Hill had taken on the task motivated by 'a potent combination of both profit and philanthropy'.[37] The disaster of the Famine meant that he had to forget any thoughts of starting to make a profit during those years, as he fulfilled what he considered to be his moral obligations to his tenants.

Not only did Hill need to look after his tenants in Gaoth Dobhair, but he also had four motherless children to raise and make provision for. They spent much of the year with him in Ballyare being looked after by their aunt Louisa while Hill travelled weekly to oversee the work in Gaoth Dobhair. After a few years of rearing his children and regularly living under the same roof as him, Louisa married her sister's widower to become the children's step-mother in May 1845. Marrying her dead sister's widower was illegal in Britain at the time and the couple had to wed in Wandsbeck, Denmark. When the ensuing controversy was discussed in parliament, Hill and his new wife were supported by friends of high standing, and so underwent no loss of social status or consequent damage to their children's prospects of advancement or marriage in Victorian high society.[38] It later came as a pleasant surprise when Louisa became pregnant and gave birth in 1849, at 44 years old, to a son, George Marcus Wandsbeck Hill.

The birth of a fifth child meant additional costs in educating and preparing the family for their places in society. Like others of their class, the Hills were expected to make good matches for the girls that would ensure their financial security and prepare the boys for careers, possibly as government officials, politicians or army officers. Hill did not always have money to hand when he wanted or needed to do things, either on his estate or in his family life, and his accounts show him borrowing and repaying money from family, friends and business associates from time to time.[39] He needed a substantial loan from his brother Marcus to pay for his daughter's wedding to Somerset Ward, son of the third Viscount Bangor;[40] and when his eldest son Arthur needed a commission to join the army, it was arranged by a family friend and his uncle Atty gave him an annual allowance.[41]

While Lord George Hill and his young family led a comfortable life and maintained a lifestyle that would have been unimaginable to his tenants, he occasionally ran into some financial problems. Normally though, he lived on his farming and estate income with some interest from investments.[42] After the devastation of the Famine years, hundreds of landed proprietors had gone to the wall and their already indebted estates were sold off by the Encumbered Estates Court. Hill did his utmost to ensure that his Donegal estate remained viable and to do that he needed higher income. When he had bought the estate and moved the tenants to the new strip farms, he had raised their rents but had allowed them to pay the old rates for several years to compensate them for their time and labour in demolishing their old homes and rebuilding them on the new strips. Similarly, he had given 'new cuts' rent free for several years to encourage young couples to take them up and develop them. The severe financial distress the tenants had suffered during the Famine had stayed Hill's hand in looking for the new, higher rents, but when the worst years appeared to be over by the early 1850s, Hill decided that it was time to collect them.

Hill had avoided confrontation before the Famine by consulting with the tenants and modifying his plans accordingly. Those who received new cuts from Hill were grateful for them, but some others were unhappy that the lands involved were lost to them as areas for occasional cultivation or blocked their access to mountain pastures. There was some simmering resentment evidenced in occasional isolated incidents from the late 1840s, but there was little widespread or sustained opposition. Not surprisingly, when Hill looked for the new rents in the 1850s tenants were unhappy to have this extra financial burden visited on them just as they were struggling to get back on their feet after the Famine.

What sparked serious landlord-tenant conflict in Gaoth Dobhair was the controversial decision by Hill and other landlords to lease large parts of the mountains to foreign sheep farmers in the mid–1850s to take advantages of the profits that could now be made from that. Such land had previously given them little return for their investments when used as commonage by their tenants. The setting of land to the big sheep farmers caused tenants to lose their traditional grazing rights on the mountain pastures. Tenant dissatisfaction grew and led to attacks by Molly Maguires and other anti-grazier actions in what became known as the Gweedore Sheep War between 1856–1858.[43]

A propaganda war was fought with local priests and tenants as fears were stoked that the introduction of the sheep farmers might be a prelude to clearances as had happened in the Scottish Highlands when sheep proved more profitable than tenants for some big landowners. Extra police were drafted into the area when shepherds were attacked and sheep started to disappear. Local people were arrested, the general population heavily fined for stealing and destroying sheep and then taxed again for the presence of the extra police. Many poor people found it difficult enough to pay their rents and the unjust imposition of the sheep and police taxes on the entire population caused widespread distress and resentment. Local Catholic clergy campaigned to draw attention to the injustice and highlighted the deprivations that resulted from paying the fines. They claimed that the landlords had long been guilty of neglecting their duties to their tenants and alleged that it was their behaviour that was the root cause of the dire poverty in the area.

The conflict eventually came to an end with a parliamentary select committee inquiry into destitution (Gweedore and Cloughaneeley) established in the summer of 1858 at which both sides gave evidence. Not surprisingly, considering its composition, the committee's 400-page report found in favour of the landlords that there was no 'destitution', as they defined it, and that the landlords were not responsible for the extreme poverty in the area. It was a hard fought and bitter campaign and Lord George Hill protested against being characterised as an avaricious or uncaring landlord. He protested that:

> I am not the person represented by this petition, for I have had to borrow £2,000 since the famine to carry out those improvements in Gweedore. I live with my family in a small house which I built, upon a small farm, in order to enable me to attend and overlook those improvements; we live in a most frugal manner, and if I get to the end of the year, able to pay the calls upon me, I thank God that I have done so. This is my avarice.[44]

When the sheep war ended, Lord George Hill made efforts to get the authorities to leave the rest of the extra taxes uncollected to prevent further unnecessary suffering. For their part, the tenants signed a letter that expressed their regret for what had happened and 'our firm determination to suppress (as far as we are able) such disgraceful proceedings for the future'.[45] In the end, taxes were left uncollected and the tenants regained rights to the mountain pastures by agreeing to a small grazing fee being included in their rents.

Hill felt personally aggrieved that many of his tenants had sided against him during the sheep war and was a less frequent visitor afterwards. Nevertheless, he bought another 1,000 acres in the parish in 1862, enlarged the hotel and continued to promote the sale of local home-knits at home and abroad. He remained involved in many charitable, cultural and church bodies and made efforts to find new ways to exploit the natural resources of the area. Gaoth Dobhair remained peaceful for the rest of Hill's life, but those few troubled years in the late 1850s and the allegations made against him have had a long afterlife.

The idea that Hill might be referred to as a hero of the Great Famine would have Canon James McFadden turning in his grave.[46] He was posted to Gaoth Dobhair in

1873 and became parish priest there in 1876, just before the death of Lord George Hill. McFadden led the the anti landlord Land League campaign of the 1870s and Plan of Campaign in Donegal in the 1880s. Although dead, Hill became one of McFadden's main targets when he became embroiled in a bitter conflict with Captain Arthur Hill, who inherited his father's estate in 1879. That struggle became violent, leading to murder, mayhem and martial law in Gaoth Dobhair where evictions by Capt. Arthur Hill were resisted by local people, led by McFadden, also known as 'The fighting priest of Gweedore'. He served six months in prison in Derry for Land League agitation and while incarcerated in Derry Gaol he wrote a pamphlet called *The Present and Past of the Agrarian Struggle in Gweedore*. Although written and published in 1889, ten years after Hill's death, McFadden damned him as much as his son whose evictions he was fighting on the ground. The language of the pamphlet was often intemperate in its attacks on the deceased Lord George Hill and helped produce a distorted view of him which has coloured some later opinion. A reading of the contemporary evidence, however, leaves the feeling that Hill did his best to be a good landlord in the extremely challenging circumstances in which he found himself. Some of his decisions and attitudes can be questioned, but there is no doubt that he did his utmost to keep his tenants alive and living at home. He may have been paternalistic or stubborn at times but, for the most part, his intentions appear to have been good-hearted. That he failed to understand his tenants' dismay at their loss of rights to their traditional mountain commonage is not surprising given his entirely different understanding of his property rights as a landlord.

During the worst of the Famine, Hill had forgiven a full year's rent, collected a reduced rent another year and had ensured emergency food supplies for his tenants. He regularly consulted the local doctor to discover who was in most need and gave money to relieve their distress. His development of buildings, businesses and services provided paid employment for hotel and estate staff, seasonal labourers, turf cutters and harvesters. The development of bridle roads and bridges through the estate gave employment and allowed easier access to grazing land and houses. Hill carried out no permanent evictions, although in a few cases he threatened to do so until tenants undertook to abide by his view of acceptable behaviour, evicting one man temporarily. In a period where mass evictions and the clearing of tenants from the land were widespread on many Irish estates, Hill's more tolerant attitude is worthy of note. Any fair reading of his actions through the years up to and including the Great Famine support a claim for Lord George Hill as a famine hero.

NOTES

1. Kathy Trent, *The Blessington Estate 1667–1908* (Dublin: Anvil Books, 2004), p. 50.
2. In the Gweedore Hotel Visitors' Book, Dombrain mistakenly gives the year as 1832 but later corrects this in a letter to the *Express* in 1858. Hill's evidence to the parliamentary select committee on Destitution (Gweedore and Cloughaneeley) confirms 1834.
3. Lord George Hill, *Facts from Gweedore,* 3rd edition (1854), pp 11–12 (1st edition, Dublin: Philip Dixon, Hardy and Sons, 1845).
4. *Ballyshannon Herald*, 24 June 1835.
5. *Facts from Gweedore,* 3rd edition (1854), p. 31.
6. *Waterford Chronicle*, 2 Nov. 1833.
7. Proinsias Ó Conluain, '*His Life and Fortune to Civilise Gweedore*', RTÉ Radio 1 documentary (1975).
8. Owen Connellan, *A Practical Grammar of the Irish Language* (Dublin: B. Geraghty, 1844), p. 6.
9. Breandán Ó Buachalla, *Béal Feirste Cois Cuain* (Dublin: An Clóchomhar 1968), p. 79.
10. Connellan to Windele, Royal Irish Academy 12/2/12/55 (ii).
11. Thomas Campbell Foster, *Letters on the condition of the people of Ireland* (London: Chapman and Hall, 1846), pp 116–28.
12. *Facts from Gweedore*, Introduction to Facsimile reprint of his fifth edition of 1887 (Belfast: Institute of Irish Studies, 1971).
13. *Facts from Gweedore* 3rd edition (1854), (1st edition, Dublin: Philip Dixon, Hardy and Sons, 1845), *Appendix III., Notice to Tenants*.
14. *Memorandum Book of Lord George Hill*, Downshire Papers, PRONI D3054/3/1/2, p. 9.
15. Ibid., p. 10.
16. *Facts from Gweedore*, 3rd edition (1854), p. 40.
17. *Report from the Select Committee on Destitution (Gweedore and Cloughaneely); together with the proceedings of the committee, minutes of evidence, appendix, and index; Minutes of Evidence HC* (412) (1857/1858), British House of Commons Sessional Papers, 1858, H.C. 412, p. 279.
18. *Destitution*, p. 262.
19. *Gweedore Hotel Visitors' Book*, Donegal County Archive, Lifford. Two volumes.
20. Asenath Nicholson, *Annals of the Famine in Ireland,* Maureen Murphy (ed.) (Dublin: The Lilliput Press, 1988) and *Ireland's Welcome to the Stranger,* Maureen Murphy (ed.) (Dublin: Lilliput Press, 2002).
21. James H. Tuke, *Report in Transactions of the Central Relief Committee of the Society of Friends during the Famine in Ireland in 1846 and 1847; with and index by Rob Goodbody* (Dublin: Edmund Burke Publishers, 1996).
22. Thomas Campbell Foster (The *Times* Commissioner), *Letters on the condition of the people of Ireland* (London: Chapman and Hall, 1846).
23. Thomas Carlyle, *Reminiscences of my Irish Journey in 1849* (London: Gilbert and Rivington, 1882).
24. Asenath Nicholson and James Hack Tuke are featured in vol. one of *Heroes of Ireland's Great Hunger.*

25. 'Death of Distinguished Persons', *The Atlas*, 26 Mar. 1842.
26. National Archives of Ireland, RLFC/3/2/7/12.
27. Sophia Hillan, *May, Lou and Cass, Jane Austen's nieces in Ireland* (Belfast: The Blackstaff Press, 2011), pp 128–9.
28. Hill to Routh, *Famine Relief Commission Papers*, 10 Sept. 1846 and 6 Jan. 1847.
29. *Northern Whig*, 12 Jan. 1847.
30. Christine Kinealy *This Great Calamity, the Irish Famine 1845–52* (Dublin: Gill & Macmillan, 1994), p. 349.
31. *Distress at Gweedore,* quoted in Hillan, pp 128–9.
32. For more on the work of the Irish Relief Association, see Christine Kinealy, *Charity and the Great Hunger in Ireland: The Kindness of Strangers* (London: Bloomsbury, 2013).
33. Irish Relief Association for the destitute Peasantry, *Distress in Ireland* (Dublin: Philip Hardy and Sons, 1847), p. 8.
34. Applications to the Irish Relief Association, 1846–1847, Royal Irish Academy, Dublin, MS 27. Q. 24.
35. Charles Trevelyan to Jones-Loyd, 18 Jan. 1847, *Correspondence Relating to Measures for the Relief of Distress in Ireland*, Jan. to Mar. 1847, British Parliamentary Papers, House of Commons, p. 64.
36. Dombrain, 16 Sept. 1846, *Gweedore Hotel Visitors' Book* 1, p. 123.
37. Breandán Mac Suibhne, 'Agrarian Improvement and Social Unrest: Lord George Hill and The Gweedore Sheep War' in *Donegal History and Society*, William Nolan, Liam Ronyane and Mairéad Dunlevy (eds) (Dublin: Geography Publications, 1995), p. 553.
38. 25 Feb. 1851, *Marriages Bill, House of Lords*, debates. http://hansard.millbanksystems.com/lords/1851/feb/25/marriages-bill.
39. *Memorandum Book of Lord George Hill*, Downshire Papers, PRONI D3054/3/1/2, pp 20, 22, 26.
40. Ombersley, AFSH: 20. Cited in unpublished work on Lord George Hill by Roy Greenslade.
41. Ombersley, Atty: 36. Cited in unpublished work on Lord George Hill by Roy Greenslade.
42. Downshire Papers, PRONI D3054/3/1/2, 6.
43. Mac Suibhne (1995).
44. *Destitution*, p. 288.
45. Cited in Mac Suibhne, p. 572.
46. Canon James McFadden (1842–1917) was born in Doochary, County Donegal, and was educated at Maynooth. He was known as 'An Sagart Mór', meaning 'The Big Priest'.

CHAPTER FOUR

SIR ROBERT GORE BOOTH (1805–1876) AND THE GREAT FAMINE IN COUNTY SLIGO

Gerard Moran

The role of the Irish landlord during the Great Hunger has been examined, analysed and assessed by historians, geographers, economists, sociologists and others, and the overall conclusion has been to portray them in a poor light, they doing little to provide relief and assistance for their starving tenants and resorting to large scale clearances from their estates.[1] They have been especially criticised for their lack of engagement in relief efforts and the evictions carried out in the aftermath of the Gregory Acre Clause (1847) which stated that tenants with holdings over one-quarter of an acre were ineligible for public assistance either inside or outside the workhouse. However, the 8,000 landed proprietors were not a homogenous group: some owned estates in excess of 100,000 acres while others held less than 1,000 acres; many resided on their estates while a minority were absentees living in England, who had little direct involvement with the running of their Irish properties. Only when a detailed examination of individual properties is undertaken, can a more definitive conclusion be arrived at, but this is difficult as the estate records are not always available and, in some cases, have been permanently lost. This does not mean that we should not assess those properties where records are available, and which show how individual landowners treated their tenants during what was the greatest calamity to affect western Europe in the nineteenth century.

The estate records for the Gore Booth property in County Sligo for the Famine period are available. At the time of the Famine, the estate comprised of 32,500 acres, making it one of the largest in the county. It was divided into two sections: the barony of Carbury that extended over 12,000 acres, and the barony of Corran of 16,000 acres, purchased in 1838 for £130,000 from the Earl of Orkney and including the town of Ballymote. The family had also inherited a valuable property in Manchester and Salford in Northwest England, which provided a sizeable rental income and was mortgaged for the purchase of the Corran lands. The property at Lissadell was situated in the Sligo Poor Law Union and comprised 53 townlands in the electoral divisions of Carney, Lissadell and Rossinver and, at the commencement of the Famine, it had an annual rental income of £4,581.[2]

In the decades prior to the Great Hunger, Sir Robert Gore Booth, who had inherited the estate in 1814, introduced improvements on his properties where the holdings were unviable and congested. In his evidence to the Devon Commission of 1843 to 1845, Sir Robert stated that no holding should be under four acres as it would not support a family.[3] He maintained that a 25 acre farm would sustain a family in comfort, but the surplus population would have to be removed to achieve this.[4] At the commencement of the Famine, the farm size on the Lissadell estate ranged from one to 25 acres with the average being from ten to 13. Twelve per cent of the holdings in Drumcliff were under five acres, while 53 per cent were between five and 15 acres.[5] From an early stage, when he took over the running of the estate, Gore Booth suggested remedial measures to alleviate the problems of poverty and congestion, concluding that radical remedies were required. In order to overcome the widespread problem of rundale, he realised that the consolidation of holdings was necessary. In 1847 he stated, 'I have at all times endeavoured to increase the size of the farms and in a manner that was consistent with justice to the individual'.[6] The Lissadell estate was scattered and resources limited, making it difficult to implement widespread changes so it was decided to concentrate on the Drumcliff part of the property and new rules and regulations were introduced including the elimination of rundale.

As with many properties, the Gore Booth estate had been let to middlemen on long leases during the Napoleonic Wars when agricultural prices were high. They sublet the farms to tenants which resulted in subdivision, congestion and poverty. In most instances, the landlord was unable to implement change until the lease expired. Only when the Famine occurred were landowners able to stamp out the middlemen system when they were unable to pay their rents, allowing proprietors to regain control over their properties. As leases fell on the Gore Booth estate, the land was divided among the smallholders and where insufficient land was available the tenants were offered farms on other parts of the property where they could be accommodated. When this was not possible, tenants received compensation for improvements that had been carried out and provided with free passage to North America. When the lease of the middleman, Mr Martin, expired in 1834 at Ballygilgan, which contained a number of sub tenants with holdings under four acres and who did not pay rent directly to Gore Booth, they were offered a free passage to North America. Those who did not take up the offer were provided with holdings at Lissadell, Cloonmullen, Ballintemple, Cartonwilliamage and other townlands. This venture cost Gore Booth £3,788, which included pulling down houses, land improvements, passage fares to North America, the construction of roads, levelling ditches and other works.[7] Despite these changes, rundale and the subdivision of holdings remained a problem with many townlands continuing to be congested and overpopulated.

The Gore Booths were regarded as landowners who promoted good agricultural practices to improve the condition of their tenants. Between 1834 and 1842, £4,000 was spent on improvements and tenants were employed on the demesne.[8] Grants were provided to drain their lands, slates were given for buildings, and timber for doors, windows and roofs. To improve communications on the estate, money was made available for the construction of roads resulting in 68 miles being laid which helped connect the more remote parts of the property.[9] Attempts to carry out improvements did not solve the problem of the non-payment of rents and was a major issue when Sir Robert took charge of the estate. By the mid-1840s, £5,796 was outstanding in rent arrears on the Lissadell property, in particular amongst those tenants with holdings under five acres, while one-quarter of the farmers on the Ballymote estate were behind with their rents.[10]

The widespread poverty and destitution in north Sligo were a result of a rapidly increasing population. Like other parts of the country, County Sligo recorded an unprecedented expansion in the decades leading up to the Famine: from 146,229 in 1821 to 180,882 in 1841. This created a population density of over 300 persons per square mile and, in some places, it was over 400, making it the highest for the country. Seventy per cent of the Irish population were dependent on the potato as their main food source by the early 1840s. As 45 per cent of the farms in the country were under five acres, the majority of the population increasingly relied on the potato to feed their families. The situation was more acute in County Sligo as 61 per cent of farms were under five acres and the population was heavily dependent on the potato despite attempts by Gore Booth and other landowners to consolidate the holdings and introduce improvements. Tenants on these holdings enjoyed a subsistence existence when the potato crop was abundant, but the threat of a calamity was never far away as happened on a number of occasions in the 1820s and 1830s. Gore Booth and other proprietors who prophesized that a calamity was inevitable because of the high dependence on the potato were proved right when reports emerged in the autumn of 1845 that the crop had failed.

In 1845, one-third of the potato crop was lost, but this did not lead to major concerns in Sligo because crop failures occurred periodically. In September 1845, the constabulary reported from Ballymote that the potato had the appearance of being plentiful, a better crop than normal.[11] However, within weeks the news became more alarming as the disease spread. By November, it was estimated that one-third of the crop was lost. The group to suffer most was the labouring population who paid their rents through their labour and depended on conacre to grow the potato which fed their families. That month, Rev. John Garrett, the vicar of Emlaghfad, reported from Ballymote that there were few good potatoes in the area and he called for public works to be introduced for the labouring classes.[12] Large parts of the barony of Carbury were also impacted with one-eighth of the crop in Rossinver and one-tenth in Lissadell destroyed.[13] In December, Sir Robert Gore Booth informed the Sligo Board of Guardians that many people would have no potatoes by the following April and the crop in Lissadell was ruined.[14]

By April 1846, the crisis with the food supply was becoming evident. John Scott, Secretary of the Sligo Relief Committee, reported that half of the crop in Drumcliff was lost and a large group of labourers had walked to a meeting of the Poor Law Guardians and begged for relief.[15] Further gloom followed over the following months. Gore Booth and his wife, Caroline, spent from May to June 1846 in London, returning in time to receive bad news about the approaching harvest.[16] In mid-July, there were reports that the new potato crop was severely affected with blight and by October it was a total failure throughout the country: the yield per acre did not exceed one ton per acre.[17] According to the Constabulary, the yield in Sligo was under half a ton per acre down from 8.3 tons the previous year.[18] The problem was compounded by 11 inches of rain in June, July and August leading to widespread blight. In August 1846, one Poor Law Guardian, Mr Gillimote stated he had examined his crop one evening and it was fine, but the following morning discovered it was severely damaged. While the stalks looked healthy, it was only when the potatoes were dug it was found they were damaged.[19] The *Sligo Champion* stated that the hopes of the poor were destroyed and 'unless God averts the evil, they have now before them another year of want and suffering, disease and misery'. It added that the unpredictability of the potato was such that an alternative food supply needed to be introduced.[20] The Corran Relief Committee stated that the potato in its area was a total disaster and called on the government to direct the Board of Works to put in place public works. It later claimed that 'multitudes are in utter destitution

... Actual starvation will visit and lay waste many of the most populous villages of this district'.[21] With no meal left to purchase, Rev. John Garrett complained that the poor people of Ballymote were 'left to the mercy of hucksters who charge enormous profits'.[22] Similar scenes were reported from north Sligo where the crop was a complete failure with people on the Palmerston estate unprepared for the crisis that lay ahead: Rev. Brennan, the parish priest of Ahamlish, stating that 1,200 families were totally destitute.[23]

The Carney Relief Committee was established in August 1846 at the behest of Sir Robert Gore Booth out of a growing concern for the plight of the cottiers and small farmers who had difficulties paying their rents and who he felt would be unable to feed their families. The government was only prepared to distribute the Indian meal, purchased secretly in the United States by Sir Robert Peel in November 1845, to the local relief committees. It was intended that the committees would purchase the corn at cost price and sell it to the people. Few tenants on the Gore Booth estate had the resources to purchase the corn even if it was sold at cost price. The government eventually gave donations to relief committees including the one at Carney so that the poorest could be fed.[24]

Gore Booth's involvement with relief operations during the Famine can be divided into four areas: as a member of the Sligo Board of Guardians; his participation with four local relief committees; the private measures implemented to aid his tenants and those on neighbouring properties; and assisting a large number of his tenants to emigrate. He was deputy chairman of the board of guardians at the outbreak of the Famine, elected for the Lissadell division, but in 1847 he resigned the seat and became an *ex-officio* guardian in order that an additional member could be added to the board.[25] He was also chairman of the Sligo Grand Jury. In December 1846, he presided over a meeting at which a presentment of £6,000 was granted for the building of the Sligo Ship Canal.[26] His attendance at board meetings appears to have been erratic during the Famine period, but this may have been due to his commitment to the local relief committees that he was involved with. In addition, Gore Booth was appointed chairman by the Lord Lieutenant of the new Relief Finance Committee of the union in March 1847 whose members included Captain Gilbert and Andrew Walker. Its primary function was to adjudicate on the ordering of relief, and it was acknowledged that Gore Booth carried out this role very effectively.[27] Like most unions, Sligo had difficulties coping with the demands which the Famine placed on it. Sir George Nicholls, the architect behind the Irish Poor Law, had informed the government in 1838 that it would be unable to cope with a famine situation. The Sligo workhouse had opened its doors to paupers in December 1841 with accommodation for 1,200 inmates, but by the autumn of 1846 was struggling to deal with rising inmate numbers and declining income. Large numbers of labourers had been admitted to the Sligo workhouse by November 1846, some having worked on the relief works but who found the wage of *8d.* a day insufficient to support their families.[28] With the cost of purchasing provisions rising and distress widespread the union came under increasing financial pressure.

By October 1846, the Sligo guardians owed £13,000 to contractors and £500 was outstanding from rates. When it was built it had cost £12,842 to complete.[29] The application to the government for a £3,000 loan was rejected, they being told to rely on their own resources. In an attempt to reduce expenditure, the guardians decided to reduce the quantity of food that the paupers received and at a meeting in November 1846, attended by Gore Booth, the support given to children aged between nine and 15 years was cut.[30] At the same time, the union was unable to collect the poor rates as ratepayers were unable to pay. Landowners were finding it increasingly difficult to meet their financial commitments as rents went unpaid by their tenants. On 23 December 1846, a meeting of landed proprietors and cess payers took place in Sligo and it was proposed that taxation for the relief of the poor should be changed to reduce the heavy burden on landowners who lived close to estates that were congested. It also called for a facility which would assist landowners aid their tenants to emigrate to North America.[31] The problem can be seen from the Gore Booth estate which encountered a major increase in the poor rate: in 1843 the rate for Lissadell was *5d.* in the £ and this rose to *6s.* in June 1847, most being paid by the landlord. Gore Booth was forced to get into debt to survive. As the English Quaker and philanthropist, James Hack Tuke, said in 1847: 'if each proprietor was responsible for the rates on his own land, he would, in many cases, soon free himself from the burden of pauperism by profitable employment of the labourers on his estate'.[32]

A further problem was the failure of many landowners to attend the weekly board meetings at a time when the Sligo workhouse was full and debt increasing. Landlords with extensive estates in the county seldom attended the meetings and a circular was sent to all landed proprietors by the Dublin authorities in December 1847 urging them to adopt a more proactive role with the relief efforts.[33] By this stage, the workhouse was under severe pressure. When the potato failed relief could only be given within the workhouse with no provision for outdoor relief. As people starved, they headed to the workhouse, resulting in the authorities being unable to cope. By February 1847, the Sligo workhouse was full and unable to accommodate any further inmates. At this point, 48 per cent of the population of the union was dependent on relief: in Lissadell, it was nearly 90 per cent, 55 per cent in Rossinver and 24 per cent in Carney.[34] New and dramatic ways to deal with the problem of overcrowding were introduced. In November 1847, 130 old and infirm inmates and their children were discharged and replaced by 250 able bodied paupers. The workhouse was overcrowded by 200 and hundreds more were desperately seeking admittance.[35] Captain Gilbert reported that many who sought entry were desperate 'and without relief cannot subsist much longer'.[36] While the workhouse was under pressure it was accepted that conditions in Sligo were more favourable than other workhouses in the country with little disease in the institution.[37] However, the situation was rapidly changing. On 26 October 1847, between 200 and 300 people assembled outside the workhouse gates asking to be admitted, but they could not be accommodated.[38] The union's financial position was also deteriorating, leaving it unable to pay its debts, while the government was demanding that the money advanced for the building of the workhouse be repaid.[39]

The financial problems put pressure on landowners like Gore Booth. As the administrative unit for the setting and collection of the Poor Law rate was the electoral division some landlords often had to pay more because of the refusal or inability of their peers to meet their obligations—something they were unhappy with. Four of the landowners in the Lissadell, Carney and Rossinver electoral divisions, Sir Gilbert King, Captain Michael Kelly, Charles Gore Jones and John Gethin, were among those unable to meet their financial payments for the Poor Law rate, placing a further strain on Gore Booth. Cormac Ó Gráda points out that one in 12 landowners at the start of the Famine were seriously insolvent and their position deteriorated rapidly with the failure of the potato.[40] Nonetheless, even as the crisis was deepening, they were widely criticised. The *London Universe* in September 1846 stated that Irish landlords displayed complete selfishness and heartlessness towards their tenants and were heedless to all criticisms.[41] Throughout 1846 and 1847, the *Sligo Champion* was extremely critical of landowners in Sligo stating that they had done nothing to provide relief for their tenants—although they had an annual rental income of £235,756, they had provided only £2,000 in aid. Praising Gore Booth, it said, 'Sir Robert and his lady are using their best endeavours to alleviate the suffering of the famine-stricken creatures in their district'.[42] Caroline Gore Booth made a number of donations, separate from her husband, which drew praise from the parish priest in Carney. On 16 February 1847, he thanked her for:

> ... [T]he most extensive, indiscriminate and unostentatious charities performed by her Ladyship, and trusting that she might be consoled by the fact that "the humble prayers of God's humble creatures are offered every night, and in every house, for the spiritual and temporal welfare of every member of her ladyship's family".[43]

In March, Lady Gore Booth donated a further £100 towards general relief in Ireland.[44] The problem which landowners faced making their poor law payments was greatest where a large proportion of the farms were small, under £4 in valuation, as they were the first to renege in paying their rent.

In addition to his work with the Sligo Board of Guardians, Gore Booth was also involved with four relief committees, acting as chairman of the Lissadell, Carney, Rossinver and Drumcliff bodies. He was also a member of the Corran Relief Committee but does not appear to have attended many of its meetings. As early as August 1846, Gore Booth was distributing relief on his estate. In February 1847, he gave £150 to the committees at Lissadell and Rossinver. Unlike a number of other major landowners in north Sligo, he was acutely aware of the suffering and depravation that existed, witnessing it on a daily basis. Landlords who did not reside on their estates had a negative impact on the local economy and this was especially the case during the Great Hunger. They tended not to have a close relationship with their tenants and depended on their agents to be kept informed, which led to 'feelings of mistrust and antipathy between owners and occupiers which ... eliminated any possibility of benevolence on the one hand and loyalty on the other'.[45] Those absentee proprietors, like Lord Palmerston, did not respond as quickly to the crisis of the potato failure on their properties. Desmond Norton points out that Palmerston and some of his agents 'were subject to various kinds of policy lags' in relation to relief, largely due to the hierarchical structure of administrating the estate with local agents, a central agency and the landlord.[46] In the early stages of the Famine, some landowners provided their tenants with relief work independent of the government measures. As Christine Kinealy points out, these tended to be landlords who resided on their estates, such as Gore Booth, and not those who were absentees.[47] In 1847, Rev. John Green, vicar of Ahamlish and secretary of the Ahamlish and Rossinver Relief Committees, informed the relief commission in Dublin that little help had been forthcoming from Palmerston and the poorest tenants were excluded from the relief works and 'are literally in a state of starvation'.[48] Even when the full impact of the Famine became apparent, these landowners were slow in coming to the aid of their starving tenants. Local relief committees were exasperated with the prevarications of some landowners. When the Corran Relief Committee wrote a circular to the landowners in their area in 1846 asking for assistance, they were disappointed that none replied. Shortly afterwards, Gore Booth indicated that he would support the population on his estate with relief and employment, allowing the committee to concentrate its efforts on the rest of the area.[49] He later sent £100 to the committee when conditions deteriorated further, it being reported that the dead were being brought out at night to be buried without coffins.[50]

Gore Booth's commitment to the relief operations in north Sligo can be measured in that he attended 70 per cent of the meetings of the four relief committees. In 1847 he told the Select Committee on Colonisation from Ireland that he often left Lissadell at dawn and did not return until after midnight in his efforts to help the starving poor of north Sligo. He attended meetings in Sligo one day a week and his involvement with the four relief committees could take up to three days each week. These exertions resulted in Gore Booth contracting famine fever in 1847, but it was diagnosed early and did not have a long-term impact and so he was able to continue his relief work after a couple of weeks convalescing. In his absence, his wife, Lady Caroline, continued distributing relief to the most destitute in the community, working from eleven in the morning till late in the evening, often in constant hail and intense cold.[51]

This took place at a time when the *Sligo Champion* was reporting on the dire conditions in the county. According to the newspaper: 'Deaths from starvation are now so numerous, that they are looked upon as a matter of course, and have ceased to create alarm, or horror in the public mind'. Want of food and starvation was only going to deteriorate because land remained untilled and the peasantry did not have the means to sow the land.[52] On 17 February 1847, the Catholic curate of Grange, Rev. Dominick Noone, named 17 people aged between 12 and 68 years who had died of starvation in Ahamlish over the previous ten days; within weeks, people were dying at a rate of seven a day in the parish.[53] There was also extreme want and fatalities in the Lissadell area. The coroner's verdict on Thomas Killernane from Drumcliffe stated that he had 'died of starvation', his stomach did not have a particle of food, was smaller than was natural and was much collapsed.[54] In the western part of Ahamlish, 425 families, numbering 2,278 people, were destitute with only 187 employed on relief works. Father Noone reported that many had not eaten a regular meal for over three weeks and were surviving on stumps of cabbage and wild berries. James Jones, one of the principal landowners in the parish, had not provided the people with any relief.[55] In Ballyconnell, there were not 20 stacks of oats among the 2,000 inhabitants. Gore Booth was informed that destitution and starvation was so great that people were dying, but the authorities did not regard the situation as extreme even though people had pawned every article of furniture and clothing to buy food. Gore Booth interceded and asked the government for a grant of £50,000 for the impoverished districts for 'the landlords of the district are unable to access [it] themselves, or pay money advanced'.[56]

The Lissadell Relief Committee included Gore Booth, two Catholic priests, Rev. Patrick O'Gara and Rev. M. Brennan, and the local Church of Ireland rector, Rev. William Jeffcott. In February, Gore Booth suggested that large boilers be purchased to make soup, each providing up to 200 gallons; and in May the committee sent boilers to Ballinfull, Cloghwhisky, Rockley, Ballyconnell, Ardtarmon and Breaghwy.[57] At the same time, he established two soup kitchens which distributed 280 gallons of soup to the poor on the Ballymote portion of the estate.[58] The Corran Relief Committee also had five soup kitchens in the area feeding 4,000 of the most needy.[59] The establishment of soup kitchens is generally regarded as one of the more beneficial aspects of relief operations during the Great Famine, which helped to save thousands of lives. They were first introduced in Cork city in November 1846 by the Society of Friends and were a cheap and effective way of feeding people. One advantage was that soup greatly reduced the incidence of diarrhoea and dysentery, which were prevalent before the introduction of the government's soup kitchens. Gore Booth saw the merits of the soup kitchens as a major relief measure in the fight against starvation and he introduced them on to his estate even before the government system was introduced.

In addition to his public obligations in helping the poor, Gore Booth also provided relief to his own tenants. He had always adopted a paternalistic approach on his estate, establishing national schools at Milltown and Castletown, a dispensary at Carney and contributions towards the building of both Catholic and Church of Ireland churches.[60] As early as November 1845, Gore Booth had established a mill at Lissadell to grind diseased potatoes and, the following January, he returned £150 of conacre rents to tenants who had lost their potato crop.[61] During the summer of 1846, Gore Booth was providing food, which included spending £1,721 in August for goods purchased from local merchants, such as Leech and Son in Sligo. It was then sold to the tenants at cost price. Between October 1846 and July 1847, a further £13,403 was spent on relief, most purchased abroad and brought to Sligo port, but some was bought locally. A further £2,427 was spent on direct relief for the tenants on his estate.[62] One-hundred-and-fifty loaves of bread were sold to people each day at cost price and 30 of the most destitute were given corn for nothing. Between late August and early December 1847, when famine conditions were extreme, Gore Booth distributed 393 tons of Indian meal, 70 tons of flour, 40 tons of whole wheat flour and nine tons of biscuit. In October 1847, the provision store at John's Point where Gore Booth kept relief provisions was broken into and a large quantity of Indian meal stolen.[63] The crew of his yacht were employed as bakers and cooks and all the household was engaged in the distribution of relief not only at Lissadell, but also on neighbouring properties. Four boilers were purchased which distributed soup on the estate.[64] In January and February 1847, Gore Booth also paid for 24 coffins so people could be buried with dignity in the north Sligo area.[65]

Gore Booth was prepared to work with other landowners to purchase and transport food from Britain and North America. From the summer of 1846 he was importing and supplying food. In October 1846, along with a number of other landowners in north Sligo, he purchased 700 tons of Indian meal in the United States which was sold to tenants at cost price.[66] In March, he joined forces with Lord Palmerston and Lord Enniskillen to buy 200 tons of Indian meal which was then distributed among the tenants on the three estates.[67] In February 1847, 174 tons of white corn was purchased in New York costing £2,300, for distribution among his tenants and those on neighbouring properties.[68] In the summer of 1847, 262 tons of seed oats, barley and wheat costing £3,941 was imported to that the tenants would have seeds for planting.[69] Gore Booth also imported food on the *Manchester* and the *Rose* in June.[70] After January 1847, all the food that he was distributing was making a loss and he was subsidizing the relief effort: it is estimated it cost him £4,212. In addition, he suffered financially, estimated at £21,742, when the cargo of food he was importing on the *Washington*, was lost at sea.[71]

While Gore Booth was providing relief for his own tenants, he quickly realised that the situation on neighbouring properties was critical. As early as 1846, he was distributing aid to Lord Palmerston's tenants on Inishmurry Island; otherwise, they would have perished.[72] The townlands with the greatest destitution in the Lissadell electoral division were Ardtarmon, Raghly, Ballintemple and Ballyconnell, but Ardtarmon was the only one owned by Gore Booth. Most of the smaller landowners were not in a position to help their tenants, lacking the resources to do so. While distress and starvation were not as great on Gore Booth's property, he made a conscious decision to aid tenants on neighbouring estates, taking responsibility for the destitute of these properties and also for the Palmerston tenants in Ahamlish.[73] Captain Henry O'Brien, a Board of Works official, highlighted the level of destitution he witnessed on those estates when he visited Carbury in March 1847. He stated that 'the children were bloated in their faces and bodies, their limbs were withered to bones and sinews, with rags on them which scarcely preserved decency, and assuredly afforded no protection from the weather'.[74] Gore Booth justified his intervention in March 1847, noting that:

> Some leased lands are in a miserable state, but the districts worse off are owned by absentee landlords or those too poor to give any assistance ... I can carry on for a little although it is a hard care to burthen [sic] one's property with debts for others—but we must keep [the] creatures alive at any cost.[75]

The problem on Palmerston's estate was that much of the land was held under the rundale system, about 60 to 80 tenants having patches of land in a townland. This resulted in the population tottering on the edge of disaster, as in the Sands area, where the people relied totally on the potato.[76] Gore Booth went to Sands two or three times a week distributing bread and medicines 'to those who must die if food be not given them'. Their condition was such that they were unable to send a child to the public works to earn money.[77] Gore Booth accompanied Captain O'Brien on his tour of the north Sligo area in February and March 1847. He wrote of the harrowing scenes that they encountered. Dozens were dying daily, he recorded:

> In the first lay ... a coffin with the owner's wife, who had died three days before, of want. The owner stood near the door having come from the public works (where he was earning 8*d*. a day) to see to burying his wife, and he told us he was about to depart 'to dig a hole to put her in, and try to get a couple of men from the works to help him carry her there'. A skeleton of a living child was in a cradle, in a corner near a fire. A woman, a neighbour, was sitting by it and rocking the cradle, and said it would be dead before the morning.[78]

O'Brien stated that the relief works were ill-geared to saving lives and showed the destitution and poverty of the area.[79] While Gore Booth was in a more favourable financial position than many of his peers, he was unable to continue providing long-term support. The lack of indebtedness in the early days of the Famine and the availability of rentals from his Manchester and Salford properties enabled him to play a more benevolent role in relief operations in north Sligo, but this could not be carried on indefinitely.

It is difficult estimate the financial contributions that Gore Booth made to relief operations, but contemporary figures place the sum between £30,000 and £80,000.[80] However, a sum of £40,000 appears more plausible, although it does not take into account the money spent on assisted emigration from the estate to North America.[81] Relief was financed in a number of ways: directly by Gore Booth himself, through contributions from friends and acquaintances, and donations from the Society of Friends. Individual donations came from Richard Calbridge of Eton who subscribed £430, the Prime Minister, Lord John Russell, who sent £100 and Lady Dunraven who forwarded £5. People also sent contributions, estimated at £685, to Lady Caroline Gore Booth.[82] This was provided at a time when little or no rental money was being received from the Sligo properties and Gore Booth was still straddled with payments on the loans that he had taken out for the purchase of the Ballymote lands in 1838. As a result, in 1847 he mortgaged the Lissadell estate for £50,000 to meet his bank repayments and to finance his emigration schemes.[83] The family's financial position was not helped by the excesses of Sir Robert's brother, Henry, who had amassed considerable debts and was having to pay maintenance for several illegitimate children he had with mistresses. He was constantly writing to Gore Booth looking for money and, in return, he was provided with partial financial help.

Gore Booth's endeavours during the Great Famine were praised by the nationalist newspaper, *The Sligo Champion*. It maintained that he was a landowner who had looked after not only his own tenants, but those on neighbouring properties, taking a philanthropic approach to his fellow man. His charitable work was also acknowledged by the parish priest of Drumcliff, Rev. Patrick O'Gara, which was unusual as many Catholic priests were extremely critical of landlords and their failure to aid their tenants. In March 1848, O'Gara told Gore Booth: 'It must be a source of great consolation to you, that, whilst other landlords were fleeing the country through apprehension of personal peril, you were deeply rooted in the affections of a grateful peasantry'.[84] Captain Henry O'Brien also acknowledged Gore Booth's work with his tenants, but he had been 'pressed to feed his neighbours' tenants'. He added: 'What he has done for the part of the country where he resides, has been so well done, that it would prove a real blessing to enable him to do more and were it not for him they would be dying'.[85] Gore Booth did not look for public recognition for his work. In an undated letter in the Lissadell papers he stated that he did not want his charitable work to be brought before the public. He insisted that 'I do what I consider only my duty, and I have at all times endeavoured to do the same, there I do not wish nor care to be vindicated in any way as an Irish landlord'.[86] Nevertheless, despite Gore Booth's attempts to assist the people of north Sligo, there was a death threat made against him in early December 1847.[87]

Landlords who desperately tried to provide for their tenants, like Gore Booth, were angry with the government's inaction, as it blamed landowners for not looking after their tenants, increasingly forcing them to shoulder an intolerable burden with the poor rates. As far as the government was concerned, local landowners were to be at the forefront of relief operations when it was not prepared to take on this responsibility.[88] While the British authorities refused to accept the accounts of death, starvation and suffering from Catholic clergymen and nationalist politicians, maintaining they were exaggerated and not a true reflection of affairs, they also rejected statements that came from resident landowners in Ireland, like Gore Booth, stating these landlords wanted the government to pay for works which would improve their estates. By late 1847, landlords like Sir Robert were no longer in a position to provide sustainable assistance to their tenants. Throughout 1848 and 1849 the *Sligo Champion* and other newspapers consistently highlighted the plight of the people and the apparent unwillingness of the government to intervene: 'No tongue could faithfully tell the amount of misery, sickness, want, wretchedness, within the dreary precincts of this doomed locality,' it avowed in May 1849.[89] By this stage, the workhouses were bearing the brunt of the relief efforts at a time when many landowners were engaged in the wholesale eviction of their tenants who had no alternative but to turn to the

Poor Law to survive. By December, the Sligo workhouse contained 2,437 inmates, 300 more than its limit, and was forced to rent six premises in the town, including the Charter House on Old Market St, to accommodate the overflow.[90]

The problems which Gore Booth encountered during the Famine years were compounded by a number of factors: the location of the estate in a county that was one of the hardest hit by the failure of the potato, the high incidence of small holdings on the property and the high level of rent arrears that had accumulated in the years preceding the calamity. However, his reaction to the crisis was not draconian, unlike many of his peers. At the time the potato failed Gore Booth was already engaged in providing his tenants with the option of locating to North America, he paying the passage fare. This was done in conjunction with the estate improvements that were being implemented. Between 1839 and 1841, 42 families, numbering 207 individuals, accepted Gore Booth's offer of assisted passage to North America, Sir Robert stating that if he had not done so 'I should have been throwing them on the world and leaving them to beg'.[91] With the coming of the Famine, he decided to continue the emigration scheme, but this was largely initiated by the tenants themselves who saw it as a way of escaping famine and starvation. Consequently, 1,600 were assisted to leave for North America between 1847 and 1848, costing £5,999.[92] Gore Booth was not prepared to send those who were industrious and improving farmers and the preference was to send families rather than individuals: as with James Murphy, his wife and seven children, ranging in age from 10 to 25 years, and Widow McGlone who was accompanied by her five children, ranging in age from 18 to 25 years. Both families arrived in St John, New Brunswick on the *Lady Sale* in July 1847.[93] These and other departures allowed the vacated holdings to be redistributed among the remaining families, thus creating viable farming units. Many of the families selected were headed by widows and also included orphans, as these groups were unlikely to carry out improvements on their holdings. It was important that the first group of assisted emigrants was carried out successfully, as the continuance of further schemes depended on their positive reports coming back to Sligo. Women tended to initiate the petitions to be assisted as they had little attachment to land and wanted a new life away from famine and death. One of the first groups sent from the estate arrived at St John on the *Aeolas* on 31 May 1847. They issued a statement that Sir Robert was 'always kind to his tenants' and they had been well cared for on the journey.[94] Gore Booth ensured the emigrants were medically fit to travel, being examined by his physician, Dr Hamilton, when they were selected and prior to their departure from Sligo port. Unlike other landowners who engaged with the emigration process, the Gore Booth's provided additional provisions on the voyage, including sending a cow on the *Yeoman* so that passengers would have fresh milk. The New Brunswick authorities had been notified of the emigrants' arrival and requested to provide them with assistance and advice on employment opportunities.[95]

Sir Robert Gore Booth played an important role in relief operations during the Great Hunger, in particular during the period 1845 to 1847. He distributed food among his tenants and actively engaged with relief committees. However, this changed after 1847 when relief became the responsibility of the Poor Law with landowners having to increasingly finance this though the poor rates, at a time when income was declining substantially as tenants were unable to pay their rents. The role of landowners like Gore Booth have been largely unacknowledged by historians. Sir Robert kept a low profile and shunned publicity, instead putting his complete energy into helping the population of north Sligo and Ballymote. Nevertheless, his tenants recognised his work and paid for the church clock in Ballymote in recognition of the relief he had provided for the people during the Famine. The memorial sent to him thanking him for saving the lives of the people can be seen in Lissadell.

NOTES

1. See Christine Kinealy, *This Great Calamity: The Irish Famine, 1845–52* (Dublin: Gill & MacMillan,1994), James S. Donnelly, *The Great Irish Potato Famine* (Stroud: Sutton Publishing, 2001); Cormac Ó Gráda, *Black '47 and Beyond: The Great Irish Famine in History, Economy and Memory* (Princeton University Press, 1999); Joel Mokyr, *Why Ireland Starved: A Quantitative and Analytical History of the Irish Economy, 1800–1850* (London: Routledge, 1985).
2. *Second Report from the Select Committee of the House of Lords on Colonization from Ireland,* HC 1847–8 (593), xvii, p. 255, q. 2599; Rentals for the Lissadell for 1843 (PRONI, Lissadell papers, D/4131/H/8).
3. *Evidence taken before her majesty's commission of inquiry into the state of the law and practice in respect to the occupation of land in Ireland* (Devon commission), HC 1845 (605), xix, p. 204, q. 70; p. 205, q. 45.
4. *Second Report from the Select Committee on Colonization,* p. 272, qs 2765–6.
5. Deidre Ryan, 'The Lissadell estate of Sir Robert Gore Booth: famine and emigration, 1845–1847' (unpublished MA thesis, UCD, 1996), pp 7, 13.
6. *Second Report from the Select Committee on Colonization,* p. 258, qs 2636–8.
7. Names of Ballygilgan tenants who received lands elsewhere (PRONI, Lissadell papers, D/4131/H/8).
8. *Second Report from the Select Committee on Colonization*, p. 259, q. 2639.
9. Ibid., p. 267, qs 2631–2.
10. Rentals for Lissadell for 1843 (PRONI, Lissadell papers, D/4131/H/8; George Dodwell's account with Robert Gore Booth for four year's rent of the Ballymote estate from the commencement to 1 May 1837 (PRONI, Lissadell papers, D/4131/H/4).

11. Sub Inspector, Ballymote to Col. Duncan McGregor, 25 Sept. 1845 (NAI, Famine Commission papers, RLFC 2/213120).
12. Rev. J. Garrett to the Lord Lieutenant, 24 Nov. 1856 (NAI, Famine Relief Committee papers, RFLC, 2/z 16462).
13. Ryan, 'Lissadell estate of Sir Robert Gore Booth', p. 16.
14. *Mayo Telegraph*, 24 Dec. 1845.
15. John Scott to the Central Relief Committee, 28 Apr. 1846 (NAI, Relief Committee papers, Sligo, RLFC 3/1/1901); *Mayo Telegraph*, 6 May 1846.
16. *Morning Post*, 7 May 1846; *Clare Journal, and Ennis Advertiser*, 29 June 1846.
17. J.S. Donnelly, 'Production, prices and exports, 1846–51' in W.E. Vaughan (ed.), *A New History of Ireland, v: Ireland under the Union I, 1801–70* (Oxford University Press, 1989), pp 286–7.
18. *Correspondence from May 1846 to January 1847 relating to the Measures adopted for the Relief of Distress in Ireland*, HC 1847 (761), li, p. 57.
19. *Mayo Telegraph,* 19 Aug. 1846.
20. *Sligo Champion*, 1 Aug. 1846.
21. Resolution of the Corran Relief Committee, 21 Aug. 1846 (NLI, CSORP, Distress papers, DP 4407).
22. Liam Swords, *A Dominant Church: The Diocese of Achonry, 1818–1960* (Dublin: Columba Press, 2004), pp 146–7.
23. Thomas Power, 'The Palmerston estate in County Sligo: improvements and assisted emigration before 1850' in Patrick Duffy and Gerard Moran (eds), *To and From Ireland: Planned Migration Schemes, c. 1600–2000* (Dublin: Geography Publications, 2004), pp 188–9. The problems on the Palmerston estate were due to the rundale system, which the landlord had started to end when the leases of middlemen expired, see Desmond Norton, *Landlords, Tenants, Famine: The Business of an Irish Land Agency in the 1840s* (Dublin: UCD Press, 2006), pp 34–6.
24. J.S. Donnelly, 'Famine and the government response, 1845–6' in Vaughan, *New History of Ireland*, pp 278–9.
25. *Second Report of the Select Committee of the House of Lord on Colonization*, p. 255, q. 2604. Sligo poor law union comprised 23 electoral divisions and had 52 guardians, 13 of whom were ex officio members.
26. *Limerick Chronicle*, 23 Dec. 1846.
27. *Sligo Journal,* 19 Mar. 1847; 27 Apr. 1848.
28. *Tyrawley Herald,* 5 Nov. 1846.
29. Fergus O'Ferrall, *John Ferrall: Master of Sligo Workhouse, 1852–66* (Dublin: Four Courts Press, 2019), p. 21.
30. *Sligo Champion*, 31 Oct. 1846; *Tyrawley Herald*, 5 Nov. 1846.
31. Resolutions of a meeting of landed proprietors and cess payers in Sligo, 23 Dec. 1846 (NAI, CSORP, 1846/O.342).
32. James Hack Tuke, *A Visit to Connaught in the Autumn of 1847* (London: C. Gilpin, 1848), p. 15
33. *Sligo Journal,* 17 Dec. 1847.
34. *Tyrawley Herald*, 25 Feb. 1847; *Distress in Ireland, Supplementary Appendix to the Seventh Report from the Relief Commission*, HC 1847–8 (956), xxix, p. 80.

35. Report of Captain Gilbert on Sligo workhouse, 24 Nov. 1848 (NAI, CSORP, 1847/O.12196).
36. Ibid., 8 Dec. 1847 (NAI, CSORP, 1847/O.12730).
37. *Sligo Champion,* 30 Oct. 1847; see also Tuke, *Visit to Connaught,* p. 16.
38. *Sligo Champion*, 29 Oct. 1847.
39. Ibid., 30 Oct. 1847.
40. Ó Gráda, *Black' 47: The Great Irish Famine*, pp 128–129.
41. Reprinted in *Mayo Telegraph*, 16 Sept. 1846.
42. *Sligo Champion*, 27 Mar. 1847.
43. This letter was quoted in a court case concerning the historic role of the family in the welfare of their tenants: 'Edward Walsh and Constance Cassidy, plaintiffs, and Sligo County Council, Judgement of Mr Justice McMahon', delivered on 20 Dec. 2010, at: www.trusts.it/admincp/UploadedPDF/201202061429140.jIreland%20Walsh%20%5b2010%5d%20IEHC%20437.pdf
44. 'Scotch and Irish Relief', *Express* (London), 26 Mar. 1847. Lady Caroline was Sir Robert's second wife, marrying in 1830, his first wife having died in January 1828in childbirth. She was the daughter of Thomas Goold of Merrion Square, Dublin. They had two sons and three daughters.
45. N.D, Palmer, *The Irish Land League Crisis* (New Haven: Octagon Books, 1940), p. 30.
46. Norton, *Landlords, Tenants, Famine*, p. 45.
47. Kinealy, *This Great Calamity,* pp 51–52.
48. Ryan, 'Lissadell estate of Sir Roger Gore Booth', p. 17.
49. Rev. J. Garrett to Famine Relief Commission, 29 7 30 Jul. 1846 (NAI, Famine Relief Commission papers, RLFC 3/1/489); Swords, *A Dominant Church*, p. 144.
50. Swords, *A Dominant Church*, p. 153; *Sligo Champion*, 13 Feb. 1847.
51. *Second Report of the Select Committee of the House of Lord on Colonization*, pp 262, 268.
52. *Sligo Champion*, 2 Jan. 1847.
53. Ibid., 20 Feb.; 13 Mar. 1847.
54. Ibid., 23 Jan. 1847.
55. Ibid., 30 Jan. 1847.
56. P. Porth? [illegible] to Sir Robert Gore Booth, 13 Jan. 1847 (PRONI, Lissadell papers, D/4131/H/8).
57. *Sligo Journal*, 19 Feb. 1847; Minutes of meeting of Famine Relief Committee (PRONI, Lissadell papers, D/4131/H/8).
58. Liam Swords, *In Their Own Words: The Famine in North Connacht, 1845–49* (Dublin: Columba Press,1999), p. 132, 148.
59. Rev. J. Garrett to William Stanley, 4 Feb. 1847 (NAI, Famine Relief Committee papers, RFLC 3/2/26/18).
60. Samuel Lewis, *A Topographical Dictionary of Ireland,* vol. 1 (rep. Baltimore, Genealogical Publishing Co., 1984), pp 266, 513, 599.
61. Ryan, 'Lissadell estate and Sir Robert Gore Booth', p. 20.
62. *Second Report of the Select Committee of the House of Lord on Colonization*, pp 206–281.
63. *Sligo Journal,* 5 Oct. 1847.
64. *Ibid.,* 10 Dec. 1847; Swords, *In their Own Words*, p. 148.

65. *Sligo Journal*, 19 Feb. 1847.
66. Power, 'Palmerston estate in County Sligo', p. 119.
67. Ibid., p. 120; Ryan, 'Lissadell estate of Sir Robert Gore Booth', p. 25.
68. Purchase of meal, 19 Mar. 1847 (PRONI, Lissadell papers, D/4131/H/8).
69. Ryan, 'Lissadell estate of Sir Robert Gore Booth', p. 26.
70. *Sligo Journal*, 4 Jun. 1847; *Nation,* 12 Jun. 1847; *Transactions of the Central Committee of the Society of Friends during the Famine in Ireland in 1846 and 1847* (Rep. Dublin, 1996), p. 354.
71. Ryan, 'Lissadell estate of Sir Robert Gore Booth', pp 24–25.
72. Jeffcott to Famine Relief Committee, 2 Dec. 1846 (NAI, Famine Relief Committee, Sligo, RLFC, 3/2/7935). Inishmurry was leased to the Wynne family until 1845–46, Norton, *Landlords, Tenants, Famine*, p. 36.
73. Ryan, 'Lissadell estate of Sir Robert Gore Booth', p. 14.
74. *Correspondence from January to March 1847, relating to measures adopted for the relief of distress in Ireland* (Board of Works series, second part), HC 1847 (97), lii, p. 180.
75. Gore Booth to Anthony ? (illegible), 3 Mar. 1847 (PRONI, Lissadell papers, D/4131/H/8).
76. *Second Report of the Select Committee of the House of Lord on Colonization*, p. 148.
77. Gore Booth to Anthony [illegible], 3 Mar. 1847 (PRONI, Lissadell papers, D/4131/H/8).
78. Quoted in Swords, *In their Own Words*, pp 147–149.
79. Ó Gráda, *Black '47*, p. 64.
80. The *Sligo Journal* stated the Gore Booth had spent £80,000 on relief operations, *Sligo Journal*, 12 May 1848.
81. £40,000 is the sum quoted in 1880 by the journalist, Finlay Dun, Finlay Dun, *Landlords and Tenants in Ireland* (London: Longmans, 1881), p. 191.
82. *Second Report of the Select Committee of the House of Lord on Colonization,* p. 282; Ryan, 'Lissadell estate and Sir Robert Gore Booth', p. 30.
83. Joe McGowan, *Constance Markievicz: The People's Countess* (Mullaghmore, Co. Sligo: Cottage Press, 2003), p. 57; Tyler Anbinder, 'Lord Palmerston and famine emigration ' in the *Historical Journal*, 44, 2 (2001), p. 451.
84. Fr Patrick O'Gara to Sir Robert Gore Booth, March 1848 (PRONI, Lissadell papers, D/4131/H/8).
85. *Correspondence from January to March 1847, relating to measures adopted for the relief of distress in Ireland*, p. 182.
86. Gore Booth to Anthony [illegible], 3 Mar. 1847 (PRONI, Lissadell papers, D/4131/H/8).
87. *Sligo Journal*, 10 Dec. 1847.
88. See Kinealy, *This Great Calamity*, p. 39.
89. *Sligo Champion*, 12, 19 May 1849.
90. *Sligo Journal*, 1 Dec. 1848; *Sligo Champion*, 23 Dec. 1848.
91. See Gerard Moran, *Sir Robert Gore Booth and his Landed Estate in County Sligo, 1814–1876: Land, Famine, Emigration and Politics* (Dublin: Four Courts Press; 2006), pp 33–34.
92. *Second Report of the Select Committee of the House of Lord on Colonization,* pp 260–1.
93. Passengers on the *Lady Sale*, July 1847 (PRONI, Lissadell papers, D/4131/H/8).
94. David J. Johnson, *Irish Emigration to New England through the Port of St John, New Brunswick, Canada, 1841 to 1849* (St John, New Brunswick, 1996), pp 214–215.
95. Moran, *Gore Booth and his Landed Estate*, pp 37–39.

CHAPTER FIVE

'A GHASTLY SPECTRAL ARMY'

Speranza (1821-1896) and The Famine Year

Christine Kinealy

WEARY men, what reap ye?—Golden corn for the stranger.
What sow ye?—Human corses that wait for the avenger.
Fainting forms, hunger-stricken, what see you in the offing?
Stately ships to bear our food away, amid the stranger's scoffing.
There's a proud array of soldiers—what do they round your door?
They guard our masters' granaries from the thin hands of the poor.
Pale mothers, wherefore weeping?—Would to God that we were dead—
Our children swoon before us, and we cannot give them bread.

Little children, tears are strange upon your infant faces,
God meant you but to smile within your mother's soft embraces.
Oh! we know not what is smiling, and we know not what is dying;
But we're hungry, very hungry, and we cannot stop our crying.
And some of us grow cold and white—we know not what it means;
But, as they lie beside us, we tremble in our dreams.
There's a gaunt crowd on the highway—are ye come to pray to man,
With hollow eyes that cannot weep, and for words your faces wan?

No; the blood is dead within our veins—we care not now for life;
Let us die hid in the ditches, far from children and from wife;
We cannot stay and listen to their raving, famished cries—
Bread! Bread! Bread! and none to still their agonies.
We left our infants playing with their dead mother's hand:
We left our maidens maddened by the fever's scorching brand:

Better, maiden, thou were strangled in thy own dark-twisted tresses—
Better, infant, thou wert smothered in thy mother's first caresses.

We are fainting in our misery, but God will hear our groan;
Yet, if fellow-men desert us, will He hearken from His Throne?
Accursed are we in our own land, yet toil we still and toil;
But the stranger reaps our harvest—the alien owns our soil.
O Christ! how have we sinned, that on our native plains
We perish houseless, naked, starved, with branded brow, like Cain's?
Dying, dying wearily, with a torture sure and slow—
Dying, as a dog would die, by the wayside as we go.

One by one they're falling round us, their pale faces to the sky;
We've no strength left to dig them graves—there let them lie.
The wild bird, if he's stricken, is mourned by the others,
But we—we die in Christian land—we die amid our brothers,
In the land which God has given, like a wild beast in his cave,
Without a tear, a prayer, a shroud, a coffin, or a grave.
Ha! but think ye the contortions on each livid face ye see,
Will not be read on judgment-day by eyes of Deity?

We are wretches, famished, scorned, human tools to build your pride,
But God will yet take vengeance for the souls for whom Christ died.
Now is your hour of pleasure—bask ye in the world's caress;
But our whitening bones against ye will rise as witnesses,
From the cabins and the ditches, in their charred, uncoffin'd masses,
For the Angel of the Trumpet will know them as he passes.
A ghastly, spectral army, before the great God we'll stand,
And arraign ye as our murderers, the spoilers of our land.
(Speranza, 'The Stricken Land', *Nation,* 23 January 1847)

Jane Francesca Agnes Elgee was born in December 1821 to a middle-class, Protestant family from Wexford, known for their allegiance to Britain and to the Anglican Church. Her father, Charles, was a solicitor; he died when Jane was 3-years-old, so she was brought up by her mother between their homes in Wexford and Dublin. Jane's background, upbringing and gender made her an unlikely candidate to become a writer for the *Nation*, a champion of the oppressed, or a gifted linguist whose translations would include Alphonse de Lamartine's *History of the French Revolution* in 1850.[1] Throughout her adult life, Jane was a radical nationalist, a political activist and spokesperson for the Irish poor. In 1845, Jane reinvented herself as 'Speranza', the

Italian word for hope. In a story recounted some years later by her protégé, William Butler Yeats, he revealed that:

> She was walking through Grafton St. (I think it was), when a great crowd came by following a hearse. It seemed as though the crowd would never end. She stepped inside a book-shop to let it pass. The crowds still streamed by. 'Whose funeral is this?' she asked the shop-boy. 'The funeral of Thomas Davis,' was the answer. 'Who was Thomas Davis?' 'A poet', was the reply. It seemed to her there must be something great and imaginative in a country where so many followed a poet to the grave. Thenceforth she began to think deeply on these matters—the result soon came in the poems of Speranza.[2]

Using a variety of pen-names, but finally settling on Speranza, Jane commenced writing for the *Nation*, a newspaper founded in 1842 to promote cultural nationalism in Ireland. One of the editors was the Catholic nationalist, Charles Gavan Duffy.[3] Recalling his first meeting with her, Duffy, who had assumed the anonymous writer of such strident poetry to be a man, stated: 'Miss Elgee was the daughter of an archdeacon of the Establishment, and had probably heard nothing of Irish nationality among her ordinary associates'.[4] When interviewed in later life, Speranza made a similar observation, saying: 'I was quite indifferent to the National movement, and if I thought about it at all I probably had a bad opinion of its leaders; for my family was Protestant and Conservative, and there was no social intercourse between them and the Catholics and Nationalists'.[5]

The *Nation* was the mouthpiece of Young Ireland, a dynamic group of both Protestant and Catholic nationalists who were increasingly moving away from Daniel O'Connell's 'Old Ireland'. Speranza sided with the former and the radicalism of the charismatic Thomas Francis Meagher and John Mitchel. An insight into her character, regardless of her youth and gender, was provided by her criticism of O'Connell and his moderate views, in a verse published in late 1847. At this stage, the Liberator was a few months dead, his final speech in parliament having been an emotional appeal on behalf of the starving Irish poor.[6] The political divisions between Old Ireland and Young Ireland intensified following his death, with Speranza's allegiances remaining with the latter. Her poem, although called, 'A Lament', expressed sorrow for his political decisions, not his death:

> He whose broad forehead was circled with might.
> Sunk to a time-serving, driveling inanity.[7]

Possibly mellowed by age or experience, on the centenary of O'Connell's birth in 1875, Speranza penned another poem to O'Connell, but one that was fulsome in its praise of Ireland's famous statesman and his final pilgrimage on behalf of the Irish people that had ended in Genoa in May 1847.[8]

Speranza's early contributions to the *Nation* coincided with the reappearance of the potato blight in Ireland. The relief measures introduced by the government in London were inappropriate and parsimonious, transforming the food shortages into a deadly famine. Speranza used her penmanship to champion the Irish poor and to highlight their hunger and oppression. These themes were evident in several of her poems, including 'The Voice of the Poor':

> Before us die our brothers of starvation
> Around are cries of famine and despair
> Where is hope for us, or comfort, or salvation
> Where—oh! Where?[9]

It closed with the starving victims pleading, 'Lord, grant us *Death!*'. The poem was printed in the Boston *Pilot* on a number of occasions, with later printings adding 'The Irish Famine' to the title.[10] It was also a theme in 'Foreshadowings':

> Woe! 'Tis the black steed of famine that cometh
> At the breath of its rider the green earth is blasted,
> And childhood's frail form droops down, pallid and wasted.[11]

Speranza's most famous poem appeared in the *Nation* on 23 January 1847. At this stage, the main form of relief being provided was through the public works, which were palpably unsuited as a form of emergency relief for a hungry people. Moreover, the weather was unseasonably cold, most particularly in the west, with snow covering the roads and hills of Connemara.[12] The east of the country was also suffering from hard frosts and intermittent snow storms, which were hampering the arrival and delivery of the mails.[13] Even as hundreds of thousands of men, women and children were trying to survive on starvation-level wages, massive amounts of food and alcohol were being shipped out of the country.[14] Entitled 'The Stricken Land', but subsequently renamed 'The Famine Year', Speranza's poem was a searing indictment of the relief policies of the British government—the 'stranger'.

> WEARY men, what reap ye? Golden corn for the stranger.
> What sow ye? Human corses that wait for the avenger.
> Fainting forms, hunger-stricken, what see you in the offing?
> Stately ships to bear our food away, amid the stranger's scoffing ...

The poem was remarkable for a number of reasons. It presented a visceral, unsanitized and rare view of the impact of famine on the human body and human spirit.[15]

Speranza depicted the starving as dehumanized and hollow forms who are no longer recognizable as people but have become, in her words, 'a ghastly spectral army'. Nonetheless, their presence and their voice remained even after their corporal death. In format and content, Speranza was breaking new ground, which represented a 'poetic experimentation', as famine and starvation described so graphically were not traditional topics for English-language poetry. Unwittingly, her powerful language and innovative format provided a model for how subsequent famines in Ireland and other parts of the empire would be viewed and described.[16]

At a time when a new revolutionary zeal was emerging throughout Europe, including Ireland, Speranza's writings were not only incendiary, but in the context of the repressive legislation introduced by the British government in 1848, treasonous.[17] The wholesale arrest of leaders of Young Ireland in the spring and summer resulted in two women—Speranza and Margaret Callan—taking over the publication of the *Nation*. In her most inflammatory writing, 'Jacta Alea Est' (The Die is Cast), published at the same time that the unsuccessful rising was taking place in Ballingarry in County Tipperary, Speranza exhorted the men of Ireland to take up arms:

> Courage! Need I preach to Irishmen of courage? Is it so hard a thing then to die? Alas! Do we not all die daily of broken hearts and shattered hopes ... No! it cannot be death you fear; for you have braved the plague in the exile ship of the Atlantic, and the plague the exile's home beyond it; and famine and ruin, and a slave's life and a dog's death; and hundreds, thousands, a MILLION of you have perished thus. Courage! you will not now belie those old traditions of humanity that tell of this divine God gift within us ... Now is the moment to strike, and by striking save, and the day after the victory it will be time enough to count our dead.[18]

By order of the Lord Lieutenant, all copies of the paper were seized.[19] Charles Gavan Duffy was wrongly accused of having written the article but, unlike other leaders of Young Ireland who were found guilty of treason and sentenced to death, he was eventually acquitted. The reason for this was that during one of the trials, from her place in the ladies' gallery, Speranza announced that 'I am the culprit, if crime it be'.[20] Speranza's gender and family connections not only protected her, but they also had protected Duffy. Although Speranza briefly disappeared from public life after 1848, she did continue to write for the revived *Nation*, albeit under different pseudonyms.[21] The Great Hunger, however, had not only killed approximately one million Irish poor, but it had also ended the nationalist aspirations of both Old Ireland and Young Ireland. Mass emigration meant that a new wave of nationalism was emerging overseas.

In 1851, Speranza married, her preferred name now being Francesca Speranza Wilde. William Wilde was born in Roscommon in 1815. Like Speranza, he came from

Ireland's minority Protestant elite. As a young man, William proved to be a brilliant doctor, specializing in what was then called 'deaf-dumbness'. William was also a gifted travel writer, antiquarian, statistician, archeologist, social historian and folklorist. Unusually for a man of his background, he spoke the Irish language fluently. William believed that culture was the glue of a nation and wanted the artistry and sophistication of Irish Celtic culture to be recognized, not just in Ireland, but internationally. He argued that the vast presence of Celtic antiquities in Ireland was equal to the treasures in ancient Greece and Rome. His 1849 publication on the beauties of the Boyne Valley proved ground-breaking in revealing Ireland's rich early history.[22]

Similarly to Speranza, William demonstrated a concern for people less well off than himself. In 1841, he opened a make-shift dispensary for the treatment of infections of the ear and eye, reserved for the poor. Within two years, more than 1,000 patients had been treated. In 1844, he took over a disused almshouse in Dublin, which became St. Mark's Ophthalmic Hospital for Diseases of the Eye and Ear. Not only did it provide free treatment to the poor, but the hospital also became an important centre of research and teaching.[23] William and his family proved to be some of the most generous financiers of the hospital.[24] In addition to his medical career and antiquarian activities, William was involved with the Irish censuses of 1841 and 1851, and, in a much-reduced capacity, in 1861 and 1871. It was as a census commissioner that William's reputation and legacy—and his knighthood—largely rested. In 1841, his role was mostly confined to interpreting medical data as a contracted assistant, not a commissioner.[25] Ten years later, William's role was magnified and although not the main commissioner, he was acknowledged to be the main author of the post-Famine census.[26] He wrote two of the most important supplements, namely, the Status of Disease and the Tables of Death. The latter provided a historic overview of pestilences and famines from the prehistoric period to 1850, thus placing the tragedy of the 1840s in its longer context.[27] He informed the readers that: 'It must not be supposed that the famine and pestilence which affected Ireland between the years 1845 and 1849 was the greatest, or the only, calamity of the kind which ever came upon us. Far from it'.[28] Wilde's Tables of Death remains 'a classic work of great scholarship, erudition and industry, and is the standard reference work in the subject'.[29]

William's interest in the impact of the Great Famine on Ireland extended beyond the census reports. In 'Irish Popular Superstitions', which first appeared in the *Dublin University Magazine* in May and June 1849, he expressed concern that so many people were leaving the country:

> There is at present a springtide of emigration from Ireland, and great is the rejoicing of those who imagine we are to be benefitted by it; the Malthusian who feared

> for the consequences of over-population (although we are inclined to believe the country was by no means overpopulated as a whole; although it certainly was most unequally populated).[30]

In the Preface to the book edition of *Popular Superstitions*, published in 1852, William explained how the losses caused by the Famine were not simply demographic:

> A wild and daring spirit of adventure—a love of legendary romance—a deep-rooted belief in the supernatural—an unconquerable reverence for ancient customs, and an extensive superstitious creed has, from the earliest times, belonged to the Celtic race. We cannot, therefore, wonder that among the but partially civilized, because neglected and uneducated, yet withal chivalrous inhabitants of a large portion of Ireland, a belief in the marvelous should linger even to the present day. It is, however rapidly becoming obliterated; never to return.
>
> When now I enquire after the old farmer who conducted me, in former years, to the ruined Castle or Abbey, and told me the story of its early history and inhabitants, I hear that he died during the famine. On asking for the peasant who used to sit with me in the ancient Rath, and recite the Fairy legends of the locality, the answer is: 'He is gone to America'; and the old woman who took me to the Blessed Well, and gave me an account of its wondrous cures and charms—'Where is she?' 'Living in the Workhouse'.[31]

Individually and collectively, writing from different political perspectives and for very different audiences, Speranza and William Wilde proved to be some of the most insightful critics of how the government's relief policies during the Famine had damaged Ireland, its people, and its culture. Moreover, emigration meant that any recovery would be a long and slow process.

Speranza and William had three children together: William, born in 1852, Oscar in 1854, and Isola in 1857. Oscar was named after the son of the legendary warrior poet, Oisín. His parents' desire to give him a name steeped in Celtic traditions was deliberate—on his birth Speranza wrote to a friend, 'He is to be called Oscar Fingal Wilde. Is that not grand, misty and Ossianic?'[32] Isola's death in 1867 devastated the family, the teenage Oscar responding by writing one of his earliest and most tender poems, 'Requiescat'.[33] Even after her marriage, Speranza continued to use poetry as a way of providing commentary on the way in which Ireland was governed. The year of Oscar's birth, 1854, was the year when Famine emigration peaked, with as many as one-quarter of a million people leaving the country. The ongoing flight from Ireland, even though the Famine had ended, worried both Speranza and William. Speranza made mass emigration—the exodus—the focus of one of her most successful poems:

> A MILLION *A DECADE*!" Calmly and cold
> The units are read by our statesmen sage;

Little they think of a Nation old,
Fading away from History's page;
Outcast weeds by a desolate sea—
Fallen leaves of Humanity.[34]

This poem, along with 'The Famine Year', became one of Speranza's most beloved and frequently quoted writings, especially as emigration and food shortages continued throughout the nineteenth century.[35] In a two-page feature in *Irish Society* in 1892, for example, this poem was reprinted to remind readers, 'how she sang of the famine and its terrible effects, followed by emigration'.[36]

The Wilde's home in Dublin became a site where the intelligentsia would gather and exchange ideas, which proved to be an important tool in rebuilding Ireland's cultural and literary confidence. The gatherings were even noted by the press in America, the Boston *Pilot* reporting, 'Their house in Merrion Square was a rendezvous for all that there was of literary and artistic eminence, beauty, wit and fashion'.[37] Speranza's generosity in hosting literary salons, or 'at homes', was another symbol of the hope that she embodied in her name and her actions. Through the weekly gatherings, the Wilde children would meet the leading intellectual writers and political thinkers of the day. The salons continued after she moved to London, regardless of her straightened financial circumstances. In this way, she cultivated an emerging generation of Irish writers including George Bernard Shaw and W. B. Yeats. The tradition of literary 'at homes' was continued by Oscar and his wife, Constance.[38]

The year 1864 proved to be an eventful one for the Wildes. In January 1864, William was knighted for his services to the Irish census and so Speranza became Lady Wilde, a title she clearly relished. One Dublin newspaper paid special tribute to William's founding and endowment of St Mark's Hospital, which, 'will, we are sure, never be forgotten by the citizens of Dublin and the poor of Ireland'.[39] In July, the University of Dublin awarded him an honorary M.D. for his services to medicine—an honor that resulted in his being described as 'the most distinguished of all Irishmen'.[40] William's accolades were marred when one of his patients, Mary Travers, persistently and publicly accused him of seduction. In her accounts of what had happened, Travers also held Speranza up for public ridicule. The salacious episode resulted in a much-publicized court case in December 1864. The jury ruled that Travers had been libeled by Speranza, but awarded her only one-farthing, while the Wildes had to pay £2,000 in court costs.[41] The public scandal damaged William's reputation and the family finances, following which he gave up his professional practice and spent more time at his summer home in Moytura, County Mayo. Nonetheless, his interest in Irish politics continued. In 1870, he attended a series of meetings to form a Home

Rule Association and acted as its first secretary. In early 1871, William was one of the main speakers at a banquet to celebrate the election of the nationalist—and former Young Irelander—John Martin, to the British Parliament.[42] When he rose to speak, 'A cheer for Speranza' was called for.[43] William died in 1876, aged 61. The family home in Merrion Square was sold and, in 1879, Speranza moved to London. There, she joined her two sons.[44] Ironically, the three remaining Wildes had become emigrants too.

The distress caused by the Travers case may have been compensated by the publication of a compilation of Speranza's poems at the end of 1864. Many of them had appeared in the *Nation* between 1846 and 1848. The publication was dedicated to her sons, Willie and Oscar, with the inscription: 'I made them indeed/Speak plain the word country. I taught them, no doubt/That country's a thing one should die for at need'.[45] Reviews in the Irish press were generally favourable, and often referred to Speranza's days in the *Nation*:

> It is not our business, in the literary portion of our paper, to say anything of the political tendencies of the poetry of Young Ireland ... The writers of the old Nation passed away, and a new generation succeeded them, some of whom carried on the work of their predecessors with a genius worthy of those who had gone before them. None of those new writers could for a moment be compared with the one whose poems, published under the name 'Speranza', week after week, delighted the readers of the paper in which they appeared. Speranza's poems have been collected and published by Mr. Duffy, and we must say that we have seldom met with a greater treat than we have had when perusing them in this new form. We have felt that we were reading poetry, and poetry of no mean order. If glowing thoughts, lofty aspirations, language of the most fastidiously correct description, and imagery of the most gorgeous nature, go far to constitute poetry, then the name cannot be denied to the productions of 'Speranza' ... The Biblical nature of her images and expressions cannot fail to strike every reader, and the clearness of her language. The certainty with which she expresses her meaning, is particularly agreeable in these days, when a certain amount of obscurity seems often to be an almost essential element in whatever is to have any claim to be looked upon as poetry.[46]

A less positive review appeared in the *Southern Reporter and Cork Commercial Courier,* which admitted that they did not approve of her politics and believed that her poetry lacked imagination. Nonetheless, they praised the realism of 'The Famine Year'.[47] A number of British newspapers also focused on the political dimension of the poems, one Scottish newspaper averring:

> We are too near the times of the famine and the rebellion and the 'exodus'. Many Irishmen, and most Englishmen and Scotchmen, will recoil from Speranza's politics, however much they may admire the form in which they are presented. Thus, it must

> happen that this lady's political poetry will not gain the sympathy of the nation, and so will fail of securing that meed of praise to which on its abstract merits, apart from political predilections and influences, it will be entitled.[48]

Sales of the publication were high, however, and a second edition appeared in 1867 and an enlarged version in 1871. In later editions, the dedication was simply, 'To Ireland'.[49]

In later life, Speranza continued to write and publish, she being partly motivated by the need to earn an income following William's death, while the land agitation had put an end to rent received from the family's properties in the west.[50] Her work continued to focus on themes with a political message. Her new poems often first appeared in *The Shamrock*, an advanced nationalist newspaper that had been founded in Dublin in 1866. Many were then reprinted in the Boston *Pilot*.[51] The imprisonment and harsh treatment of the Fenians, a republican movement founded in the wake of the Great Hunger, led Speranza to again take up her poetic pen:

> HAS not vengeance been sated at last?
> Will the holy and beautiful chimes
> Ring out the old wrongs of the past ...
> Will the eyes of the pale prisoners rest
> Once again on their loved mountain scenes ...[52]

Speranza's continued political involvement led one Irish newspaper to write of her in 1892, 'She pleaded in prose and verse for the liberation of the Fenian prisoners in '67; she sympathized with the Land League movement, and now the Home Rule cause has in her an ardent supporter'.[53] Additionally, Speranza wrote on topics as diverse as women's suffrage and the role of Irish America in winning independence for Ireland.[54] She also proved to be a role model for the next generation of women activists. Fanny Parnell, a poet and gifted sister of Charles Stewart Parnell, was likened to Speranza, with comparisons drawn between 'The Famine Year' and Parnell's poem, 'Hold the Harvest'.[55] Although she was based in America, Fanny's poems were widely printed in the Irish press, much to the chagrin of the British government, leading one nationalist paper to observe, 'Miss Fanny Parnell, in a few months, has won as deep a place in the hearts of the Irish people – as "Speranza" won in '48'.[56] Maud Gonne, who personally travelled to County Mayo to organize relief during the food shortages of the 1890s, was called 'The New Speranza'. In 1900, Gonne penned the polemical 'The Famine Queen', in which she accused Queen Victoria of overseeing a deliberate policy of starving her Irish subjects.[57] Her fiery rhetoric was reminiscent of the language used by Speranza 50 years earlier.

In 1881, from her London home, Speranza reconnected with traditional Irish folklore, publishing the delightful 'Ancient Legends, Mystic Charms and Superstitions of

Ireland'.[58] It drew largely from her husband's earlier research and on interviews with the older generation of Irish peasants. Speranza's love of Ireland was evident in the Preface:

> In a few years such a collection would be impossible, for the old race is rapidly passing away to other lands, and in the vast working-world of America, with all the new influences of light and progress, the young generation, though still loving the land of their fathers, will scarcely find leisure to dream over the fairy haunted hills and lakes and raths of ancient Ireland.
>
> I must disclaim, however, all desire to be considered a melancholy *Laudatrix temporis acti*. These studies of the Irish past are simply the expression of my love for the beautiful island that gave me my first inspiration, my quickest intellectual impulses, and the strongest and best sympathies with genius and country possible to a woman's nature.[59]

The book concluded with 'Sketches on the Irish Past' that included some of William's writings. The publication also returned to themes that had informed much of Speranza's writing and politics: the Famine and emigration. She lamented the continuing mass emigration, a theme that she and William had often written about:

> A million of our people emigrated; a million of our people died ... The echoes of the old tongue—is dying out at last along the stony plains of Mayo and the wild sea-cliffs of the storm-rent western shore. Scarcely a million and a half are left of people too old to emigrate, amidst roofless cabins and ruined villages, who speak that language now. Exile, confiscation, or death, was the final fate written on the page of history for the much-enduring children of Ireland.[60]

Yeats, who in 1888 would draw on earlier work by the Wildes and publish *Irish Fairy Tales and Folk Lore*, was generous in his praise:

> She [Speranza] is doing good work in setting down in good English Sir William Wilde's great collection of folk lore and legend. Sir William Wilde employed peasants in all parts of Ireland to gather together everything in the way of charm or fairy tale. Old men and women, too, when going away cured from his hospital, would ask leave to send him eggs or fowl, or some such comfiture, and he would bargain for a fairy tale instead.[61]

Speranza's book was brought out in America in 1887, one review pointing out that: 'The ancient legends and traditions, which were at one time the themes of every homestead in the country, are now rapidly dying out, and if not recollected and published under these auspices, would soon be forgotten'.[62] Yet again, Speranza, building on earlier work by William, was helping to honour the traditions and customs of the poor people of Ireland.[63] Her connection with Ireland and Irish authors continued through the work of the Irish Literary Society, founded in London in 1893, with Speranza as its first vice-president.[64]

Speranza's earlier poems and prose was frequently reprinted, especially her writings associated with the Famine period. 'The Die is Cast', outlawed in 1848, found new generations of readers, with even a conservative English newspaper admitting, 'As a sample of blood-stirring English prose it still retains its place in a number of collections, and especially those issued on the other side of the Atlantic'.[65] Did Speranza regret any of her earlier actions or words? When it was brought to her attention by Home Rule MP, T.D. Sullivan, that extracts of 'Jacta Alea Est' were being reprinted to inspire new generations of nationalists, she responded:

> Thanks for the volume and the number with Jacta Alea Est, but I cannot read it. It recalls too vividly that evening when I wrote it —no, I did not write it, I dashed it on the paper phrase by phrase as I walked up and down the room in the light of a glorious sunset, with a glow as bright, of pride, and hope, and expectation in my heart and brain. No, I cannot read now. I cannot calmly tread the ashes of that once glowing past.[66]

That Speranza remained indelibly linked with the Famine was evident, with her poems often reprinted in the nationalist press. She was also referenced in a review of Rev. O'Rourke's 1875 publication, *The Great Famine*, with the first stanza of her now-famous poem to explain to a new generation the tragedy that had occurred 30 years earlier.[67] On the other side of the Atlantic, Speranza continued to be remembered for her role in Young Ireland and her poetry of 'the Famine and the Exodus'. A review of her writings in the Boston *Pilot* in 1879 noted, 'Her sympathy for her country's sufferings in these days is only equaled by her scorn of those whom she blamed for letting such things be. How her indignation blazes forth at the coolness with which the loss of a million of her countrymen is taken'.[68] Speranza's second son, Oscar, also declared his support for Irish independence and his awareness of Ireland's sad history.[69] In 1887, in pursuit of financial security, he took on the role of editor of *The Ladies' World*, which he renamed *The Woman's World*, and set about transforming it to be 'representative of the thought and culture of the women of this century'.[70] Early on, Oscar was offered a poem on the Famine for publication, which he described as being 'full of power and pathos'. It prompted him to explain to the unnamed author:

> How tragic the stories of the Irish Famine are! My father worked all through it, and afterwards wrote the Blue Book on it for the Government. He used to tell me marvelous tales about it. I am very glad you have taken one of the incidents of it for a poem.[71]

During these years, Oscar was increasingly identifying with his Celtic origins. Reviewing Oscar's writings in 1891, fellow Irishman, W.B. Yeats despaired of English people's 'complete inability to understand anything he says', adding, 'We should not find him so unintelligible—for much about him is Irish of the Irish. I see in his life and works an extravagant Celtic crusade against Anglo-Saxon stupidity'.[72]

Oscar's three very public trials in 1895 and his imprisonment for 'gross indecencies' brought public disgrace on a family that had given so much to Ireland, her history and culture. Oscar's time in prison led to two masterpieces of literature. Speranza had always believed that poets were agents of social and political change, and Oscar realized this ambition in his best-known poem, *The Ballad of Reading Gaol*. His intellectual debt to his parents was acknowledged in the viscerally raw, *De Profundis*—also written while in prison: 'She [Speranza] and my father had bequeathed me a name they had made noble and honoured, not merely in literature, art, archaeology, and science, but in the public history of my own country, in its evolution as a nation'.[73] The Great Famine had been a key component in Ireland's evolution towards independence, and Speranza and William had each made a distinctive and lasting contribution to providing an understanding of this tragedy.

Speranza died in February 1896, while her beloved son Oscar was languishing in Reading Gaol. Dubbed the 'National Poetess of Ireland', Speranza's later years were marred by poverty, scandal and personal tragedy.[74] During her lifetime, she was described as 'the world-famed "Speranza", dear to Irish hearts, whose patriotic poems and lyrics are familiar household words wherever the liberty-inspired genie of English literature are used and appreciated'.[75] When she died, Oscar had been incarcerated for just over eight months; Speranza had been denied permission to visit him and he was refused permission to attend her funeral. Many newspapers in Britain and Ireland noted her passing. As the *Wexford People* explained:

> Her connections, her faith, her position in society, all seemed to forbid any connection with the popular movement which enveloped Ireland in the forties. But she was first attracted and then swept away by the enthusiasm of the hour ... The poems of Speranza have in them no trace of feminine softness. This young girl denounced the enemies of Ireland and lamented her woes in verses as stern and majestic as the strain of a Hebrew prophet. The awful disaster of the Famine is reflected in all its horror in her verses.[76]

Jacta Alea Est was also frequently referenced, as a tribute to the lasting impact of Speranza's words.[77] The Boston *Pilot*, an admirer of Speranza during her long career in the public eye, was fulsome in their recognition of her championing the poor of Ireland:

> Lady Wilde devoted her talents to the cause of her country, and as service to the vanquished seldom meets with recognition from the victorious, her admirers have chiefly been among the ranks of the defeated. But, after all, where should a poet or patriot look for better reward than in the hearts of the poor and friendless? It was something for this woman, wellborn and tenderly nurtured, to see and feel, as she did, the utter desolation of the poor.[78]

Regardless of such accolades, Speranza's funeral was inconspicuous, with only her son, William, his wife and one other person in attendance—a friend of Oscar who laid a wreath on his behalf.[79] Speranza was buried in Kensal Green Cemetery in London, in common ground, with no headstone. Still incarcerated and refused permission to attend the burial, Oscar paid the funeral expenses. Poignantly, for a woman who had lived much of her long life in the public eye, it had been her wish that she should be buried 'quite privately'.[80]

Oscar died in a hotel in Paris in 1900, tragically of an untreated ear infection that he had developed while in prison. His three years since being released had been mostly lonely and poor. It was a poignant irony that a family who had devoted so much time highlighting issues to do with social justice and economic dislocation, would die in relative obscurity and, in the case of Speranza and Oscar, poverty. For a family that spoke so much on the negative impact of emigration and their dislike of imperial rule, Speranza and her two sons had created new lives in England and when they died, were buried outside of Ireland. Only William was buried in Dublin.

Jane Elgee Speranza Wilde continues to defy easy definition or categorization. Born into a life of privilege in Ireland as one of the Ascendancy class, she was cheered by the poor people of Dublin when she appeared in public.[81] Speranza's final years would be spent in poverty and social stigmatism, which ended with her burial in an unmarked grave in London. Her long life was colourful and rife with contradictions. An unwavering critic of the British government, she was presented at court, attended balls and soirees in Dublin Castle and fully embraced the title bestowed on her husband in 1864. A devoted wife and mother, she also continued to define herself through her written work and through her self-chosen name, Speranza. In her lifetime and following her death, she remained controversial. Her writings, especially in regard to Irish history, have not always found favour with modern biographers. In a 2017 publication on nationalist writings of the nineteenth century, she was accused of standing 'uneasily at the border of colonial subject and ethnological colonizer, a doubled representation that continues in her 1887 ancient legends'.[82] Both she and William were also impugned for a 'stunning elision of the claims of recorded history through rhetorical preterition'.[83] Seen through the prism of the Famine, however, the reputation of the Wildes is less ambiguous. For 50 years, Speranza remained in the public eye as a result of her politics and her publications, making her one of the most prolific and enduring members of the original Young Ireland. Like many of its founders, she was a Protestant nationalist, but she combined this with her feminism and her social consciousness, which differentiated her from many of her class and gender. Her poems on the Famine and its impact—most notably 'The Famine Year', 'A Voice for the Poor', and 'Exodus', captured the spirit of the age that she had lived through and the divide between the helpless, hopeless condition of the poor and the clinical detachment of officials and politicians. The constant reprinting of her poems in the decades after 1852 meant that, in the words of Melissa Fagan, Speranza became 'a kind of memory bank' for the tragedy of the Famine years, a reminder of the tragedy that had changed Ireland forever.[84] Yet Speranza, in both her chosen name and her prolific writings, offered the Irish people hope that better days lay ahead.

Born into privilege and part of a Protestant elite in Ireland, Speranza, William and Oscar Wilde spent their final years either in isolation, exile, poverty or public disgrace. Fortunately, their multiple contributions to literature, history, medicine, famine studies, cultural nationalism and social justice, outlived them. Although less than 600 words in length, Speranza's poem, 'The Famine Year', written in January 1847, did not diminish in power over the intervening decades. In it, Speranza laid bare the suffering of the Irish, especially of women and children, while laying the blame firmly at the feet of 'the stranger' who had misgoverned Ireland for centuries. Her fearless defence of the vulnerable and voiceless during the Famine made her their hero, a role that she relished and that she also deserved.

NOTES

1. Although beloved and respected during her lifetime, her reputation as a poet and a nationalist (and even as a mother) suffered following Oscar's fall from grace. Her reputation is being restored, see, Eibhear Walshe, *Jane Wilde* (Brighton: Edward Everett Root, 2020).
2. W.B. Yeats, 'The Celt in London', Boston *Pilot* (hereafter *Pilot*), vol. 52, no. 39, 28 Sept. 1889. Yeats was the *Pilot's* London correspondent.
3. The other founders were Thomas Davis and John Blake Dillon. Speranza originally used the pen-name John Fanshawe Ellis, leading Duffy to assume she was a man.
4. 'From a History of Young Ireland by Charles Gavan Duffy', *Weekly Freeman's Journal*, 9 Aug. 1884.
5. 'Our Irish Portrait Gallery. Lady Wilde', *Irish Society* (Dublin), 9 Jan. 1892.

6. 'Destitute Persons (Ireland) Bill', House of Commons Debates, 8 Feb. 1847, vol. 89, cc. 943–945. O'Connell warned parliament that unless they acted 'not only liberally, but generously', one quarter of the Irish population would be lost.
7. This poem, 'A Lament', was published in the *Nation* on 5 Dec. 1847. It was not included in the anthology.
8. 'Daniel O'Connell. HIBERNIAE LIBERATOR AD LIMINA APOSTOLORUM PERGENS GENOAE OBDORMIVIT', *Pilot*, vol. 38, no. 19, 8 May 1875.
9. Lady Jane Francesca Agnes Speranza Wilde, *Poems by Speranza* (Dublin: M. H. Gill & Son, 1864), p. 14.
10. The poem was printed in the *Pilot*, vol. 32, no. 9, 27 Feb. 1869; 'The Voice of the Poor. The Irish Famine', *Pilot*, vol. 37, no. 38, 19 Sept. 1874.
11. Wilde, *Poems*, 'Foreshadowings', pp 18–19.
12. 'News of the Day', *Vindicator*, 13 Feb. 1847.
13. 'Ireland', *Morning Post*, 12 Feb. 1847.
14. Christine Kinealy, 'Food exports from Ireland, 1846–1847' in *History Ireland*, issue 1 (spring 1997), vol. 5, 32–36.
15. The anthology included a translation (by William Wilde) of the 1739, 'A Lament for the Potato'. In a number of accounts, it was incorrectly stated that Speranza had made the translation, eg, *Pilot*, vol. 46, no. 46, 17 Nov. 1883.
16. Amy Martin, 'The Skeleton at the Feast. Lady Wilde's Famine poetry and Irish international critiques of food scarcity', in Christine Kinealy, Jason King and Ciarán Reilly, *Women and the Great Hunger* (Hamden: Quinnipiac and Cork University Press, 2016), pp 150–8.
17. Christine Kinealy, *Repeal and Revolution. 1848 in Ireland* (Manchester University Press, 2009).
18. The editorial appeared in the *Nation* on 29 July 1848.
19. Lord Clarendon had issued a Proclamation a few days earlier outlawing the 'seditious press'.
20. This story was repeated often, 'The New Knight and his Lady', *Belfast Morning News*, 10 Feb. 1864; 'Obituary', *Pilot*, vol. 59, no. 7, 15 Feb. 1896.
21. She used the pseudonyms 'A' and 'Stella and Vanessa', see *Nation,* 30 Nov. 1850.
22. William R. Wilde, *The Beauties of the Boyne and its tributary, the Blackwater* (Dublin: James McGlashan, 1849). 'It was Wilde who first identified the tumuli at the Bend of the Boyne as the Brugh na Boinne of early Irish literature. It was he who first noted the crannog or artificial lake-dwelling at a former lake at Lagore, Co. Meath', in 'The surgical intellect of the senior Wilde', *Irish Times*, 19 May 2001.
23. Mark T. Watts, 'Sir William Wilde 1815–1876: royal ophthalmologist extraordinary', *Journal of the Royal Society of Medicine*, vol. 83, March 1990, pp 183–4; Peter Froggatt, 'William Wilde and the 1851 census of Ireland', in *Journal of Medical History,* 1865, 9 (4), 302–24, p. 314.
24. 'The Governors of St. Mark's Ophthalmic', *Freeman's Journal*, 29 Oct. 1861. His three young children also supported their father's venture. The same report acknowledged

donations received from 'Master William Wilde, one pound; Master Oscar Wilde, 10*s*; Miss Isola Wilde, 10*s*'.

25. Peter Froggatt, 'Sir William Wilde, 1815–1876. A centenary appreciation. Wilde's place in medicine', in *Proceedings of the Royal Irish Academy*, vol. 77, 1977, 261–278, p. 264.
26. The Chief Census Commissioner in 1851 was William Donnelly, the Registrar-General of Marriages.
27. *The Census of Ireland for the year 1851. Part V. Tables of deaths. Vol. I.*, 1856, British Parliamentary Papers (BPP), XXIX.
28. Ibid., *Part I. Showing the area, population and number of houses by townlands and electoral divisions,* BPP, 1852–3, XCI, p. 144.
29. Froggatt, 'Wilde and the 1851 census', p. 306.
30. 'Irish Popular Superstitions', *Dublin University Magazine*, vol. xxxiii, no. cxcvii, 541–60, p. 547.
31. W.R. Wilde, Preface, *Irish Popular Superstitions* (Dublin: James McGlashan, 1852).
32. Speranza to unnamed correspondent, quoted in Richard Ellman, *Oscar Wilde* (New York: Alfred A. Knopf, 1988), pp 16–17.
33. The poem appeared in Oscar's first collection of poetry and was singled out for praise, 'Oscar Wilde', *Dublin Evening Telegraph,* 13 Sept. 1881. A copy was displayed in the Chelsea home of Oscar and Constance, 'Mrs Oscar Wilde at Home', *Portadown News,* 1 Dec. 1894.
34. 'Our Irish Portrait Gallery. Lady Wilde', *Irish Society,* 9 Jan. 1892.
35. It was frequently reprinted in the Boston *Pilot*, e.g., *Pilot*, vol. 33, no. 53, 31 Dec. 1870.
36. 'Our Irish Portrait Gallery. Lady Wilde', *Irish Society,* 9 Jan. 1892.
37. Ibid., 'Oscar Wilde. Something about his parents and his poems', vol. 45, no. 2, 14 Jan. 1882.
38. 'Mrs Oscar Wilde at home', *Portadown News*, 1 Dec. 1894.
39. 'Sir William Wilde', *The Evening Freeman*, 29 Jan. 1864.
40. 'Honour to Medical Man', *Belfast Morning News*, 28 July 1864.
41. 'Court of Common Pleas. Mary Josephine Travers v. Sir William Wilde and Lady Wilde', *Dublin Daily Express*, 17 Dec. 1864; *The Irishman*, 24 Dec. 1864.
42. He preceded this by quoting Thomas Davis, 'Banquet to J. Martin. Esq., MP', *Freeman's Journal*, 7 Feb. 1871.
43. 'The Meath Election', *Dublin Weekly Nation*, 11 Feb. 1871. During his long speech, William briefly referred to his own ill-health.
44. After Oxford University, Oscar relocated to London. Willie Wilde (1852–99) had been called to the Irish bar. In 1879, he and his mother moved to London where he worked as a journalist. He was constantly in debt.
45. Lady Jane Wilde, *Poems by Speranza* (Dublin: James Duffy, 1864).
46. 'Poems by Speranza', *Dublin Evening Post*, 7 Mar. 1865.
47. *Southern Reporter and Cork Commercial Courier*, 23 Mar. 1865.
48. 'Poems by Speranza', *Caledonian Mercury*, 24 June 1865.
49. *Poems by Speranza* (Lady Wilde), New Edition (Dublin: M. H. Gill & Son, 1871), p. v.
50. The article referred to her straightened financial circumstances, 'Lady Wilde's New Book', *Pilot*, vol. 50, no. 21, 21 May 1887.

51. 'The Travers and Wilde Scandal', *Maidstone Telegraph,* 1 July 1865; 'St Patrick's day poem – new from Speranza, "Sparks from the Forge"', *Flag of Ireland,* 25 Mar. 1871; 'New poem by Speranza, "Antigone"', *The Irishman*, 6 May 1871; Ibid., 'Poem by Speranza', 22 Mar. 1873. Many of these poems first appeared in the *Shamrock.*
52. 'The Prisoners, Christmas 1869', appeared in the 1871 edition of *Poems*.
53. *Irish Society* (Dublin), 31 Dec. 1892.
54. Lady Wilde, 'The Bondage of Women', in *Social Studies* (London: Ward and Downey, 1893), pp 1–27; Lady Wilde, *The American Irish* (Dublin: William McGee, 1882).
55. See Christine Kinealy, 'When History and Hope Rhymed. Fanny Parnell: Nationalist, Feminist and Patriot Poet', in Mary Kelly (ed.) *Navigating Historical Crosscurrents in the Irish Atlantic: Essays for Catherine Shannon* (Cork University Press, 2022), pp 86–106.
56. 'The Poet of the Irish Land War', *Pilot*, vol. 44, no. 4, 22 Jan. 1881.
57. Christine Kinealy, 'The Real Famine Queen? Maud Gonne and Famines in the 1890s' in Kinealy and Gerard Moran, *Famines before and after the Great Hunger* (Quinnipiac and Cork University Press, 2020).
58. Lady Wilde, *Ancient Legends, Mystic Charms and Superstitions of Ireland. With Sketches of the Irish Past* (London: Ward and Downey, 1881), p. 327.
59. Ibid., p. xii.
60. Ibid., p. 327.
61. W. B. Yeats, 'The Celt in London', *Pilot,* vol. 52, no 39, 28 Sept. 1889.
62. Ibid., 'Lady Wilde's New Book', vol. 50, no. 21, 21 May 1887.
63. Ibid.
64. 'Inaugural Meeting', *Flag of Ireland*, 11 Mar. 1893.
65. 'Politics and Persons', *St James's Gazette*, 6 Feb. 1896.
66. 'Literary notes', *Canterbury Journal, Kentish Times and Farmers' Gazette*, 7 Mar. 1896; *Linlithgowshire Gazette*, 14 Mar. 896.
67. 'The Great Famine' reviewed in the *Nation*, 5 Feb. 1875.
68. *Pilot*, vol. 42, 12 Apr. 1879.
69. '53 days of court proceeds', *Dublin Daily Express*, 13 Feb. 1889; *Freeman's Journal*, 21 Feb. 1889. Oscar attended the Parnell Commission in 1888–1889 a number of times.
70. Oscar to Helen Sickert, 27 May 1887, Merlin Holland (ed.) *Oscar Wilde. A Life in Letters* (London: Fourth Estate, 2003), p. 103.
71. Ibid., Oscar to an unidentified correspondent, [September 1887], p. 104. According to Holland, the poem was never published, 'possibly because of the increasingly sensitive issue of Irish home rule'.
72. 'Oscar Wilde's last book. Review by W.B. Yeats', *United Ireland*, 26 Sept. 1891.
73. Oscar Wilde, *De Profundis* (London: Methuen, 1924). It was written as a letter when Oscar was in prison and published posthumously in 1905.
74. 'Death of Lady Wilde', *Wexford People*, 8 Feb. 1896; *Kerry Sentinel*, 8 Feb. 1896. Her death was widely noted in the British press, 'Death of Lady Wilde', *Huddersfield Daily Chronicle*, 6 Feb. 1896; 'Lady Wilde', *The Queen*, 15 Feb. 1896. Her now-disgraced son, Oscar, was

rarely mentioned in British newspaper reports, with a few exceptions, 'Death of Oscar Wilde's Mother', *Edinburgh Evening News*, 5 Feb. 1896.

75. This article, reflecting on Oscar's parents, was written following the release of his book of poems, 'Oscar Wilde', *Dublin Evening Telegraph*, 13 Sept. 1881.
76. *Wexford People*, 8 Feb. 1896.
77. 'Death of Lady Wilde', *Freeman's Journal*, 6 Feb. 1896.
78. 'Obituary', *Pilot*, vol. 59, no. 7, 15 Feb. 1896.
79. 'The Late Lady Wilde', *Freeman's Journal*, 8 Feb. 1896.
80. Geraldine McDermottroe, 'A tribute to Speranza – Lady Wilde', in *The Wildean*, no. 9 (July 1996), 5–10.
81. *Dublin Weekly Nation*, 4 July 1863.
82. Patrick R. O'Malley, *Liffey and Lethe: Paramnesiac History in Nineteenth-Century Anglo-Ireland* (Oxford University Press, 2017), p. 168.
83. Ibid., p. 168.
84. Melissa Fagan, *Literature and the Irish Famine 1845–1919* (Oxford: Clarendon Press, 2002), p. 165.

International Involvement

CHAPTER SIX

'UNMITIGATED, HOPELESS PAIN'

William Rathbone V (1787–1868) and the Great Hunger

Christine Kinealy

Like many people involved in philanthropy during the Famine, William Rathbone V had no direct connection with Ireland. Yet, in 1847, Rathbone was the person chosen by Captain Robert Bennet Forbes to oversee the difficult task of disbursing the cargo of the relief ship, USS *Jamestown*. Despite Rathbone's role on both sides of the Irish Sea in assisting and defending victims of the Great Hunger, his involvement is largely ignored both in Famine historiography and in biographies of the Rathbone family.[1] His involvement in the voyage of the *Jamestown*, however, provides insights into the difficulties in providing private relief in the midst of a famine, while reinforcing the international and ecumenical nature of such benevolence.

Rathbone was born to a wealthy merchant family in Liverpool, a city indelibly associated with enslavement, but both his father and grandfather—also William Rathbone—were founding members of the Society for the Abolition of the Slave Trade, established in the city in 1788.[2] Rathbone grew up to a life of privilege but the guiding principle of each Rathbone generation was that:

> They looked on business as a means to an end, as a way of providing funds to enable them to pursue other interests and, in doing so, they carried over into business, their social-consciousness and moral integrity. Their principles demanded that the pursuit of profit, though justifiable, was not the sole aim of business transactions.[3]

Rathbone was an ardent abolitionist too, even though much of his family's early wealth had been based on American cotton. By the 1840s, this trade was neither dependable nor lucrative, but Rathbone blamed his own 'defects and deficiencies' for a drop in revenue.[4] It was left to his sons, William Rathbone VI and Samuel Greg Rathbone, to revive the family's fortunes and to develop more trading links in the east, most notably with China.[5] Like many involved in the abolition movement, Rathbone was an advocate of temperance.[6] It appears that he first became acquainted with Father Mathew, Ireland's 'apostle of temperance', when the priest travelled to Britain in 1843, where he administered 'the pledge' (not to drink alcohol) to thousands of people in Glasgow and Liverpool. In the latter city, Father Mathew was hosted by the Rathbone family and William, despite being a Unitarian, attended Catholic Mass in St Patrick's Church, to mark the official launch of the campaign.[7] Rathbone's admiration for the Irish priest continued and, in August 1846, he, along with a number of prominent Irish landlords, contributed to an annuity fund to allow Father Mathew to continue with the temperance movement.[8] Rathbone had other associations with Ireland, which gave an insight into his political sympathies. In early 1836, he was one of the prominent city officials to welcome Daniel O'Connell to Liverpool, a city known for its ties to the Orange Order, to slavery and its support for the Conservative Party.[9] Both Rathbone and O'Connell were strong supporters of the abolition of slavery. Moreover Rathbone, a religious non-conformist, had been an ardent champion of the campaign for Catholic Emancipation. In this regard, he was following a family tradition of compassion for Ireland. In July 1799, William Rathbone IV had written to a friend expressing sympathy with oppressed people everywhere, including 'our Brethren at home, and particularly so with ill-fated, oppressed, and unhappy Ireland'.[10] Like his predecessors, Rathbone was also active in local politics, being elected a Liberal councillor for the city in 1835 and serving as mayor in 1837. In the years that followed, Rathbone became a leading advocate of the public health movement, working alongside pioneering figures such as local doctor, William Duncan. Liverpool then had the unenviable reputation of being the unhealthiest city in the United Kingdom.[11] Rathbone, like Duncan, recognized the importance of cleanliness in promoting good health. In 1842, building on an initiative by Kitty Wilkinson, Rathbone persuaded the Corporation to open public baths and wash-houses at rates that even the poorest could afford to pay.[12]

Liverpool, with its multiple maritime links to Ireland, and as the main port of embarkation to North America, quickly became absorbed into suffering associated with the crop failure in Ireland. The first appearance of the blight in 1845 and the accompanying shortages had led to a petition to the city's mayor to convene a public meeting to request that the government intervene to assist the Irish poor. Liverpool's Mayor, David Hodgson, however, was notorious for his anti-Catholic views, and had refused to convene the meeting.[13] His intransigence was reported in Irish newspapers.[14] Instead, a meeting was convened by a number of tradesmen to support Ireland. During the discussion, several of them likened the scarcity in Ireland to poverty in Britain, for which they partly blamed the Corn Law legislation.[15] Rathbone, one of the main speakers, suggested that the government should address the deficiencies that existed throughout the whole of the United Kingdom. At the end of the meeting, Rathbone received three cheers, suggesting a level of influence and popularity amongst the people of Liverpool that transcended party politics.[16]

It was the much-publicized voyage of the USS *Jamestown,* transporting supplies from Boston to Cork in spring 1847, that brought Rathbone directly into contact with the suffering in Ireland. The relief ship was commanded by Captain Robert Bennet Forbes, who was much-respected on both sides of the Atlantic Ocean.[17] The American Congress had given permission for both the *Jamestown* and the *Macedonian*—two ships-of-war—to be used for this purpose. In preparation for her 'voyage of mercy', armaments had been removed from the *Jamestown* to facilitate loading on 17 March.[18] In early February 1847, Forbes contacted Rathbone, explaining that he had volunteered to bring donations to Ireland on behalf of the Committee of Relief and was waiting for Congress to grant permission. By doing so, he could ensure there were no delays and that minimal costs would be incurred. He concluded by saying that after Cork, 'I may have time to cross the channel and shake hands with my friends in Liverpool'.[19] In early March, Forbes reported to Rathbone that Congress had placed the *Jamestown* at his disposal and he wanted to put its cargo in the hands of an agent of the Society of Friends in Cork.[20] In advance of the journey, Forbes also made contact with fellow New Englander, Joshua Bates, a successful merchant who was a senior partner in Baring Brothers in London.[21] Both Bates and Barings were associated with the work of the British Relief Association.[22] He was also a business contact and friend of the Rathbone family.[23] In his correspondence, Forbes referred to Rathbone as 'our mutual friend'.[24]

Rathbone was the person chosen by Forbes to ensure that the mission of the *Jamestown* was fulfilled. On 13 March, only a few days before loading commenced, Forbes made a direct appeal to Rathbone:

> Knowing your character as a philanthropist to be unsurpassed, I have to request that you will act as agent, take such measures to have the cargo of the *Jamestown* properly distributed as may suggest themselves to you, and particularly to procure the assistance of any vessels of war or of the revenue to take the cargo out. It will consist of 500 barrels more or less of provisions; 4,000 barrels Indian meal in casks and handy drilling bags; 2,000 bushels of beans and peas, in suitable packages; 1,500 barrels bread; 5,000 bushels of Indian corn in barrels and bags, the weight of which will be about 800 tons.

He explained this request for assistance on the grounds that, 'I wish to have everything done to relieve me from labor at Cork, as well as all glorification'.[25] Being chosen to assist in this philanthropic endeavour came as a surprise to Rathbone, however. In early April, he wrote to his eldest son, William, saying that he had been 'put in a great fuss by the receipt of a letter from R. Bennet Forbes' who was bringing a frigate to Cork laden with 8,000 barrels of provisions for Ireland and Scotland. Forbes's letter had informed Rathbone that the distribution would be put under the control of a committee, which was 'to be named and prepared by me, and [I am] also to arrange with government to receive the property and prepare the conveyances to be at Cork'. He admitted to his son, 'You may well conjecture my consternation at this responsibility'.[26] Rathbone's sense of duty, however, was stronger than any disquietude he felt. He informed William that he had already contacted Henry Labouchere, the Chief Secretary for Ireland, and Bates of Baring Brothers, to arrange for storage for the cargo and its disbursement using small crafts and vessels. The *Jamestown* was expected to arrive on 15 April, and Rathbone closed his letter by saying, I am thinking of going to Cork myself'.[27]

In the days leading up to the sailing, Forbes contacted Rathbone a number of additional times. In addition to discussing the cargo, Forbes, who was now describing Rathbone as his 'agent and adviser', asked him to locate ballast—not coal—for the homeward journey. In all of these undertakings, Rathbone would be assisted by Baring Brothers from their bases in London and Liverpool.[28] A few days before the departure, Forbes again contacted Rathbone with a practical suggestion about working with a partner in Cork:

> In regard to the manner of distributing the cargo, I would say I shall be governed by your better judgment, and have only to say if the 'learned Blacksmith', Mr. Elihu Burritt, is near you and you should concur with me and the Committee that he would be a suitable person to be joined with yourself or your agent in the actual distribution, I shall be pleased to have you confer with him—he would give us a history of the state of the sufferers and would work zealously in the cause. If he cannot give time to it, or if it would not be agreeable to you to have him assist you or your agent, and he should be coming home about the 1st May, I shall be glad to have him return with me in the *Jamestown*.[29]

Burritt was an interesting choice. Born in Connecticut in 1810, he was known as 'the learned blacksmith' because, despite his humble origins, he had taught himself to be fluent in a number of languages. A noted supporter of abolition, temperance and pacifism, he had travelled to England in the summer of 1846.[30] In Liverpool, he made contact with both William Rathbone and his younger brother, Richard, the

President of the Liverpool Peace Society.[31] Burritt had spent three days in Skibbereen in February 1847, curtailing his stay when he fell ill with what he suspected was famine fever. The published account of his stay helped to sustain international sympathy on the suffering in west Cork.[32] Burritt decided not to return to America in 1847 and so he did not accept Forbes' offer of travelling home onboard the *Jamestown*. Instead, he remained in Europe, promoting his message of world peace, mixing with some of the leading progressives including Frederick Douglass and the Rathbone family.[33] When Burritt finally left England in October 1849, it was William Rathbone who chaired the farewell meeting.[34]

Even as the *Jamestown* was making its way across the Atlantic, selected copies of Forbes' correspondence were appearing in the Irish press, making him and Rathbone household names.[35] The *Jamestown* arrived in Cork at 5.00pm on 12 April, and anchored in White Bay, only 15 days after setting sail and earlier than had been predicted.[36] Its appearance was noted in the press in Ireland and in Liverpool, the *Liverpool Journal* reporting: 'To our respected townsman, Mr. William Rathbone, has been confided the distribution of this immense stock of provisions, and for this purpose, no doubt, he will shortly proceed to Cork'.[37] On 16 April, the *Liverpool Mercury* informed its readers:

> Our philanthropic townsman, William Rathbone has proceeded to Cork, in pursuance of the wishes conveyed to him across the Atlantic, to assist in the arrangements for an impartial distribution to the necessitous in Ireland, of the bounty which is transmitted to that distressed country from the United States. We should like to see Mr. Rathbone meeting Mr. Forbes, when the latter has fulfilled his amateur task steering the *Jamestown*, sloop of war, into the harbour, with her welcome freight on board.[38]

Rathbone was accompanied by his wife, Elizabeth, and second son, Samuel.[39] In Cork, they made the Imperial Hotel their base. One of the first local people Rathbone contacted was fellow abolitionist, Isabel Jennings.[40] He also renewed his acquaintance with Father Mathew, the well-known temperance advocate and friend of the local poor. Father Mathew personally guided the Rathbones and Forbes through the poorest districts in the city.[41] Forbes referred to what he witnessed as a 'valley of death and pestilence'.[42] Some years later, Rathbone reminisced about this encounter with the Cork priest:

> Of our first meeting I remember little; but the pleasing impression of his frank, genial bearing, his clear open countenance—the general impression of goodness and power which his whole appearance and manner conveyed was very strong.[43]

Following Rathbone's arrival in Cork, a meeting was convened on the afternoon of Saturday, 17 April, at the Cork Institution, to discuss with both Forbes and Rathbone the best way of disposing of the cargo and forming a committee of distribution for this purpose. The meeting was attended by some of the most influential members of Cork society, including: Lord Francis Bernard, the third Earl of Bandon and local Conservative MP from 1842 to 1856; Archdeacon Samuel Kyle, an Anglican minister who held this position from 1833 to 1876; Dean Horatio Newman, Anglican Dean at Cork Cathedral from 1842 until his death in 1864; the Very Rev. Thomas Barry, V.C., parish priest in Bantry; Rev. William Hallinan, parish priest in Ballinhassig; Rev. J. MacNamara; Very Rev. Theobald Mathew, the famed temperance advocate; Rev. William O'Sullivan, Roman Catholic Curate in Cork City and secretary of the Relief Committee since 1846; Major N. Ludlow Beamish, a retired military officer and member of a successful family of brewers; Thomas Lyons, a local Justice of the Peace; William Fagan, part of a family of successful butter merchants who, a few months later, would be elected as a Repeal candidate to parliament in the General Election; Dr. Robert Lyons, a Cork-born physician; Nicholas Marshall Cummins, author of a powerful letter to the London *Times*, published on 24 December 1846; and his cousin, John James Cummins, a banker one of the founders of the British Relief Association. The Cummins family provided free storage for the cargo of the *Jamestown* until it could be distributed. Archdeacon Kyle, Dean Newman, Beamish and Fagan were also active members of the Cork Relief Committee that, over the summer months, was providing an average of 16,000 free rations of soup a day.[44]

At the meeting, Lord Bernard was called to the chair and Beamish spoke first, stating that it needed to be made clear that the *Jamestown's* cargo was for the whole county of Cork, not just the city. He wanted this to be announced as soon as possible, fearing that otherwise even more people would flock into the city to seek relief. To avoid any divisions or misunderstandings, Rathbone asked for Forbes to outline his vision for the cargo. Forbes responded that:

> ... [T]he donations in the *Jamestown* and in the *Tartar*, which was on her way hither, were given by all classes from the servants of a family, up to the very richest who put their hands deeply in their pockets—from all classes of Christians except Catholics. But the reason they got nothing from the Catholics was that they had sent their contributions through their priests—perhaps the best mode. The wish of the donors was that the distribution of the food should be entrusted to a committee comprising of persons of all sects. They did not expect that their small mite would go far to relieve Ireland, but they wished to sow the sentiment broadcast throughout the nation. (Hear, hear.) They did not wish to attach more weight to it than it deserved,

> but they wanted the world to know the aim they sought, in sending a vessel of war on a mission of mercy. (Hear, hear).[45]

Forbes further explained that even if Catholics in Boston had not been directly involved in providing the *Jamestown's* cargo, the mission had the support of the Catholic hierarchy. Forbes carried with him a letter from Rev. John Bernard Fitzpatrick, the Bishop of Boston,[46] to Rev. Dr John Murphy, the Bishop of Cork, praising the actions of Forbes and hoping that this would be the first of many cargoes.[47] However, Bishop Murphy was not destined to read this letter as he passed away on 1 April, only days before the arrival of the *Jamestown*.[48] Murphy was 75 years old and his death was attributed to water on the chest. The poor of Cork had lost a powerful and able spokesperson.[49] During the meeting, Forbes made it clear that *Jamestown's* cargo was for County Cork only, with subsequent cargoes being sent to adjoining counties. He was especially anxious that the committee's supplies should reach people that government relief could not. It was a glaring admission that official relief was not saving lives. Forbes also suggested the committee should be called the New England Committee to make the origins of the donations clear. The suggestion that Rev. William Whitelegge, a local Unitarian minister, should be invited to join the committee was enthusiastically endorsed by Forbes on the grounds of religious inclusivity and because he, too, was Unitarian.[50]

The newly formed committee of distribution met again on the afternoon of Monday 19 April in the Cork Institute. Major Beamish presided. Because so many of the American donors were members of the independent Methodist community it was decided that more members of that persuasion should be included in the committee, so it was enlarged to include the Earl of Mount Cashell and Messrs. Logan, Bergin, Harvey and Ballard. Although Rathbone attended, he took no part in the heated discussion as to whether the city should receive any of the relief—something that Father Mathew vigorously supported on the grounds that the distress was so extensive. The issue was resolved by the government officer, Captain Delves Broughton, who suggested that the hams which had been part of the cargo, be sold and the money used to purchase more 'suitable food' for the poor, some of which could be distributed in the city. The additional suggestion by Broughton not to include the district occupied by Lord Mount Cashell in the distribution on the grounds that 'it has resident landlords who should be made to do their duty, and not come here seeking gratuitous relief' was not well received by several members of the committee. Mount Cashell took the suggestion as a personal insult, saying, 'This is all ill feeling towards me. We have ten thousand wretched people looking up towards us; and God knows I have done all in my power'.[51] The discussion was a powerful reminder that as welcome as the cargo of the *Jamestown* was to the people of Cork, in the starving condition of Ireland there were many competing forces who wanted to benefit from it, and that private relief could make the difference between life and death.

Any feelings of ill-will or dissent were absent that evening when Forbes and Rathbone attended a soirée at the Temperance Institute on Academy Street, which was closely associated with the work of Father Mathew. Less than 18 months earlier, Frederick Douglass had spoken at this venue on 'Temperance and Slavery'.[52] Over 300 people attended the soirée and when Forbes and Rathbone entered, they were cheered enthusiastically 'and both seemed moved by their greeting'. Isaac Varian, a local manufacturer, abolitionist and supporter of Young Ireland, was called on to preside and his first salutation was to 'the Queen'[53]—loyalty to the monarchy being commonplace even amongst radical Repealers. Forbes then spoke with his trade-mark modesty and reticence, although he revealed that the day before he had travelled to Blarney and kissed the famous Blarney Stone.[54] He did not mention that he had also been given a gift of a cow, which would eventually travel back to Boston with him.[55] Forbes informed the meeting that three more relief ships were being sent from Boston, one of which was destined for Scotland, but he expected that even more would be sent when the success of the *Jamestown's* journey was known.[56] Not only were the people of Boston cheered. Father Mathew suggested that their friends in England should be thanked, he then calling on Rathbone to speak. Rathbone's response included a frank admission of his political views regarding the government of Ireland:

> Mr. Chairman, Ladies, and Gentlemen, if my friend Mr. Forbes, who came from the United States loaded with mercy, with peace, and prosperity, be astonished that his name should be received so warmly, well may I be astonished, who am only his secretary and here at his bidding, and truly may I say that I am unprepared to thank you except with the fullness of my heart (cheers). I hope that all here will allow that there are in England men whose hearts beat warmly for justice to Ireland (great cheering)—men who think that her green fields, her intelligence, and her heart demand that she should obtain that justice (cheers). I know that a great deal of the misery of Ireland is owing to the misrule imposed upon her by my countrymen; but, gentlemen, I hope that in proportion to the burden put on you will be the elasticity of that spirit which rises superior to it (hear, hear, and loud cheers). When I hear the eloquent words and the good feeling which proceed from the lips of your chairman—when I see around me many who have met here on different occasions from this, who are united together in the bonds of self-denial to raise their intellects and increase their knowledge, I feel that the regeneration of Ireland is now indeed beginning, and that if our American friends who come now to see the suffering of this country—to see her in her sufferings languid and low, with her

> children perishing around—if they come again ere many years pass over your heads, and I will hope my friend, Captain Forbes, will live to see it, then they will hear the anthem of 'Patrick's Day' sung by Irishmen, with full bellies, with well clad backs, and with souls to make a right use of the blessings which Providence will bestow on them (loud cheers). I thank you with my heart and soul, and I beg you to believe that there are Englishmen banded together to fight the battle of civil and religious liberty for Ireland, that they are respectable and respected, and intelligent men, and that they will continue, as long as God gives them life, to fight that battle—to obtain for Ireland that justice which she demands at the hands of England (tremendous cheering).[57]

Privately, some aspects of the meeting disturbed Rathbone. The following day, he sent a letter to Ralph Varian, Isaac's brother, who had presented a closing address at the soirée. Although expressing his appreciation of the event, Rathbone cautioned Varian about criticizing British officials publicly:

> Delighted and gratified by the meeting last night, the heart and intellect which were called forth in honour of Mr Forbes and his blessed mission, and heartily responding to the sentiments of your own excellent speech, yet I must express my deep and lasting regret at the feelings expressed, and responded to by some, respecting her Majesty's Ministers.
>
> I must leave it to abler pens to discuss the wisdom of their measures, but I do solemnly and religiously protest against that condemnation of their motives, which the greater searcher of hearts can only know.
>
> Of some of them I can speak from my own knowledge that their minds are full to exhaustion, of the thought of how to alleviate the appalling misery of Ireland, their hearts swelling beyond the power of expression with the desire to do so. Englishmen must blush and hide their faces at the *past* misrule of Ireland, but Patriots, Friends of your starving country, do not, in the name of the common Father of us all, do not, I entreat you, destroy their power to redeem that past.[58]

Nor was Varian the only person to be chastised. Rathbone informed his son, William, about a 'remonstrance of mine against a Catholic clergy man' whom he felt had spoken out of place at the gathering, but he added that, as the clergyman's speech had not been reported, it was 'therefore unnecessary on my part to protest against'.[59] Rathbone's comments provide an insight into the complex politics of being an Englishman who supported justice for Ireland, yet still believed that the government's relief policies were being enacted for altruistic reasons. Moreover, as the first letter was printed in the local newspapers, it was clearly a viewpoint that Rathbone was willing to be made public.

On the morning of Tuesday, 20 April, Forbes breakfasted with William and Elizabeth Rathbone in the Ursuline convent in Cork.[60] The convent, which was located in Blackrock, had been founded by Nano Nagle in 1771 and the community had moved to those premises in 1825.[61] The Sisters had helped to pioneer the use of fine needlework and lace embroidery that was adopted by other Irish convents to provide famine relief.[62] It was not Rathbone's only involvement with local nuns: 'Mr and Mrs Rathbone of Liverpool', through Father Mathew, had donated £2 to the Sisters of Mercy on Rutland Street in aid of the servants' asylum. Captain Forbes donated ten shillings to the same cause.[63] However, Forbes' time in Ireland was coming to an end. On his penultimate day in the country, he hosted 200 people on board the *Jamestown*, being mindful to only serve modest refreshments.[64] In the evening, Forbes held a private dinner in Cobh (Cove) for about 20 relief officials, including Rathbone.[65]

Before leaving Cork on 22 April, Forbes handed responsibility for all the remaining decisions regarding relief to Rathbone.[66] Forbes had received many accolades during his short time in Ireland and both Forbes and Rathbone received letters from various government officials acknowledging their assistance, including ones from the Earl of Bessborough, the Lord Lieutenant of Ireland,[67] Henry Labouchere, the Chief Secretary, and Charles Trevelyan, Secretary of the Treasury. Forbes described their contents as 'very gratifying'.[68] Forbes added his own tribute to Rathbone:

> I cannot close my remarks without stating that Mr. William Rathbone, a merchant of long standing of Liverpool, whom I consulted by letter, early in the stage of my proceedings, not only met me at Cork himself, devoted to the business I had enlisted him in, but he brought his excellent lady, his son and a secretary to assist and cooperate with me in carrying out the benevolent views of the donors, and I would respectfully suggest the passage of a resolution, by the Committee, particularly thanking him for his personal sacrifices and for his attention to your business.[69]

No sooner had Forbes left Ireland than Rathbone's committee realized that their initial work on distribution had met with an unforeseen problem. Earlier discussions had been based on the assumptions that the committee had 800 tons of relief to distribute, but they became aware that Forbes had promised part of the cargo at the request of private individuals. Consequently, only approximately 600 tons of relief remained in their hands.[70] At a meeting on 24 April, the new situation was debated at length. There was also discussion about what to do with the hams that were part of the cargo—several members of the committee wanted to sell them in order to purchase more suitable food for the use of the poor, but they were reminded that the now-absent Forbes had been unequivocally opposed to any of the cargo being sold. Interestingly, Captain Broughton, the government agent, believed the hams would be wasted on the poor who would not know how to cook them and who, he claimed, were 'delighted' with a diet of stirabout anyway.[71] This assertion regarding the palates of the local poor was vigorously challenged by Father Mathew, who stated: 'He did not know any people who liked good things better than the Irish when they could get them'. Rathbone, who rarely intervened during these discussions, inserted a practical note, by pointing out that it would take ten days to sell the hams 'and in the meantime thousands were dying', a comment that was applauded by other members of the committee.[72] A decision was made that hams should be included in the relief sent to the localities in Cork. The logistics of distribution were also discussed. Regarding its dispersion inland Captain Broughton again intervened, to advise against asking the government for assistance, stating: 'it would be a matter of great disgrace to them if they allowed the Government to be solicited on that point. He was sure the country gentlemen would willingly lend their horses and carts'.[73] Regarding the question of how they could ensure that such a variety of foodstuffs could be shared equitably, again Rathbone responded pragmatically, offering to pay £15 from his fund to employ somebody to create an accurate list of foods available, but pointing out: 'It was quite evident they would satisfy nobody—they did not expect it: all they could do was to distribute the food as quickly as possible'.[74] Privately, Rathbone also took it upon himself to raise the funds to pay for Forbes's return journey to Boston, as it seemed unlikely the British government would cover this expense. Instead, he appealed to the American Chamber of Commerce, so that 'Mr Forbes might not have to expend any money in Cork'. William junior was charged with liaising with this body.[75]

Rathbone hoped that with Forbes's departure there would be a lull in associated activities. At this stage, Rathbone was working from 8.00 am in the morning until midnight on *Jamestown* business but was still unable to get through all the work that he had to do. Yet, despite feeling overwhelmed, he admitted, 'I feel I am in the right place'.[76] Rathbone privately observed to William junior that, 'Nothing can exceed the extraordinary union of bad and good, of mean and generous, in the people of this district', but adding that he had never witnessed before such 'devotion and zeal'. He singled out the Quakers for praise, describing their involvement and organizational abilities as 'admirable'. He also commended Captain Broughton, Thomas Jennings (Isabel's father) and the Beamishes for their 'excellent' assistance. On a personal level, Rathbone paid tribute to his wife and son, Samuel, for their support.[77] Elizabeth, in turn, singled out some of the local women, including Isabel Jennings, who had done all that they could do to assist the committee.[78] The names of these women, however, did not appear in the official records.

A few days following Forbes's departure from Ireland, the Rathbones travelled to Limerick, via County Kerry. Rathbone was already familiar with distress in the latter place, as both he and Forbes had received heartfelt entreaties for assistance from Father John O'Sullivan, the parish priest of Kenmare.[79] O'Sullivan had even travelled to Cork for a private meeting with Rathbone, but returned to his 'unfortunate parishioners' empty-handed.[80] In Limerick, Rathbone wanted to arrange for the anticipated arrival of the *Tartar* and the distribution of her cargo in the south-west of the country.[81] As was so often the case, it was the Society of Friends who came forward to volunteer, leaving Rathbone feeling confident that he would soon be able to leave Ireland.[82] After Limerick, the Rathbones returned to Cork for a day before travelling to Liverpool. Elizabeth was relieved, admitting, 'most truly thankful shall we all be to turn our faces homeward'.[83]

Before returning to Liverpool on 4 May, Rathbone wrote to Major Beamish, the vice chairman of the New England Committee, thanking the committee for their hard work, but also making a few practical suggestions about how to proceed after he had left. Regarding the 18 packages of clothing that had been sent, to avoid imposition or the clothes ending up with pawnbrokers, he recommended that they be entrusted to two ministers, the Rev. Trench in Schull and Rev. Edwin Thomas in Annascaul, near Dingle. These men lived in some of the poorest districts and knew the local people well. Rev. Frederick Trench was Anglican curate in Cloughjordan but had travelled to Schull in early 1847 when he heard about the distress there. He worked closely with the local Catholic priest, Father James Barry, to bring relief to the distressed people.[84] In regard to Rev. Thomas in County Kerry, Rathbone said, 'he has resided there 30 years, and thus knows every individual. I know him to be liberal in his views, indefatigable and judicious in his efforts, and that on him alone the whole weight of the district rests'.[85] Rathbone suggested that if there were any surplus supplies left after the agreed allocations had been made, they should be handed to Major Beamish and Marshall Cummins to distribute as they saw fit, perhaps working with the local coastguard. With his usual graciousness he added, 'These, must, however, be considered merely suggestions, and not as requests'.[86]

At a meeting on 8 May, Rathbone's letter was discussed by the committee. It was revealed that far from there being a surplus as Rathbone had anticipated, there was a 'considerable deficiency', which had placed the committee in 'a very embarrassing position, for orders had already gone out to the great number of country districts, and the consequence would be that great disappointment would arise'.[87] Marshall Cummins stated that he was especially embarrassed and took responsibility for the over-estimate of the contents of the cargo, which had been based on the ship's manifest showing a greater number of goods than had actually landed. He estimated the shortfall to be in the region of 30 to 40 tons of foodstuffs. In regard to a suggestion that the Society of Friends be asked to make up the deficiency, Beamish responded that he had already written to Rathbone asking if he could use his contacts with other relief ships to assist. Again, the rights and wrongs of giving relief to the city of Cork were discussed, with those who resided in the city arguing that the distress of the poor was as extreme as in the surrounding countryside. Even though lists had already been drawn up, the committee was continuing to receive new requests, leading Cummins to despair that, 'every gentleman seemed to fancy that the particular place or parish where he happened to reside was to have a separate grant'.[88] Even more frustrating to the committee was the indiscriminate way in which grant applications were submitted. Cummins lamented:

> Some of the applications which had been lately addressed to him on this subject were couched in the most extraordinary terms, and amongst the rest from parties who, at the very moment, had orders in their pockets from the British Association stores at Haulbowline. Although not exactly connected with these proceedings, he might have observed that most unjustifiable attacks had been made on the Association in the public papers for hoarding their stores, whereas the parties to blame were those who hoarded the orders upon these stores and then came begging to other societies.[89]

In contrast, the Archdeacon of Cork pointed out that several districts containing large numbers of distressed people had been totally overlooked in the scramble to receive assistance. He believed that 'in times of such general distress the selection was difficult and embarrassing'. The discussion provided a number of unpalatable insights into the difficulties of so much relief being provided by volunteers working for unregulated bodies, while trying to make up for deficits in government relief.

The final meeting of the New England Committee took place on 3 July. At this stage, all supplies had been disposed of and the accounts were ready to be wound up.[90] The previous weeks had brought even further bad news. Part of the corn in the cargo was found to be bad, further reducing the stores available. Also, much to the shame of the committee, an appeal for a small testimonial to be raised on behalf of Captain Forbes failed to generate any income.[91] The benevolence of the people of New England, however, had not ended with Forbes's departure. In mid-May, the *Tartar*, under the command of Captain Russell, arrived in Cork, carrying supplies that did not fit on the *Jamestown*. Again, Rathbone was in charge of its disbursement, the contents being sent to the adjoining counties of Kerry and Limerick.[92] Over the next few weeks, Rathbone oversaw the arrival of the *Reliance* from Boston, the *Thames* from Georgia, and the *Macedonian*, under the command of George de Kay, which had sailed out of New York but was largely supplied by the people of Boston and Portland, Maine.[93] Relief ships also arrived from New York and Delaware, the contents of which were put under the aegis of the Mayor of Cork, Andrew Roche.[94] In mid-May, the *Morea*, laden with provisions from Boston, valued at £6,000, arrived in Glasgow, leading the *Freeman's Journal* to comment:

> The gratitude of our unhappy people has attempted to find expression but we are conscious that all that could be spoken must fall far short of what should be (and we hope is) felt ... Truly the generosity of the noble hearted Americans is above all praise. They are at this moment engaged in a most expensive war, and yet, to judge from their acts towards Ireland and Scotland, one would suppose that they had nothing to think of except how best to succour the needy at this side of the Atlantic.[95]

The paper referred to Forbes's Scottish antecedents, and the fact that he had hoped to visit the country and oversee the distribution there himself. Instead, he had returned to Boston to oversee more relief shipments, leaving everything else in the capable hands of Rathbone.[96]

From his home in Liverpool, Rathbone kept an eye on proceedings of this and other cargoes.[97] He informed the relief committee in Glasgow that he would ensure that all aid would be given 'free from religious or party differences'.[98] He also assured John Clow, the Treasurer of the Liverpool Committee for Subscriptions to Scotland, that:

> In regard to the manner of distributing the cargo of the *Morea*, I have to say that the desire of the Boston donors, no doubt, is, that the donations coming as they do from all classes of Christians and men of all political parties, should be put into the hands of parties not having any particular bias as a committee, and I understand the gentlemen selected are of the character alluded to—bearing in mind that we want it distributed as far and as wide as the small quantity will admit, so as to do the most good, and at the same time inculcate the sentiment of relief from New England.[99]

Rathbone's work on behalf of the donors in New England did not go unnoticed on the other side of the Atlantic. Josiah Quincy, the Mayor of Boston and Chairman of the New England Relief Committee, personally thanked Rathbone for his assistance, to which the Liverpool philanthropist responded:

> It was a great privilege to my family and myself, though in so humble a way, to be admitted as fellow labourers in a cause ... for which the world has reason to bless and thank you ... no thanks are needed for helping the commander of the *Jamestown*. The obligation was on our side in being allowed the opportunity of association with one who is held in such deserved estimation by his fellow citizens.[100]

Privately, however, Rathbone had already written to his friend, Forbes, admitting, 'the sojourn in Ireland was one of unmitigated, hopeless pain, but how could we do less for our own part, when you were making such great sacrifices?'.[101] He believed that the Irish poor would continue to require external assistance until the harvest. In contrast, he had heard from his contacts in Scotland that they expected to complete the year with a surplus of relief provisions.[102] Sadly, the 1847 harvest in Ireland, although relatively blight free, was small. Moreover, changes in government relief provision meant that Irish poverty was to be alleviated through the mechanism of the amended Poor Law and thus, by local taxation. From their home in Liverpool, the Rathbones were kept informed of the deteriorating conditions in Ireland by their friend in Cork, Father Mathew.

In summer 1847, Rathbone was engaged with multiple aspects of the Liverpool's civic and municipal life, happily leaving the running of the family business to his sons.[103] His activities included supporting fellow Liberal candidates in the approaching General Election,[104] and being part of a committee to erect a statue to William Huskisson, a former MP for Liverpool who had been killed in 1830 at the opening of the Liverpool and Manchester Railway.[105] Dominating all local news in Liverpool, however, was the mass exodus of the poor from Ireland into the city. By May, over 13,000 were arriving daily, with the number continuing to rise. The influx of famine refugees, often diseased, concerned the local authorities, particularly Poor Law officials and medical practitioners.[106] By the time of Rathbone's return from Cork, the Liverpool authorities were putting in place measures to return Irish 'paupers' back to Ireland, and were hoping to average 12,000 returns a day.[107]

Rathbone's time in Ireland had clearly made an impact on him. Shortly after returning to Liverpool, he attended an emergency meeting 'to consider how the Town was to be saved from the desolating inroads of famishing multitudes from Ireland'.[108] When the mayor, in his opening statement, contended that the Irish poor should be maintained by Irish landlords and Irish property in their own country, he was greeted with loud cheers.[109] Rathbone injected a note of sympathy for the Irish poor, informing the meeting that:

> He had been for the last few weeks in Ireland witnessing all its horrors, and he was sure no one who had not seen it could realize to his imagination those poor wretched victims, literally dying in the streets and lying by the hedges, with all the marks of dissolution in their countenances. He had been seeing such scenes of misery and wretchedness in Ireland, that he hardly knew whether his mind was his own. He had literally been lying in the hotel and hearing the groans of the dying during the night, and going out and witnessing in the streets of Cork during the day, people lying down and dying, so common an occurrence that they were passed unheeded.[110]

Displaying sentiments similar to those expressed by James Hack Tuke and other members of the Society of Friends, Rathbone defended the integrity of the Irish poor while exposing the intrinsic cruelty of the public works:

> Many of the preceding speakers had spoken of the poor of Liverpool, but he wished to be allowed to say one word for the poor of Ireland, and one word against the hardheartedness of Irish landlords (Hear, hear.) He had been, for the last four weeks, or nearly so, in Ireland, witnessing all the horrors there, and one who had not seen them could not picture to themselves these poor wretched creatures, dying in the streets and in the hedges, with all the looks of destitution on their faces. He had seen people willing to work, carrying spades on their shoulders, and yet they could get none. He had heard the overlooker saying to a man, 'You are not equal to your work'. 'How can I be so?' was the reply, 'when I have a wife and eight children to support from eight shillings a week, and I cannot see them starve'. The superintendent said, 'You are an excellent man, and I will make you superintendent' but it was too late for, two days after, the man was dead. He died in consequence of working for his family and not taking proper support. He had been told by the same overlooker that the only way to make the men take proper support was not to let them go to their meals—not to let them go even to the soup shops, but to bring their food to them and see that they ate it, or else it would all go to their families and they would not be fit for their work.[111]

From Liverpool, both William and Elizabeth Rathbone maintained a frequent correspondence with Father Mathew who, in turn, kept them appraised of the deteriorating situation in Ireland and the suffering caused by delays in opening government soup kitchens over the summer of 1847.[112] Rathbone responded to his heartfelt plea by arranging for 300 barrels of flour to be sent to Cork, with Father Mathew promising, 'I shall carefully husband, dispensing their valuable contents like a precious treasure'.[113] In the subsequent months, Father Mathew continued to send regular reports of 'unhappy Ireland' to Liverpool, primarily to Elizabeth. In early February 1848, the priest reported on the cruel consequences of the Gregory Clause, in excluding the poorest people from receiving Poor Law relief.[114]

In 1848, the international relief effort on behalf of Ireland that had saved so many lives in the previous year had largely dissipated, forcing the main relief organizations to end their involvement. Some individual donations continued but on a much-reduced scale. William Rathbone continued his association with Cork by privately sending money to Father Mathew, which the priest used to provide employment. In February, Father Mathew informed Rathbone that:

> On the part of the rising generation of my generation, I thank you for your ardent desire to infuse into them a spirit of self-respect and industry ... a young Ireland, prosperous and happy, will delight your eyes on your next visit to Ireland.[115]

As the year progressed, Rathbone continued to assist Father Mathew, both from his own purse and from money entrusted to him from benefactors in Boston and other parts of America. A gift of £50 made in April 1848 was used to purchase seed, the priest explaining:

> Though not an advocate for the extensive cultivation of potatoes, I am of opinion that, to enable our destitute people to recover from the effects of the late calamity, no other food could be so easily had to supply their many wants this season.[116]

In July, Father Mathew reported optimistically about those who had benefited from the Rathbones' money: 'They are now able to support themselves by the fruits of their industry. I saw last week, as I passed through the country, many luxuriant fields of potatoes and turnips, from seed I was enabled to distribute'.[117] His optimism was short-lived. On 13 August, he informed Rathbone:

> I regret that the melancholy task of announcing the total destruction of the potato crop has devolved upon me. The blight appeared three weeks back; but it seemed confined to particular places, and affected only the stalks; since then, wet weather has been so constant, the blight has become general, and the tubers are rotting with frightful rapidity.[118]

Father Mathew felt especially troubled as he had encouraged the poor people to cultivate potatoes and had provided relief to them on this basis. The consequence, he believed, was that 'Thousands, who have endured every privation rather than surrender their little farms, and consign their wives and children to the hopeless support of a workhouse, are now in despair'.[119] As he travelled through the countryside, he observed, 'the wretched people bathed in tears. I could only mingle my tears with theirs'.[120] Rathbone's support was not confined to assisting Father Mathew. At the beginning of 1849, the Board of the Cork Poor Law Union offered their thanks for 'the courtesy and attention' with which he had responded to their enquiries about sending female workhouse inmates to New Orleans. The scheme had been abandoned, but it was Rathbone who had been their trusted advisor.[121]

The deteriorating situation in Ireland was set against a backdrop of rising political tensions. By the summer of 1848, support for Ireland was again at risk as the Chartist threat in Britain, and the rise of the Irish Confederates (formerly Young Ireland), alarmed the British government that the United Kingdom might become part of the European 'year of revolutions'.[122] Despite his liberal politics, Rathbone feared an alliance between these two radical groups, explaining to his daughter in late July:

> 100,000 Irish in Liverpool unemployed, and Chartists to join, are fearful materials for mischief ... our open docks and warehouses leave us much at the mercy of the

> incendiary ... The English law is defective, we cannot search for arms when we know where they are; we cannot incarcerate the leaders, though preaching rebellion or virtually such, though not legally; nor can we enter the houses where clubs we know meet, and the most inflammatory and rebellious language is used; yet Liverpool is the high road to and from Ireland, a post which a general would say the country's safety required to be guarded; yet her Majesty's Ministers leave us very much to ourselves, and in some degree tie our hands by their reserve.[123]

While no major uprising took place in Ireland in 1848, the political unrest in the country did decrease sympathy for the Irish poor.[124] A return of blight meant that, as Rathbone told his son, over winter the poor would again face 'real distress'; moreover, 1849 brought a new deadly disease to the ports of Britain and Ireland—cholera.[125]

Forbes continued to correspond with the Rathbone family following his return to Boston.[126] He also remained in the eye of the British public. In July 1849, the Liverpool Shipwreck and Humane Society presented a gold medal to Forbes, 'for his courage and humanity in leaping overboard from the *Europa*, on the occasion of the late fatal collision, and assisting to save the lives of the passengers on the unfortunate vessel'. The newspaper report went on to say that: 'Mr. Forbes is an intimate friend of Mr. W. Rathbone, and was the means of sending, through that gentleman, to Ireland and the Western Islands of Scotland, an immense supply of provisions, of the value of £60,000, during the year of famine, an act of generous humanity which ought never be forgotten'.[127] The connection between the two men continued in a further way. In spring 1863, at the height of the American Civil War, Forbes' brother, John Murray Forbes, a Boston businessman and supporter of Abraham Lincoln, visited England to protest against the building of ships to be used by the Confederate Army.[128] After visiting the American Consulate, he then called on the Rathbone family who advised him about how to stop this activity.[129] The mission was successful.[130]

The friendship between the Rathbones and Father Mathew also endured beyond the years of famine. In 1849, on the eve of undertaking a two-year temperance tour of America, Father Mathew stayed with the Rathbones in Liverpool at their beautiful home, Greenbank.[131] Before departing from the English port, Mathew administered the pledge to hundreds of men and women at the Hibernian school on Pleasant Street. Rathbone agreed that anybody who visited the priest at Greenbank could also receive the pledge.[132] From America, Father Mathew continued to write to Elizabeth informing her of his progress, his health—and his controversial decision not to comment on the question of slavery.[133] Even from 3,000 miles away, the Rathbones continued to send financial support to Mathew, especially when he was unable to pay his bills.[134] Their kindness led Father Mathew to tell Elizabeth that he loved her like a sister.[135] William Rathbone's continued connection with Cork was evident in other ways. In June 1852, he was a guest at the opening of the prestigious National Exhibition in the city.[136] It was a joyous occasion and a tribute to the resilience of the local people who had turned their fortunes around in the five years since Rathbone's earlier visit. Father Mathew's final stay with the Rathbones was in 1855. At this stage, he was in poor health although he had spent several months in Madeira trying to recuperate. The relationship between the Rathbones and the priest only ended with the priest's death in December 1856. Mathew's biographer wrote of this relationship that 'no friends whom he had known at any period of his career were truer, more generous, or more unwearying and unselfish in their kindness towards him, than the Rathbone family. Their friendship never wavered or failed during his life'.[137]

William Rathbone died in February 1868. His obituaries were long and effusive, as was fitting for one associated with many of the social reforms that had taken place during his life-time. While his philanthropy and support for progressive issues such as the abolition of slavery were mentioned, his involvement in the Great Famine was not.[138] Even newspapers based in Cork, the landing place of the famed *Jamestown*, omitted to mention his crucial role during the dark years of the late 1840s.[139] A telling insight into how beloved he was to the people of Liverpool was that, within days of his death, subscriptions were made to honour him with a memorial.[140] Rathbone's political and philanthropic legacy lived on in his son and heir, William Rathbone VI, who was elected Liberal MP for Liverpool in the same year that his father died.[141] Ironically, he lost the seat in 1880, because he refused to take a pledge to support Irish Home Rule—a stance he subsequently reversed.[142] One the younger Rathbone's lasting legacies to the city was the creation of a system of district nursing, which he funded himself.[143] Moreover, during the 'forgotten famine' in Ireland of 1879 to 1882, Rathbone junior assisted in raising money for an emigration scheme introduced by James Hack Tuke in Connemara.[144]

The success of the voyage of the *Jamestown*, while prompted by the generosity of people in New England, was achieved through the cooperation of generous benefactors located in Boston, Cork, London and Liverpool. While Captain Forbes has, appropriately, been frequently commemorated as the hero of this voyage of mercy, the part played by Rathbone, aided and assisted by his friend, Father Mathew, was also an example of heroism and altruism. The fact that Rathbone was singled out by Forbes to complete his mission is perhaps not surprising given his life-time commitment to philanthropy and public service. However, his compassion and common-sense added a humanity to the process that were his trademark, whether he was dealing with the poor in Liverpool or in Cork. William Rathbone was part of Liverpool's commercial merchant elite, but it was as a philanthropist, a social reformer and a political progressive that he made his most lasting contributions. In Ireland, his sympathetic benevolence, his pragmatism and his wisdom helped to save many lives, making him one of the Famine's unsung heroes.

NOTES

1. For example, Rathbone is not mentioned in Timothy J. Sarbaugh, '"Charity begins at Home". The United States government & Irish Famine relief 1845–1849' in, *History Ireland*, issue 2, vol. 4 (summer 1996), 31–35; nor is he mentioned in many articles relating to the *Jamestown*: Aedín Ní Bhróithe Clements, Irish Studies Librarian, Notre Dame, 'Recent Acquisition: American Foreign Aid during the Great Famine in Ireland', https://sites.nd.edu/rbsc/recent-acquisition-american-foreign-aid-during-the-great-famine-in-ireland/ ; Rathbone was not mentioned in a brief discussion in the British parliament, 'The *Jamestown*', House of Commons Debates, 29 April 1847, vol. 92, cc 127–128; a biographer of the Rathbone family, Sheila Marriner in *Rathbones of Liverpool, 1845–73* (Liverpool University Press, 1971), makes no mention of Rathbone's involvement in the Famine, support for abolition, or friendship with Forbes and Father Mathew, not does a biography written by one of his descendants, Eleanor F. Rathbone, *William Rathbone. A Memoir* (London: Macmillan, 1905).
2. Rathbone, *A Memoir*, p. 8.
3. Marriner, *Rathbones*, pp 3–4.
4. On the occasion of William Rathbone VI's 21st birthday, his father apologized for not being able to give him a portion of his inheritance, William Rathbone V to his son, Greenbank, Liverpool, 9 Feb. 1840, University of Liverpool Special Collections and Archives (U of L), Rathbone papers (RP), MS ix. 3. 7. Duty, character and restraint were constant themes in William and Elizabeth Rathbone's letters to their sons.
5. Marriner, *Rathbones*, p. 7.
6. Like a number of other temperance advocates, however, he did drink wine.
7. John Furnival, *Children of the Second Spring: Father James Nugent and the work of childcare in Liverpool* (Leominster: Gracewing, 2005), p. 202. Both Rathbone and his father were originally members of the Society of Friends but severed their connections. Rathbone, *Memoir*, p. 41.
8. 'Mathew Annuity Fund', *Globe,* 4 Aug. 1846.
9. The occasion was even reported in the Irish American press, see 'Splendid reception of Mr. O'Connell in Liverpool', Boston *Pilot*, vol. 2, no. 11, 12 Mar. 1836.
10. Quoted in Rathbone, *Memoir,* pp 21–22.
11. See Christine Kinealy, 'Dr William Duncan of Liverpool', in Christine Kinealy, Jason King and Gerard Moran, *Heroes of Ireland's Great Hunger* (Quinnipiac and Cork University Press, 2020), pp 131–146.

12. Edward H. Gibson, III, 'Baths and Washhouses in the English Public Health Agitation, 1839–48', in *Journal of the History of Medicine and Allied Sciences*, vol. 9, no. 4 (Oct. 1954), 391–406, p. 394.
13. 'The Mayor and Roman Catholics and Dissenters', *Statesman and Dublin Christian Record,* 17 July 1846. When Prince Albert visited Liverpool in summer 1846, Hogdens only invited Church of Ireland ministers to meet him, adding to the religious tensions in an already divided city. See, James Allanson Picton, 'Memorials of Liverpool', *Nineteenth Century* (London: Longmans, Green and Co., 1875), pp 500–501.
14. 'Great Meeting of the inhabitants of Liverpool to address Sir Robert Peel on the threatened scarcity of food in Ireland', *Freeman's Journal*, 3 Dec. 1845; *Wexford Independent*, 3 Dec. 1845.
15. The existence of the Corns Laws in the United Kingdom kept the price of imported corn, and hence bread, artificially high and out of the reach of the poor.
16. 'Great Meeting of the inhabitants of Liverpool to address Sir Robert Peel on the threatened scarcity of food in Ireland', *Freeman's Journal*, 3 Dec. 1845.
17. See Catherine Shannon, 'William Bennet Forbes', in Kinealy et. al., *Heroes*, pp 39–53.
18. Robert Bennet Forbes, *The Voyage of the Jamestown on Her Errand of Mercy* (Boston: Eastburn's Press, 1847), p. 8.
19. Forbes, Boston to Rathbone, 28 Feb. 1847, Forbes, *Voyage*, pp xxvi-xxvii
20. Forbes, Boston to Rathbone 11 Mar. 1847, Forbes p. xxvii.
21. Joshua Bates (1788–1864) was a senior partner of Baring Brothers from the late 1820s until his death. He was a Bostonian who managed the firm's American business. The Baring Archive: https://baringarchive.org.uk/history/biographies/joshua_bates
22. Christine Kinealy, *Charity and the Great Hunger. The Kindness of Strangers* (London: Bloomsbury, 2013).
23. Rathbones's eldest son, William jnr (later William Rathbone VI), worked in the Counting House in Barings in London under Bates's supervision in 1840, Rathbone to William jnr, 16/17 Mar. 1840 (U of L., RP), MS ix. 3. 9.
24. Forbes, Boston, to Joshua Bates Esq. London, 11 Mar. 1847, Forbes, *Voyage*, p. xxviii.
25. Ibid., Forbes, Boston, to Rathbone, Liverpool, 13 Mar. 1847, pp xxviiii- xxx.
26. Rathbone, Liverpool to William jnr, 7 Apr. 1847 (U of L., RP), MS ix. 3. 25.
27. Ibid.
28. Forbes, Boston to Baring Bros, Liverpool, 23 Mar. 1847, Forbes, *Voyage*, p. xxxi.
29. Ibid., Forbes Boston to Rathbone, Liverpool, 23 Mar. 1847, pp xxxii-xxxiii.
30. Elihu Burritt (1810–1879) was also promoting an Ocean Penny Postage during his time in Europe.
31. Elihu Burritt, Browns Hotel, Liverpool, to Richard Rathbone, 6 July 1846, Central Connecticut University Archive, Elihu Burritt Library, Burritt Letters.
32. Elihu Burritt, *A Journal of a Visit of Three Days in Skibbereen* (London: Charles Gilpin, 1847).
33. Burritt and Rathbone attended a meeting in Manchester to support the final repeal of the Corn Laws, at which William Cobden and John Bright were present, 'Final repeal of the Corn Laws: Great Banquet at Manchester', *The Albion,* 5 Feb. 1849.

34. 'Elihu Burritt', *Christian News*, 18 Oct. 1849.
35. 'Relief from America', from *Cork Southern Reporter*, reprinted in *Freeman's Journal*, 15 Apr. 1847.
36. 'Welcome Tidings', *Southern Reporter and Cork Commercial* Courier, 13 Apr. 1847.
37. 'Honour to America' in *Liverpool Journal*, reprinted in *Freeman's Journal*, 14 Apr. 1847.
38. 'Brief notes on various topics', *Liverpool Mercury*, 16 Apr. 1847.
39. Elizabeth Greg Rathbone (1790–1882) was a daughter of Belfast-born, Samuel Greg, who owned the successful Quarry Bank Mill near Manchester. Part of the family's wealth came from slave plantations in the Caribbean. Elizabeth and William married in 1812. Their second son was named Samuel Greg Rathbone (1823–1903).
40. The Jennings family hosted Frederick Douglass during his stay in Cork in October 1845 and he and Isabel developed a close friendship, see Christine Kinealy *Frederick Douglass and Ireland. In his own words* (London: Routledge, 2018).
41. John Francis Maguire, *Father Mathew. A biography* (London: Longman, Green, Longman, Roberts, & Green, 1865), p. 412.
42. Quoted in Shannon, *Forbes*, p. 4. The chapter also describes the poverty in Cork and Forbes's interactions with the city.
43. Rathbone to John Francis Maguire, 1863, Maguire, *Father Mathew*, p. 413.
44. 'City of Cork. Official Relief Committee', *Cork Examiner*, 29 Sept. 1847.
45. 'The American relief supplies meeting at Cork Institution', *Southern Reporter and Cork Commercial Courier*, 20 Apr. 1847.
46. Boston-born John Bernard Fitzpatrick (1812–1866) who had been created Bishop in 1846, was active in raising money and sympathy for victims of the Famine. Also, see chapter on Deer Island by John McColgan.
47. Bishop Fitzpatrick, Cork to Right Rev. Dr Murphy, Cork, 27 Mar. 1847, reprinted in *Southern Reporter and Cork Commercial Courier*, 15 Apr. 1847. Born in 1772, Murphy had been Bishop of Cork since 1815.
48. 'Death of Right Rev Dr Murphy Bishop of Cork', *Cork Examiner*, 2 Apr. 1847.
49. 'Death of Right Rev. Dr. Murphy', *Dublin Weekly Register*, 3 Apr. 1847.
50. 'The American relief supplies meeting at Cork Institution', *Southern Reporter and Cork Commercial Courier*, 20 Apr. 1847.
51. 'Distribution of the cargo of the *Jamestown*', *Cork Examiner*, 21 Apr. 1847.
52. Kinealy, *Douglass*, passim.
53. 'Honour to America', *The Pilot*, 26 Apr. 1847.
54. 'Honour to American Soiree to Captain Forbes at Temperance Institute', *Freeman's Journal,* 22 Apr. 1847.
55. *Some Interesting Boston Events* (Boston, Mass.: State Street Trust Co., 1916), p. 66.
56. 'Honour to American Soiree to Captain Forbes at Temperance Institute', *Freeman's Journal,* 22 Apr. 1847.
57. Ibid. Although Rathbone's speech was not included in the report in the *Tipperary Vindicator*, 24 Apr. 1847, the paper referred to it as 'an excellent address'.
58. William Rathbone, Imperial Hotel, Cork, to Ralph Varian, 20 Apr. 1847, *Southern Reporter and Cork Commercial Courier,* 20 Apr. 1847.

59. Rathbone, Cork, to William jnr, 21 Apr. 1847 (U of L., RP), MS ix 3 26.
60. Forbes, *Voyage*, p. 11.
61. 'Sisters of the Irish Ursuline Union', at: www.ursulines.ie/ursulines-blackrock/
62. Melissa Fegan, '"This most humane commerce": Lace-making during the Famine', in Marguerite Corporaal, Oona Frawley, and Emily Mark-Fitzgerald (eds) *The Great Irish Famine: Visual and Material Culture* (Liverpool University Press, 2018), pp 110–127.
63. 'Thanks', *Southern Reporter and Cork Commercial Courier'*, 4 May 1847.
64. Shannon, *Forbes*, p. 47.
65. Rathbone, Cork, to William jnr, 21 Apr. 1847 (U of L., RP), MS ix. 3. 26.
66. Forbes, *Voyage*, p. 20.
67. Bessborough died on 16 May 1847, while serving as Lord Lieutenant. He was replaced by Lord Clarendon.
68. Forbes, *Voyage*, p. 21.
69. Ibid., p. 26.
70. 'New England Relief Committee: Allocated the cargo of the: Jamestown', *Southern Reporter and Cork Commercial Courier*, 27 Apr. 1847.
71. Stirabout was made with soaking Indian Corn (maize) in milk, or more usually water. In Asenath Nicholson's' *Annals of the Famine in Ireland* (1851), she was scathing about the use of stirabout, describing it as a 'frightful formidable'.
72. 'New England Relief Committee: Allocated the cargo of the Jamestown', *Southern Reporter and Cork Commercial Courier*, 27 Apr. 1847.
73. Ibid.
74. Ibid.
75. Elizabeth, Cork, to William jnr, nd [c. 17 Apr. 1847] (U of L., RP), MS ix. 3. 28.
76. Ibid., Rathbone, Cork, to William junior, 21 Apr. 1847, MS ix. 3. 26.
77. Ibid.
78. Ibid., Elizabeth, Cork, to William jnr, nd [c. 17 Apr. 1847], MS ix. 3. 28.
79. See Chapter on 'John of Kenmare' by Colum Kenny.
80. Father John O'Sullivan to Forbes, Kenmare 21 Apr. 1847, Forbes, *Jamestown,* pp cvii-cix.
81. Elizabeth, Cork, to William jnr, 21 Apr. 18 47 (U of L., RP), MS ix. 3. 26; Ibid., Elizabeth, Limerick to William junior, nd, Friday, MS ix. 3. 27.
82. Ibid., Elizabeth, Cork, to William junior, no date, Saturday evening, MS ix. 3. 29.
83. Ibid., Elizabeth, Limerick, to William jnr, nd, Friday [possibly 30 Apr. 1847], MS ix. 3. 27.
84. At a meeting of the Skull [sic] relief committee on 22 June 1847, Father Barry introduced a resolution thanking the Rev. Trench, 'At a meeting', *Cork Examiner*, 19 July 1847. Rev. F.F. Trench featured in the classic account, *Realities of Irish Life* (1868), written by his cousin, W. Steuart Trench.
85. 'New England Relief Committee', *Southern Reporter and Cork Commercial Courier*, 11 May 1847.
86. Ibid.
87. Ibid.
88. Ibid.
89. Ibid.

90. Ibid., 26 June 1847.
91. 'New England Relief Committee', *Cork Examiner*, 5 July 1847.
92. More American Benevolence, *Wexford Independent*, 19 May 1847.
93. *Transactions of the Society of Friends during the Famine in Ireland in 1846 and 1847* (Dublin: Hodges and Smith, 1852), Appendix VIII, pp 346–348.
94. Mayor Edwards Hackett died in office in April, 'Death of Mayor of Cork', *Cork Examiner*, 16 Apr. 1847.
95. 'American Generosity. Scotland', *Freeman's Journal*, 15 May 1847.
96. Ibid.
97. 'Highland Relief Committee', *Glasgow Courier*, 27 Apr. 1847.
98. Rathbone to Glasgow Relief Committee, 12 May 1847 (U of L), Letter Book of New England Relief Society, William Rathbone papers (LB), MS PRV 1. 167.
99. 'American generosity. Scotland', *Freeman's Journal*, 15 May 1847.
100. William Rathbone to the Mayor of Boston, 18 June 1847 (U of L, LB), MS PRV 1. 167.
101. Ibid., Rathbone to Forbes, 3 June 1847.
102. Ibid.
103. Marriner, *Rathbones*, p. 9.
104. 'Lancashire South', *The Evening Chronicle*, 11 June 1847.
105. 'Monument to Huskisson', *Liverpool Mail*, 10 July 1847. William Huskisson (1770–1830) had voted for the abolition of the slave trade in 1807, but when MP for Liverpool, he bowed to the pressure of local merchants by opposing the abolition of slavery.
106. 'Liverpool and the Irish. The Health of the Public', *Manchester Courier and Lancashire General Advertiser*, 12 May 1847; 'Select Vestry', *Liverpool Mail*, 15 May 1847.
107. 'Removal of Irish Paupers to Ireland', *Liverpool Mail*, 10 July 1847.
108. 'Influx of the Irish Poor into Liverpool', *Liverpool Mercury*, 14 May 1847.
109. Ibid.
110. Editorial, *Hull Advertiser and Exchange Gazette*, 14 May 1847.
111. 'Influx of the Irish Poor into Liverpool', *Liverpool Mercury,* 14 May 1847.
112. Father Mathew, Cork to Elizabeth Rathbone, 23 July 1847, Maguire, *Father Mathew*, p. 434.
113. Ibid., Mathew, Cork to Elizabeth Rathbone, 26 Aug. 1847, p. 435.
114. Ibid., Mathew, Cork to Elizabeth Rathbone, 7 Feb. 1848, p. 450.
115. Father Mathew to William Rathbone, 26 Feb. 1848 (U of L, LB), PRV 1. 67.
116. Father Mathew, Cork to Elizabeth Rathbone, 5 May 1848, Maguire, *Father Mathew,* p. 451.
117. Ibid., Father Mathew, Cork to Rathbone, 21 July 1848. p. 452.
118. Ibid., Father Mathew, Cork to Rathbone, 13 Aug. 1848, p. 452.
119. Ibid.
120. Ibid.
121. 'Cork Poor Law Union', *Cork Examiner*, 12 Jan. 1849.
122. Christine Kinealy, *Repeal and Revolution. 1848 in Ireland* (Manchester University Press, 2010).
123. Rathbone to Mrs. Paget, 23 July 1848, quoted from John Belchem, 'Liverpool in 1848: image, identity and issues', Paper read on 19 March 1998, at: www.hslc.org.uk/wp-content /uploads/2017/05/147–2-Belchem.pdf, p. 18.

124. 'The English Labourer's Burden', *Punch*, 24 Feb. 1849.
125. Rathbone to Rathbone jnr, 29 Sept. 1848 (U of L., RP), MS ix. c. 35a.
126. Elizabeth Rathbone, Liverpool to William jnr, New York, 28 Dec. 1848 (U of L., RP), MS ix. 4. 43a. William jnr visited Forbes while in America, on one occasion delivering a gift of Cheshire Cheese from his father.
127. 'Collision at Sea', *Aberdeen Herald and General* Advertiser, 14 July 1849.
128. Rathbone, *Memoir*, pp 196–197.
129. Sarah Forbes Hughes (ed.), *Letters and Recollections of John Murray Forbes* (Boston: Houghton, Miflin and Co., 1899), pp 6–9.
130. Ibid., p. 92.
131. Maguire, *Father Mathew*, p. 461; 'Father Mathew', *Kerry Examiner*, 18 May 1849.
132. 'Departure of Rev. Father Mathew', *Liverpool Mercury*, 25 May 1849.
133. Father Mathew, Mobile, Alabama, to Mrs Rathbone, 8 March 1850, Maguire, *Father Mathew*, pp 491–492; Ibid., 3 May 1850, p. 493.
134. Ibid., Father Mathew to Elizabeth Rathbone, 9 July 1850, p. 502.
135. Ibid., Father Mathew, St. Louis to Elizabeth Rathbone, 20 Oct. 1850, p. 509.
136. 'National Exhibition in Cork', *Belfast News-Letter*, 14 June 1852.
137. Maguire, *Father Mathew*, pp 411–412.
138. 'The Late William Rathbone of Liverpool', *Leicester Chronicle*, 8 Feb. 1868; 'Death of Mr William Rathbone, *Liverpool Weekly Courier*, 8 Feb. 1868; 'A brief epitome of the history reforms from 1787 to 1868', *Liverpool Daily Post*, 1 April 1868.
139. There was no mention of his involvement in the *Jamestown* in 'Death of Wm. Rathbone of Liverpool', *Cork Examiner*, 5 Feb. 1868; 'Death of William Rathbone of Liverpool', *Clare Journal, and Ennis Advertiser,* 13 Feb. 1868.
140. 'General News', *Newry Reporter*,15 Feb. 1868.
141. Rathbone jnr continued as Liberal MP for 11 years, in a city that was a bastion of the Conservative Party, Rathbone, *Memoir*, pp 222–223.
142. 'Lord Randolph Churchill', *Oxfordshire Weekly News*, 7 Apr. 1880; Rathbone, *Memoir*, pp 307–317, 415–417.
143. 'History of District Nursing', https://historyofdistrictnursing.wordpress.com/1858–1874/
144. Rathbone, *Memoir*, pp 408–410. Rathbone described working with Tuke as 'one of the pleasantest parts of his work', also see, Gerard Moran, *James Hack Tuke,* in Kinealy et al. *Heroes*, pp 3–20.

CHAPTER SEVEN

HIGHWAY OF HEROES

Unsung First Responders to Irish Famine Refugees in Upper Canada

Mark G. McGowan

Highway 401 is the major artery that links the southern section of the Province of Ontario from the Quebec border in the east, to Windsor on the Detroit River in the west. Once known as the Macdonald-Cartier Throughway, the Government of Ontario renamed the road 'The Highway of Heroes,' to commemorate the Canadians who were killed in the Afghanistan conflict. The Canadian men and women who died in that military action had no sense that they were heroes; most simply thought they were doing their jobs as soldiers, journalists, and military support. Much the same could be said of the men and women who served Irish refugees along that same route, 170 years before. While the super highway of today did not exist, the thoroughfares of the 1840s in Upper Canada (as Ontario was known) were dirt and corduroy roads, the Saint Lawrence and Ottawa Rivers, Lake Ontario, and a network of canals in the interior of the province.[1] In 1846, when the first Irish refugees arrived after sojourning at Grosse Île, Quebec City, and Montreal, they were assisted by men and women along a transportation network that either brought them to Upper Canadian settlements or provided an easy access route to their friends, family, and imagined fortunes in the United States.[2] For the Canadians who responded—police constables, women religious, healthcare workers, emigration agents, priests, and teamsters—there are few public monuments today commemorating their service. These were ordinary settler Canadians who undertook extraordinary things for these Irish newcomers. This chapter represents a modest nod to those men and women who left few records of their lives behind, and never expected public accolades for the work that they did along these highways of heroes.

The passage of Famine migrants from Ireland to British North America has been well documented. Between 1846 and 1851 tens of thousands boarded ships, some of questionable quality, on their journey to begin a new life in British North America. The year 1847 stood out as the year when the most Irish ventured to what is now Canada; some 110,000 people left ports in the United Kingdom for Quebec (90,000), New Brunswick (17,000), and the other of Britain's Atlantic colonies. By the end of that year, which marked the highest mass migration of Irish to British North America in history, about one-fifth of the migrants had died.[3] Some died at sea; others died in the quarantine stations at Grosse Île, Partridge Island, or Middle Island on the Miramichi. Still more died in hospitals, fever sheds, tent encampments, and along the highways and byways of Canada, searching for shelter or for the comfort of family and friends who had migrated earlier. Historians may never be able to establish an exact number of the dead because of so many migrants buried in mass graves, unmarked graves by roadsides, and the simple fact that registers of those whose deaths and burials were recorded are incomplete, fragmentary, or lost. In gathering the fragments that have survived, however, researchers may have come to recognize the importance of the record-keepers and their associates who made heroic efforts to care for the sick, accommodate the healthy, and provide direction for those journeying further into the interior of Upper Canada.

Once migrants had cleared the hospitals, sheds and the quarantine station at Pointe-Saint-Charles in Montreal they had at least four options. First, to elect to stay in Montreal, where there was a large Catholic community of French and pre-Famine Irish citizens. Secondly, they could opt to travel south via the Richelieu River to St-Jean and eventually the United States. The next two options were to move northwest via the Ottawa River or southwest via the Saint Lawrence River to Upper Canada. This western section of the United Province of Canada was the new frontier, with cheap available farmland available in the Huron Tract near Lake Huron and other 'back counties', employment on canal improvements on the Niagara Peninsula, or opportunities in the growing cities of Bytown (Ottawa), Kingston, Toronto, or Hamilton.[4] The population of the province was nearly 456,000 and growing at a staggering rate. By 1851, it would be 952,000, with Toronto as its largest urban centre at over 20,000 people.[5] Irish Catholics might be disturbed by the fact that they had left the very Catholic 'Lower Province (Quebec)' for the overwhelmingly Protestant Upper Canada, where the Loyal Orange Order held sway over politics and community life in both rural and urban areas. There was considerable opportunity to be had for farmers, merchants, and artisans in Upper Canada, and pre-Famine Irish migrants had established a well-defined settlement grid, particularly in rural areas. Many other Irish emigrants, however, simply used Upper Canada as a way station, as they moved across the Niagara frontier to New York State, or through Windsor to Michigan, Ohio, and beyond.

At each stage of their pilgrimage, however, the Irish were met by private citizens, religious men and women, and public servants who provided aid, particularly to the sick and dying. The most obvious network of assistance was the Canadian Emigrant Agency and the Boards of Health established at each major port-of-call in the province. The first Chief Emigrant Agent for the United Province of Canada was Alexander Carlisle Buchanan, a native of Tyrone, Ireland, who was headquartered at Quebec City, the main entrepot for migrants. In 1838, Buchanan was replaced by his nephew A.C. Buchanan, Jr, who became one of the most important civic officials during the period of the Famine migration.[6] The younger Buchanan was assisted by Anthony B. Hawke, who was responsible for the entire Upper Canadian territory. Under Hawke, there was a network of Emigrant Agents employed by the Canadian Government to manage the arrivals of emigrants in Bytown, Cobourg/Port Hope, Kingston, Toronto, and Hamilton.[7] In June 1847, the Legislative Assembly of the United Province of Canada mandated that each community establish a Board of Health to manage the considerable needs of sick and impoverished immigrants. In a large city such as Toronto, with close to 20,000 inhabitants, city councillors had already established a Board of Health, and so, in June, board members were scrambling to find suitable hospital facilities.[8] In smaller centres the task of providing for emigrants fell to both Boards of Health, and, in the smallest villages, to the local police department. The boards reported directly to the Provincial Secretary, Dominick Daly, for reimbursements for their expenditures and for general directions. It was only when having dual systems of emigrant assistance was deemed inefficient that, in August 1847, both networks in Upper Canada came under Hawke's supervision.[9] From his headquarters in Kingston, Hawke's department was ultimately responsible for transporting migrants from the major ports of call, triaging the sick migrants once they arrived, assuring that there were adequate hospitals and sheds established by the Boards of Health for the migrants, and that healthy and able-bodied migrants were quickly transported, free of charge, to centres where they might find employment.

Prior to 1846 and the completion of canal works west of Montreal, the standard route to the interior had been up the Ottawa River to Bytown. Named after British Colonel John By, who had supervised the building of the Rideau Canal, linking the Ottawa and Saint Lawrence Rivers from Bytown to Kingston, Bytown itself was a lumber town and service centre to its agricultural hinterlands in the Ottawa Valley. There was a pre-existing Irish population in the town and region who bore a questionable reputation not necessarily of their own making. In the 1830s, Irish bush workers and raftsmen, labelled 'Shiners', had terrorized the town during their annual timber drives from the forests in the Upper Ottawa Valley.[10] Those citizens who remembered the violence of the Shiners would be wary of the new flood of Irish coming into the town, particularly the sick and impoverished refugees during Black '47. But receive them they did under Hawke's local agent G.R. Burke, who worked tirelessly with the local Board of Health and Catholic Church agencies to meet the demands of migrants arriving in Bytown.[11] One small comfort for the Irish Catholics arriving by the hundreds was that Bytown was one of the largest Catholic enclaves in Upper Canada, where, according to Bishop Michael Power of Toronto, in 1847, 6,662 of the population of the 8,100 inhabitants were Roman Catholic.[12] In recognition of the growing Catholic presence in the city, in June 1847, Pope Pius IX created the Diocese of Bytown, to serve both sides of the Ottawa River north of Montreal to Temiskaming.

The key players in emigrant reception in Bytown were the Sisters of Charity or Grey Sisters, under the leadership of Mother Elisabeth Bruyère. The Greys had been founded in Montreal as the Soeurs de Charité by Marguerite Youville in the eighteenth century. As a non-cloistered order their charter demanded that they serve the poor, orphans, and elderly through health care, charitable aid, and education. In 1844, the Coadjutor Bishop of Kingston, Patrick Phelan requested a contingent of sisters from Montreal to serve the growing community of Bytown.[13] Although only having professed her vows in 1841, and at the age of 27, Bruyère had led a team of four sisters to Ottawa, in 1845,[14] and for a short time they were known as the Grey Sisters of the Cross.[15] Much has been written about the heroic work undertaken by the Grey Sisters in Montreal, during the Famine. The Bytown Sisters, however, soon to be known as the Soeurs de Charité d'Ottawa (SCO) were one of many groups of the Montreal Greys who brought their works of service to other parts of Canada, including orphan care in Quebec City and education and health care in the fur trading centre on the Red River in present day Manitoba.[16] Bruyère's Grey's built a convent and established a hospital (Hôpital Génèral) in an old house; they soon became front line servants to the incoming Irish. Their hospital work also included service in the hastily erected fever sheds on Sussex Street at Nepean Point, overlooking the Ottawa River, not far from their motherhouse.

The Grey Sisters worked closely with local priest Father Adrien Telmond, chief medical officer Dr Edward Van Courtland, and Emigrant Agent G. R. Burke to accommodate the massive flow of Irish migrants disembarking at Bytown. During 'Black

'47' the Grey's hospital accommodated 600 patients, at least 125 of whom succumbed to typhus.[17] Sixteen of the 20 sisters also contracted disease, two young postulants very seriously, but none died.[18] According to Bruyère, they were simply overwhelmed and there were fears that the fever sheds themselves were too close to the Grey's school and convent. Although now formally independent of the mother house in Montreal, Bruyère confided to Mother Elizabeth McMullen, the Grey Sisters' superior there, that:

> Notre Père [Telmond] ne veut pas que nous soignions les émigrés attients de maladie contagieuse chez nous á cause de l'école et des Soeurs. Il a offert aux agents [de l'immigation] de bâtir le hangar des émigrés sur notre terrain et nous le s soignerons lâ mais il craint que ces Messiuers ne le veulent pas. Priez ma bonne Mère pour cette bonne oeuvre ne nous échappe pas.[19]

Notable among Bruyère's efforts to assist the Irish was the management of orphan children who were housed at the General Hospital. This is not surprising since she herself was virtually orphaned when her father, Charles Bruguier died at sea, and she looked after her two younger brothers when her mother went out to work.[20] In fact, one of Bruyère's first tasks after taking vows was the supervision of the Grey's Montreal orphanage. In Bytown, however, the Grey Sisters used the hospital as the principal site of orphan placement, especially for local French-Canadian families who needed a young Irish boy or girl for domestic service or farm labour. In the surviving ledgers for the hospital, it appears that the Greys took care of 56 children in 1847, alone. The fate of these Irish orphans in Bytown resembled much of what had happened to orphans cared for by the churches and religious orders in Lower Canada. Of the 56 children who landed at the Grey Sisters' facilities in Bytown, only three were registered as Protestants, demonstrating both the overwhelming Catholic character of the migration and its orphans and that local Protestants, lacking in their own facilities, depended on the generosity of the Greys to admit all children, regardless of creed. Bruyère's workers did not segregate the Protestant children from the Catholic. As had been the case in Lower Canadian orphan asylums, however, the term orphan held many meanings; the Sisters placed at least five children with family members, including mothers and fathers, who likely left their children with the Sisters while they sought employment, shelter, and food. Mortality rates were also very high, as had been the case in Quebec and Montreal, with close to one-in-five children dying in the care of the Sisters.

The one striking characteristic of the Bytown orphans was that despite the high number of pre-Famine Irish inhabiting the Ottawa Valley, none came forward to assist in 'taking in' an orphan. The placements were entirely within French Canadian homes but limited to only five families. A certain 'Madame Labreche', for example, took 20, or over one-third of the children. While there are no records surviving to substantiate the possibility that she kept them all, one suspects that she became an intermediary for the further distribution of the children in the community. In addition, for the children who remained behind, there was the opportunity for them to be educated, albeit briefly, in the fledgling school, established in 1845, by the original group of Grey Sisters. On the whole, what is clear about the Irish experience in Bytown was the gargantuan humanitarian effort exhibited by the Grey Sisters under Bruyère's leadership. Without their infirmary, hospital, and orphanage, the Irish deaths in the future capital of Canada would have been much higher.

Table 1: Orphan Placement in Bytown, 1847 N=56

	Male	Female	Infant	Total (%)
Placed With Mother or Father	1	2	0	3 (5.4)
Placed with Relative	1	1	0	2 (3.6)
Left on Own	1	4	0	5 (8.9)
Placed with French Canadian	16	19	0	35 (62.5)
Placed with Irish Canadian	0	0	0	0 (0.0)
Died in Hospital	2	7	2	11 (19.6)
Total	21	33	2	56 (100.00)

Source: City of Ottawa Archives, Sisters of Charity (Grey Nuns), General Hospital Ledger, Bytown, 1847.

If Bytown held out few prospects for work or shelter, Irish refugees had several options. They could take boats up the Ottawa River to Renfrew County on the west bank of the river, or Pontiac County on the east bank. Both counties had been heavily settled with Irish migrants before the Famine and there would be the prospects of farm work for the newest Irish arrivals. At Mount Saint Patrick, where the local Catholic priests served Irish farmers in Bromley and Admaston townships, there was already a sense of the devastation wrought by the potato blight in their former home. A native of County Mayo, Father John McNulty rallied local farmers, raftsmen, business owners and woods workers at the nearby timber shanties to donate to the Famine relief fund.[21] In 1847, he covered the area sometimes travelling 50 to 100 kilometres in the snow-filled woods and tapped as many people that he could for

Famine assistance. Naturally, the Irish dominated his list of donors, but there were also notable contributions from French Canadians, English settlers, and indigenous peoples from their traditional territories at Golden Lake.[22] Given McNulty's strong support for victims of the Famine both in Ireland and in the Upper Ottawa Valley, it comes as no surprise that many migrants elected to halt their journey and settle in Admaston and the area near Mount Saint Patrick.[23]

The vast majority of Irish migrants in Bytown, who chose to leave the care of Bruyère and Van Courtland, headed southwest along the Rideau Canal to Kingston. It was only 15 years earlier that hundreds of Irish sojourners completed the building of the canal, linking Bytown and Kingston, many at the cost of their lives through malaria and fever. The project, which linked the Ottawa River, Rideau River, Rideau Lakes, and Cataraqui River, was intended by the British military to be an interior transportation corridor, which would be far enough from the border of the United States to avoid potential attack. While the Irish migrants, prior to the Famine had used this route as the principal waterway from Montreal to Bytown, and into the interior, by 1847 canal improvements on the Saint Lawrence River west of Montreal made for a more direct route from the Lower Province to Kingston. In 'Black '47' Irish refugees from Montreal were more apt to take this faster route west, via steamer and Durham boat from the Lachine rapids along the Saint Lawrence River to Kingston, a trip of about 30 hours.[24]

At each town along the Upper Canadian bank of the river, Boards of Health or police detachments were present to assist the sick and dying. It was in Cornwall, West Williamsburg, Matilda, Prescott, Brockville, and Picton, where Irish migrants would make their first and sometimes last landing in Upper Canada. Local first responders were often overwhelmed. On 7 July 1847, for example, Charles Post in the town of Cornwall reported to Secretary Daly that he had been forced to build an additional shed, in order to house the migrants. The tiny hospital was crowded with 24 patients, mostly Irish, suffering from typhus, typhoid, and dysentery.[25] The Board of Police at Prescott was desperate for suitable buildings, but the Provincial Government was unwilling to defray costs for shed or leasing hospitals space, which the Provincial Secretary regarded as a local matter.[26] While Daly was willing to cover the cost of a physician at West Williamsburg, after a request from the Board of Police, he was unwilling to advance the Board of Health in Belleville for medical supplies, doctors' bills, and food, even though the Board Chair admitted that the 'Town has no means at its disposal for the purpose'. Daly firmly held the official policy of reimbursing only when money was spent by Boards of Health.[27] With this correspondence in mind, those leaders in the local reception areas of Upper Canada were, despite their best intentions, often thwarted in their charitable and medical assistance to Irish migrants because of the bureaucratic rigidity in the Provincial Secretary's Office.

Kingston became the principal dispersal centre for migrants into the interior of the province. The former capital of the United Province of Canada, Kingston also was a significant market centre for its eastern portion, as well as the site of one of Britain's most important military installations in the Canadian interior, Fort Henry. Kingston was situated at the eastern end of Lake Ontario (an enormous inland sea, stretching some 7,340 square miles just a little over 25 per cent of Ireland's land mass), between Canada and New York State, making the 'limestone town' a key transportation hub in Canada West. As directed by emigration agents, boats from Montreal and from the Rideau Canal dispatched their passengers at the Kingston wharves. Hawke's employees then triaged the emigrants quickly, with the sick being moved to the two local hospitals or to fever sheds located at Emily and King Streets, in the west of the town.[28] Healthy emigrants, once disembarked, were quickly re-boarded on steamships belonging to the Royal Mail Steamship Company, at the expense of the government, and were transported to points west: Niagara, Hamilton, or Toronto. If the latter port was the final destination, emigrants could depart the ships at smaller towns and villages near the northern shore of Lake Ontario: Picton, Belleville, Cobourg, Port Hope, Darlington, and Port Whitby. Conditions on the steamships were often poor, with emigrants either crowded in the hold or exposed to the elements on the upper decks. Some migrants, who could not get themselves on board, were crowded into open barges, towed by the steamer. According to one eyewitness on one such steamer 'The poor creatures ... were crowded together like herrings in a barrel, and many had difficulty gasping for a breath of fresh air'.[29] The correspondent continued his description by likening the conditions on board this steamer as akin to slave ships arriving in America.

While Hawke and municipal officials would eventually investigate the conditions on these contracted ships, the pressing matter was how to cope with the crush of emigrant numbers in Kingston. The Protestant community led by Mayor Thomas Kirkpatrick, and the Catholic community led by Coadjutor Bishop of Kingston, Patrick Phelan, worked in co-operation to assist the mostly Catholic emigrants.[30] Although sometimes referred to as the 'Derry of Canada', Kingston's religious communities demonstrated rare moments of ecumenical co-operation, both within the town, and in their donations to relief efforts in Ireland.[31] Despite the appearance of public co-operation between the churches, many rank-and-file Protestant citizens expressed their resentment to this massive Catholic migration; complaints were particularly loud from Kingstonians living in the precinct adjacent to the fever sheds where the sights and odours of the fetid shelters were most apparent.[32] There was also a minor confrontation at Brewery Wharf, where emigrants landed, between Father Bernard Higgins and the overtly anti-Catholic crew of the ship *Princess Royal*, but the trouble and its aftermath were diffused after an investigation led by the local constabulary and supported by Kirkpatrick and Phelan.[33] Generally speaking, the Catholic Church had always been prominent in Kingston, which, in 1826, became the first Catholic diocese in Upper Canada (now Canada West), and its first bishop, Alexander Macdonell, was noted as a loyal Tory sympathizer with military credentials.[34] In 1826, Macdonell, a fierce imperialist and Tory, was appointed the first Catholic bishop of Upper Canada, and asserted the respectability of his Catholic flock. After the rebellions of 1837–1838, which he opposed, the local Orange Lodges drank to his health.[35]

After Macdonell's death, in 1841, the Catholic presence in the city continued to grow. Through the agency of Macdonell's successor, the sickly Bishop Remi Gaulin (1841), and his ties with Bishop Ignace Bourget in Montreal, Gaulin invited the Religious Hospitallers of St Joseph to establish a hospital in Kingston.[36] This order of women religious had deep roots in Canada, having been founded by Jeanne Mance in 1659, in order to establish a hospital in the French colonial settlement of Ville Marie (later Montreal).[37] In 1845, Gaulin's duties had fallen to his Coadjutor Bishop, Patrick Phelan, a native of Kilkenny, who welcomed Mother Amable Bourbonnière, the founding superior, and four other Sisters, who would soon reside in a house on Brock Street in the centre of the town, purchased by the diocese for £750 for the Sisters' health care and orphanage projects.[38] The Sisters had arrived by steamer from Montreal in civilian clothes and were hosted by the Sisters of Notre Dame, who housed them and gave them the opportunity to don their religious habits. Although cloistered and French-speaking from Montreal, the Sisters, led by Mother Bourbonnière, successfully petitioned Phelan to allow them semi-cloistered status so that they could do their medical work more effectively within the community.[39]

Upon arrival, Bourbonnière and her sisters began the construction of the Hôtel-Dieu Hospital, using funds provided by a wealthy Montreal patron, Madame Josephine Perras. The hospital was still incomplete in the spring of 1847, when the Irish emigrants began to arrive by the thousands. The men's wing of the hospital was still in need of a roof. Bourbonnière cultivated excellent relations with the Protestant Female Benevolent Society, which operated the fledgling General Hospital, the Kingston Board of Health, and Mayor Kirkpatrick. These alliances produced mutual benefits for all concerned including the exchange hospital supplies, food, and patient transfers between the Hôtel-Dieu and the General Hospital.[40] This cooperation included daily visits by the Sisters to what they termed 'the English Hospital' for supplies or to pick up Catholic children who had arrived at that facility.[41] The Sisters accepted aid from 'Miss Burnel', the daughter of a local Protestant Minister, who generously delivered linens to the Hôtel-Dieu.[42] The Provincial Government also offered a subsidy of £1 per month per child, for those institutions willing to open their doors to children who appeared orphaned in great numbers in the local fever sheds.[43] Orphans were accommodated by the Sisters prior to 1847, but local clergy ventured to the sheds and gathered up Irish children, who were eventually joined by other orphaned children, some of whom had been at the Kingston General Hospital.

The Annalist of the Hospitaller Sisters recorded one such poignant arrival of Irish orphan children. On Christmas Eve, 1847, Monsignor Angus Macdonell, nephew to the deceased bishop, delivered 71 more children to Bourbonnière and the Sisters at the Hôtel-Dieu , who were not prepared in the slightest. To that point they had very few children they would have classified as orphans, and very little space or furniture to accommodate almost six dozen more waifs. As the RHSJ Annalist wrote, Macdonell did so: 'to save the poor children from misery and the danger they were in of losing their souls'.[44] Such a statement reveals the concern the Church had for both the physical welfare of the Irish orphans and for the possibility that they might fall into the wrong hands in a Protestant town.

Even by the Sisters' own admission, what greeted the children at the Hôtel-Dieu that evening was less satisfactory than had been hoped. The Annalist commented that 'Misery was depicted on the countenance of these poor little unfortunates several of whom had been sick and very much neglected or rather abandoned'.[45] The walls of the institution were still un-plastered and there were less than half as many beds as would be needed by the 71 children. The beds were reported to be full of vermin. There was not even an adequate dining facility for them as they gathered for their Christmas Eve supper. The Sisters erected a makeshift table consisting of two barrels supporting a collection of loose boards from a bed. The Annalist continues:

> The children had to sit down on the floor around the stove, they were chilled with cold and we served them by rows, as we had not sufficient dishes to serve them all at once, for the little girls, we got the dishes from the orphan girls ward, whom we had before the Emigrants came, and took the top of a bed, otherwise set on trestles for a table.[46]

The 71 children formed seven rows of 10 to match the seven bowls, plates, and flatware made available to them. As one child ate and cleaned the dishes, the next one took his/her place and shared the Christmas feast. After all the children had eaten, they retired to the ward, two and three to a bed, although the Annalist commented that the sisters: 'were very sorry to put them in such disgusting beds'.[47]

After Christmas, Bourbonnière was in close contact with Protestant women in the community, who assisted in improving the conditions in the makeshift orphanage. The Annalist reported that local women offered to sew new clothes for the children. The Mother Superior, evidently talented with a needle, worked throughout the night of Boxing Day to repair and remake clothes for the little girls, who comprised about half of the new batch of orphans. Several of the boys were reported to have been covered with scabs, but 'they were hardly recognizable after they were better and were cleaned up'. Bourbonnière, whose talents also extended to pharmacology, prepared an ointment that proved effective on the sores and scabs.[48] Underscoring this entire effort at the Hôtel-Dieu was the co-operative spirit exemplified by the RHSJs and the leading Protestant women in Kingston. By the end of the sailing season, it is likely that as many as 70,000 migrants passed through Kingston, with estimates ranging between 1,200 and 1,500 for those who died in the sheds constructed at King and Emily Streets.[49] The Catholic Cathedral records that its priests buried 1,234 persons that year, 989 of whom were immigrants, which included 289 children.[50]At the end of the sailing season, those indigent families, widows, and single men who were released from hospital would be housed in Kingston's new House of Industry.[51] As had been the case in Bytown, the emigrant relief effort landed primarily on the shoulders of an order of women religious, who worked co-operatively with local authorities and with other women to serve the emigrant Irish with whatever resources they had. Shaken by the huge numbers of Irish who sought refuge with them, Amable Bourbonnière had risen to the task, with the tragic loss of Sister McGorrian, a novice who worked among those infected with typhus.[52]

For his part, Hawke saw to it that as few of the emigrants who needed to ever saw the town of Kingston. The sick were moved to the sheds and the hospitals while the majority of the seemingly healthy migrants moved on to ports at the western end of Lake Ontario. On route, migrants disembarked at Port Hope and Cobourg with the promise of employment or land in the area around Peterborough, which had been settled by Peter Robinson's settlers from Tipperary and Cork in the 1820s. Some Irish migrants intending to stop at Port Whitby had a major detour backwards when their luggage was mistakenly put off at Port Darlington several miles to the east.[53] The ultimate destination was Toronto, where, in the sailing season of 1847, over 38,000 migrants would land, most of them Irish. The city of Toronto contained roughly 20,000 people, around 3,000 of whom were Irish Catholics who had migrated to Canada prior to the Famine.[54] In many ways, 'Muddy York,' as the former Upper Canadian capital was called, was on the cusp of becoming the leading metropolitan centre in Canada West. Situated on the north shore of Lake Ontario, it had a large and defensible harbour, protected by a wide peninsula that extended from the eastern side of Toronto Bay, where the Don River emptied, and stretched almost to the western banks of the lake, where a wide channel was flanked by a mound that locals called Gibraltar, and the ramparts of Fort York on the mainland. Toronto was a natural hub for small industries, a service centre for its vast agricultural hinterland, the site of a university (founded in 1827), and the market centre for the burgeoning grain trade in the province. Despite its reputation as being dominated by the scions of the Loyal Orange Order, Toronto and its hinterland provided hope for a new life for many of the Famine refugees.

Steamers with emigrants were restricted to one dock, Dr Rees' Wharf, where they would be met and triaged by Hawke's Toronto agent, Edward McElderry. While much has been written on the work of many 'Famine Heroes' in Toronto, including the Roman Catholic Bishop, Michael Power, and medical officer Dr. George Grasett, McElderry's work during Black '47 has largely gone un-noticed.[55] Born in County Tyrone, McElderry emigrated to Canada, likely in the late 1830s.[56] He was a member of St Paul's Roman Catholic parish, where he would later serve as a trustee, and become acquainted with Bishop Power. Little else is known about McElderry other than he was married to Rose Anne Lawlor, with whom he had seven children, with an eighth on the way in 1847. In the mid 1840s, he was associated with O'Connell's repeal movement and was a noted participant in local meetings of the Repeal Association in Toronto.[57] Power, who was also interested in constitutional reform in Ireland, must have taken a liking to McElderry because it was the Catholic bishop who recommended him to Hawke for the position of Emigration Agent in Toronto. For his part, Hawke admitted that he did not know McElderry well: 'He is no great scholar, but I have always found him to be zealous and correct'.[58] This is a massive understatement, because, in the absence of a women's religious order in Toronto until the autumn of 1847, McElderry, next to Power, was the most visibly active Catholic dedicated to emigrant aid in the city.

For emigrants arriving in Toronto, McElderry and his staff would have been the first Torontonians they sighted. McElderry had made sure that there were appropriate temporary sheds at the wharf for passengers who required shelter from the elements or a place where they could wait before being triaged away from the harbour. McElderry, city constables, and medical staff, would inspect passengers as they were herded off the steamers. The healthy would be given travel vouchers, signed by McElderry, to remove them from the city quickly at the government's expense.[59]

The vouchers are valuable historical documents in and of themselves as they contain the names of passengers, baggage accompanying them, and the destination of the cart. McElderry sent Irish migrants to the rich farmlands of Holland Landing to the north, Brantford to the southwest, the city of Hamilton to the south, and to the Niagara Peninsula (See Table 2).[60] The intention was to avoid turning Toronto into a refugee camp, risking the spread of disease, while targeting areas where Irish migrants might be employed on farms, clearing lands for crops, or maintaining the Welland Canal works near Niagara. Most of the migrants, perhaps just over 26,000, met by McElderry in 1847 were quickly cleared from the city, and as had been anticipated, many of these emigrants had plans to leave Canada entirely and move on to family and friends already settling and sojourning in the United States.

Table 2: Fate of the Emigrants Landing at Toronto, 1847

Total Emigrants to Toronto	38,560	%
Sent Niagara & Hamilton	26,700	69.2
Sent to Country by Land	8,950	23.2
Died in Emigrant Lodgings/Emigrant Hospital	1,124	2.9
Remaining in Hospital	413	1.1
Convalescent Hospital	210	0.5
Remain in Emigrant Sheds	293	0.8
Remain at Widow/Orphan Asylum	89	0.2
Lodging in the City	781	2.0

Source: *Mirror*, 18 February 1848. Report up to 1 February 1848.

McElderry triaged a second group, some 4,355 sick and dying persons, to be taken to the Toronto Emigrant Hospital at the corner of King and John Streets, several city blocks north of the wharf. In the spring the city council had preferred that the emigrants be isolated on Toronto's peninsula on the other side of the harbour, to protect Toronto's citizenry. The scheme proved to be impractical and the Toronto General Hospital, in the western precinct of the city, became the emigrant hospital on a temporary basis. Now, Irish migrants suffering from dysentery, typhus, and other ailments, found themselves at the 'new' Emigrant Hospital, which very quickly became overcrowded. Constable Jonathan B 'Toby' Townsend was in charge of the hospital complex and filed reports with the local Board of Health. A series of chief medical officers, including the unfortunate George Grasset, MD, were in charge of the medical matters at the hospital. Overwhelmed by the numbers of persons at the hospital, the Board of Health recommended to the city that sheds be built on the land adjacent to the hospital, and by the end of the season, 16 of these sheds had been constructed.[61] Overwhelmed by the numbers being treated in the hospital, McElderry begged Hawke for more funds to extend the general hospital building, but Hawke, regarding such capital projects as beyond the mandate of his agency, refused. Nonetheless, he did send McElderry £125 to support the work of the medical staff.[62]

McElderry was simply indefatigable. He worked directly with emigrants, advocated for them with the health and civic authorities, oversaw improvements to emigrant reception areas, and managed to supply free travel to areas of potential employment. Stephen De Vere, the Irish landlord who accompanied his tenants to Canada, met with McElderry in Toronto and offered this assessment of him as:

> One of the best authorities in Canada ... [he stated] that the demand for laborers on the part of the Farmers, would have absorbed the entire year's emigration into Upper Canada, unexampled as it was in numbers, if the infectious disease among them had not naturally disinclined the Employers from taking them into their Families.[63]

De Vere confirmed McElderry's concern to employ the emigrant Irish in Upper Canada and to triage the sick out of the travellers, lest they boomeranged back to Toronto having been shunned by locals. De Vere added in the letter that 'I never saw greater zeal or intelligence than his: and to his utter recklessness of danger and discharge of duty, he owes his early death'.[64]

Edward McElderry died on 29 October 1847 having suffered from dysentery and fever, likely contracted from the emigrants with whom he was working and compounded by exhaustion.[65] The Kingston *Whig* commented that his 'discharge of his onerous duties was universally acknowledged and was only equaled by his kindness to the poor people who came under his charge'.[66] He left his widow, Rose Anne, and their seven children destitute, and Rose Anne having yet another mouth to feed when the new baby was born. Bishop Power could not advocate for her because he died on 1 October. De Vere asked if Lord Elgin would secure a pension for McElderry's widow.[67] Similarly, Hawke, in a moment of compassion, argued that Rose Anne ought to be given a pension for the loss of her husband who had done so much, even given his life for the Irish in Toronto.[68] The Colonial Office refused, with the Governor's General's Secretary, Robert B. Sullivan, transmitting the message that many in the province had sacrificed much and died in service of the emigrants.[69] Even a petition from Rose Anne herself failed. Hawke then argued that McElderry had been paid too little at 10 shillings per day, and that it should be increased retroactively to 15 shillings and given to the family.[70] Whether Rose Anne received Hawke's estimated £46 in backpay is unknown, but she likely received at least the amount in unpaid wages of £30 8*s* owed to her.[71] Whatever the sum, Rose Anne, having secured the rights of custody to her eight children, left Toronto with her children and settled in Guelph, about 60 miles west of Toronto. Today, the McElderrys are remembered at the large family plot still prominent in St Joseph's Cemetery, and by a commemorative stained-glass window to the McElderry family in the Church of Our Lady, a cathedral-like church which towers over the town. In an ironic twist of opinions, during Hawke's pleading the case to Elgin's secretary, Sullivan, he eulogized McElderry as:

> a good man in every relation of his life and has certainly fallen a victim to his duty. Had he less zeal he would have given himself time to recover from the effects of fever, but he persisted in working beyond his strength and the dysentery set in fatally.[72]

Public health works that had been advocated by McElderry, Power, Grasset, and Mayor William Henry Boulton, continued, long after the first three had died. In the summer and autumn of 1847, the Board of Health, under the watchful eye of Hawke's department, established a Convalescent Hospital and a Widow and Orphans Asylum. Both institutions relieved the pressure on the overcrowded conditions at the Emigrant Hospital and Sheds. At the Widow and Orphans Asylum, both Protestant and Catholic leaders arranged for the placement of 197 orphaned children into the homes of families, artisans, farmers, and businesses in Toronto, the adjacent rural counties, and as far east as Essex County, just across the Detroit River from the State of Michigan. Municipal officials in Toronto made certain that every child who was placed in a situation of indenture would receive compensation for work done, proper clothing, and food and lodging.[73] Given its unique municipal powers, the city attempted to guarantee that Irish orphans were not turned into unpaid domestic and field labourers, as had been the case in other parts of British North America. At the end of 1847, of the estimated 38,560 emigrants who arrived in Toronto, about 75 per cent were Irish according to Constable Townsend of the Board of Health.[74] The total dead numbered 1,124 of the total emigrant arrivals, or roughly under 3 per cent. About 757 were buried in the Catholic cemetery ground at St Paul's Church, while those identified as Protestants, some 305, were interred at St James Anglican Cemetery. The rest were buried in unmarked graves in Potters Field.[75] With only about 2,000 remaining in Toronto, it is clear that Hawke and McElderry's efforts to move the emigrants away from Toronto worked in the short term.

Beyond Toronto, the waterways and roadways revealed more tales of individual heroism. In Brantford, for example, the local Anglican Minister, James Campbell Usher, took mercy on Mary Willis and retained her as a cook in his rectory. He must have been moved by Mary's harrowing tale. She and her husband, John, and their five children left their farm in Tipperary and set sail to Canada on the *Jessie*, leaving Limerick on 28 April 1847. They were one of many Protestant families fleeing the Famine and searching for a new life, likely among Tipperary residents who had already made homes in Upper Canada prior to the Famine. At Limerick, the first of many tragedies struck. Diagnosed with possible ship's fever, the Willis' youngest son was left behind in Ireland, while the family moved on. During their 56 days at sea, two more of the Willis children, the eldest son and 10-year-old Martha, died. When the Willis family arrived at the Grosse Île quarantine station near Quebec, their 17-year-old daughter Mary was forced to leave the ship and died in the lazarettos on the island. By the time they reached Toronto, only Mary survived with her husband and last remaining son likely having succumbed to disease at the fever sheds of King and John Streets. Mary alone lived to tell the tale of her vanquished family. It appears that in his compassion, the Reverend Usher made a home for her.[76]

There are probably many more stories of charity and mercy yet to be told. Historians are hard pressed to uncover them because most ordinary people in the nineteenth century went about their daily labours leaving few reminiscences, diaries, or testimonies from which their actions and ideas can be reconstructed. While scholars can detect general patterns of behaviour from routinely generated records like censuses, marriage registers, tax assessments, and legal records, these sources only provide a social skeleton. The fleshy bits are those derived from newspaper clippings, letters, memoirs and, in a later period, photographs. The rich, powerful, wealthy, and the chattering classes will have their stories told. It is unfortunate that the stories on the ground, of persons like Bruyère, McNulty, Bourbonnière, McElderry, or Usher, are often found accidently, or in the spaces hidden within the larger narratives. At least in the cases cited above, and their ties to their Christian faith, one might conclude that they acted heroically because they believed they were called to do so as witnesses to the Gospel. Perhaps their response was akin to that of Charles Donlevy, editor of the *Mirror*, an Irish Catholic paper published in Toronto. Donlevy begged Toronto's citizens not to flee the city but to help the emigrants:[77]

> Are the charities of our Holy Religion dried up? Are our bowls of compassion closed against the cries of our people? Look sir at the squalor and the haggard aspect of the poor creatures. Look at their fleshless bodies, and bloodless faces—at their despair, and mental torpor—at their unwashed and unclothed persons, and say we are doing

> our duty ... Sir, there is not an Irish family in this City that could not find some old vestments which would serve these people ... The dogs licked the sores of Lazarus at the rich man's gate, and were more merciful than their master. We have less commiseration than the rich man's dogs.[78]

Whatever their intentions, they stepped up and served the Irish in their time of need, and, in the case of McElderry, sacrificed a life. These were just ordinary people capable of doing extraordinary things; they were illuminating signs on a highway of heroes.

NOTES

1. From 1791 to 1841, the original Province of Ontario was known as Upper Canada and Quebec was known as Lower Canada. The Act of Union of 1840, effective in 1841, created the United Province of Canada with two sections, Canada East (formerly Lower Canada) and Canada West (formerly Upper Canada). Unfortunately for historians, in the common vernacular the old provincial names stuck, and the new ones were used only in legal conventions and in political circles. The capital of Upper Canada had been York (Toronto) and the capital of the United Province in 1841 was Kingston. This arrangement did not last long as the capital moved from city to city until it rested in Bytown (now Ottawa) in 1858. In 1867, the Dominion of Canada was formed as a confederation of four provinces: Ontario, Quebec, New Brunswick, and Nova Scotia.
2. Arthur G. Doughty, ed., *The Elgin-Grey Papers, 1846–1852* (Ottawa: J.G. Patenaude, 1937), vol. 1, Lord Elgin to Earl Grey, 13 Aug. 1847, pp 63–4.
3. Mark G. McGowan, *Death or Canada: The Irish Famine Migration to Toronto, 1847* (Toronto: Novalis, 2009); Mark G. McGowan, *Creating Canadian Historical Memory, The Case of the Famine Migration of 1847* (Ottawa: Canadian Historical Association, 2008). The most helpful primary documents for statistics can be found at Library and Archives Canada [LAC], Colonial Office Fonds, CO 384/82, Reel 1746, *Eighth General Report, Colonial Land and Emigration Commissioners, 1848* (London: William Clowes and Sons, 1848).
4. Robert C. Lee, *The Canada Company and the Huron Tract, 1826–1853: Personalities, Profits, and Politics* (Toronto: Natural Heritage Books, 2004).
5. At: www150.statcan.gc.ca/n1/pub/98–187-x/4064809-eng.htm#part4
6. Lisa Chilton, *Receiving Canada's Immigrants: The Work of the State Before 1930* (Ottawa: Canadian Historical Association, Immigration and Ethnicity in Canada Series, No. 34, 2016), p. 14. See also, Rebecca O'Reilly, 'In a Situation of Great Distress: The Emigrant Agency, Poverty, and the Irish in 19th Century Upper Canada' (Unpublished MA Thesis, University of Guelph, 2006).
7. Archives of Ontario [AO] RG. 11, 1–0–3, Toronto Emigration Papers, A.B. Hawke Letterbook, 11 Apr. 1847. In total, Hawke paid his emigrant agents in Bytown (G.R. Burke), Cobourg/Port Hope (A.B. Hawkins), Toronto (E.M. McElderry), and Hamilton (L.P. Palmer) one pound sterling per day. Emigrant physicians were paid variously: Dr

Thomas Robinson (Kingston) £50, Dr Dickenson (Hamilton) £30, and Dr Van Courtland (Bytown) £25, for the entire season (1 May to 1 November). Letterbook, Hawke to All Subagents, Apr.1847.

8. Colleen Towns, 'Relief and Order: The Public Response to the 1847 Famine Irish Migration to Upper Canada' (Unpublished MA Thesis, Queen's University, Kingston, 1990), p. 25. See also *British Colonist*, 12 June 1847. AO, Emigration Papers, RG 11, 1–0–3, Copy of Letter, Dominick Daly to Mayor W.H. Boulton, 7 June 1847.
9. Wesley B. Turner, 'HAWKE, ANTHONY BEWDEN,' in *Dictionary of Canadian Biography*, vol. 9, University of Toronto/Université Laval, 2003– www.biographi.ca/en/bio/hawke_anthony_bewden_9E.html.
10. Michael Cross, 'The Shiners War: Social Violence in the Ottawa Valley in the 1830s,' in *Canadian Historical Review* 54, no. 1 (March 1973), 1–26.
11. AO, RG 11, 1–0–3, End of Year (1846) Report, 31 Dec. 1846.
12. ARCAT, Michael Power Papers, AA10.10, Copy of letter from Michael Power to the Propaganda Fide, Rome, 12 Apr. 1847. Also Archives of the Sacred Congregation of the Propaganda Fide [APF], Scritture riferte nei congress. America Settentionale. Canada ecc. Dal 1841–1848, vol. 5, Bishop Power to PF, 12 Apr. 1847; PF to Power, 12 June 1847.
13. Until 25 June 1847, Bytown and the Upper Canadian side of the Ottawa River was part of the Diocese of Kingston.
14. Soeur Paul-Émile (Louise Guay), 'BRUYÈRE, ÉLISABETH', in *Dictionary of Canadian Biography*, vol. 10, University of Toronto/Université Laval, 2003. At: www.biographi.ca/en/bio/bruyere_elisabeth_10E.html.
15. Réal Dumas, 'Religious Communities and Institutes,' in Pierre Hurtubise, Mark G. McGowan and Pierre Savard (eds.), *Planted By Flowing Water: The Diocese of Ottawa, 1847–1997* (Ottawa: Novalis, 1998), p. 189.
16. Rita McGuire, GSIC, 'The Grey Sisters in the Red River Settlement, 1844–1870,' Canadian Catholic Historical Association', in *Historical Studies*, 53 (1986), 21–37.
17. Soeur Paul-Émile (Louise Guay), 'BRUYÈRE, ÉLISABETH', in *Dictionary of Canadian Biography*, vol. 10, University of Toronto/Université Laval, 2003. At: www.biographi.ca/en/bio/bruyere_elisabeth_10E.html. Michael McBane, *Bytown: Elisabeth Bruyere & the Irish Famine Refugees* (Ottawa: Michael McBane, 2022).
18. Soeur Paul-Emile, sgc, "Mère Elisabeth Bruyère: fille de l'Ēglise et femme d'oeuvres," La Société Canadienne d'histoire de l'Ēglise Catholique, *Rapport*, 29 (1961), pp 55–56.
19. Emilien Lamirande, *Elisabeth Bruyère: Fondatrice des Soeurs de la Charité d'Ottawa* (Montreal: Bellaramine, 1998), 167.
20. Soeur Paul-Emile, 'Mère Elisabeth Bruyère', pp 51–52.
21. Carol Bennett, McCuaig, *People of St. Patrick's* (Renfrew: Juniper Books Ltd, 1993), p. 8.
22. *Bytown Packet*, 8 May 1847.
23. Edward J. Hedican, *After the Famine: The Irish Family Farm in Eastern Ontario, 1851–1881* (Toronto: University of Toronto Press, 2020) and Carol Bennett (ed.), *The Founding Families of Admaston, Horton, and Renfrew Village* (Renfrew: Juniper Books, 1992).
24. Towns, 'Relief and Order', p. 47.

25. RG 5 C1, vol. 204, p. 17,264; Provincial Secretary, Numbered Correspondence, 1844–1867, Cornwall Emigration Returns to Daly, 6/7 July 1847.
26. Ibid., vol. 207, Board of Police, Prescott, to Day, 14 June 1847 and Daly to Board of Police, Prescott, 29 June 1847.
27. Ibid., vol. 206, Belleville Board of Health to Daly, 23 July 1847, and Daly to BH of Belleville, 31 July 1847; also vol. 204 West Williamsburg Superintendent of Police to Daly, 15 July 1847.
28. Towns, 'Relief and Order', pp 5, 67.
29. *Globe*, 25 Aug. 1847.
30. Phelan was the titular bishop of Carrhae and did not officially become Bishop of Kingston until 1857, the year Bishop Remi Gaulin died. In reality, Phelan was in control of the diocese as of 1845, when Gaulin retired. Andre Chapeau, OSB, Louis-Philippe Normand, OMI, and Lucienne Plante, CND (eds.), *Evêques Catholiques du Canada/Canadian R.C. Bishops, 1658–1979* (Ottawa: Research Centre in Religious History of Canada, 1980), pp 35–6.
31. *British Whig* (Kingston), 31 July 1847.
32. Nancy McMahon, 'Les Religieuse Hospitalières de St. Joseph and the Typhus Epidemic, Kingston, 1847–1848', CCHA *Historical Studies* 58 (1991), p. 47.
33. *British Whig*, 11, 18, 21 Aug. 1847.
34. Jane Errington, *Greater Kingston: Historic Past, Progressive Future* (Burlington: Windsor Publications, 1989), 59; Louis J. Flynn, *Built on a Rock: The Story of the Roman Catholic Church in Kingston, 1826–1976* (Kingston: Roman Catholic Archdiocese of Kingston, 1976), pp 5–8. Brandon Corcoran and Laura J. Smith, 'Bishop Macdonell and the Friends of Ireland: Mixing Politics and Religion in Upper Canada', Canadian Catholic Historical Association, *Historical Studies*, 79 (2013), 7–23.
35. *Lord Durham's Report* (1839), Gerald M. Craig (ed.) (Toronto: McClelland and Stewart, Carleton Library Series, 1963), p. 98.
36. McMahon, 'Les Religieuse Hospitalières', pp 41–2.
37. Cornelius J Jaenen, *The Role of the Church in New France* (Toronto: McGraw-Hill Ryerson, 1976), pp 11–12.
38. Errington, *Greater Kingston*, 122. See also: https://rhsjstjoseph.omeka.net/exhibits/show/hdhk-175/founding-of-hdhk
39. McMahon, 'Les Religieuse', p. 46.
40. Ibid., p. 46; Brian S. Osborne and Donald Swainson, *Kingston: Building on the Past* (Westport, ON: Butternut Press, 1988), pp 128–9.
41. Religious Hospitallers of St Joseph (Kingston), Archives [hereafter RHSJA], Typescript History/Memoire, p. 19.
42. RHSJA, Annals of the Hotel Dieu, Kingston, typescript, vol. 1, 26 Dec. 1847.
43. Ibid.
44. Ibid.
45. Ibid.
46. Ibid.

47. Ibid.
48. Ibid.
49. Towns, 'Relief and Order), p. 123. The number appears a little high given the recorded deaths, the expeditious way migrants were moved through the port, and the fact that just over 38,000 made the next stop in Toronto.
50. Archdiocese of Kingston, St Mary's Cathedral, Register of Baptisms, Marriages, and Burials, 1843–1849. The Catholic Church recognized 1,234 deaths in 1847. Of these, 989 were identified as 'emigrants' and of these, 289 were children. The emigrants were almost all Irish, with 328 (33.2%) being identified by county of origin.
51. *British Whig*, 18 Dec.1847; and Queens University Archives, House of Industry, Inmate Registers, 2262-Box 7, Ledger 1, Dec. 1847-July 1848.
52. RHSJ Archives, Annals, vol. 1, pp 12–13.
53. *Globe,* 19 June 1847.
54. The numbers are contested for this period. In the 1842 Census of Canada West, Toronto was not parsed out from the Home District in which it was located. There were 83,301 persons in the district of whom, 17,985 were of Irish birth, and 8,500 were Roman Catholic. In the 1848 Census, the city was included indicating that of the 23,503 citizens, only 1,965 claimed Irish birth and 5,903 were Roman Catholics. When adjusting for the Irish who may have stayed in the city after the sailing season of 1847, one concludes that the local Irish population on the eve of the Famine was probably around 3,000, by birth and descent. *Census of Canada, 1665–1971*, vol. 4 of the *Census of Canada, 1870–1871*(Ottawa: I.B. Taylor, 1876), pp 134–135, 165–166, & Table 11.
55. Laura J. Smith and Robert G. Kearns, 'Dr. George Grasett: Toronto's Response to the Typhus Outbreak of 1847,' in Christine Kinealy, Jason King, and Gerard Moran (eds)' *Heroes of Ireland's Great Hunger* (Hamden, CT: Quinnipiac University Press/Cork University Press, 2021), pp 163–76. Mark G. McGowan, 'Bishop Michael Power of Toronto (1804–1847): A Reluctant Hero,' in Kinealy, King & Moran (eds), *Heroes*, pp 191–204; Mark G. McGowan, *Michael Power: The Struggle to Build the Catholic Church on the Canadian Frontier* (Montreal & Kingston: McGill-Queen's University Press, 2005).
56. www.ancestry.ca/family-tree/person/tree/72711300/person/30261195542/facts?_phsrc=cPz184&_phstart=successSource
57. *Mirror*, 2 Feb. 1844.
58. AO, RG–11 1–0–3, Emigration Papers, Hawke Letterbooks, Hawke to A.C. Buchanan, 11 Apr. 1847
59. LAC, RG19-D–5, vol. 2532–5, Emigrant Service Fund, 1843–1847. See: Laura J. Smith, 'We have scattered them far and wide: Transporting Indigent Irish Emigrants in the Canadas, 1843–1847,' in Christine Kinealy and Gerard Moran (eds), *Irish Famines before and After the Great Hunger* (Hamden, CT: Quinnipiac University Press/Cork University Press, 2020), pp 77–99.
60. *Mirror*, 18 Feb.1848. The report includes some of the few surviving statistics of McElderry's internal migration targets.
61. See McGowan*, Death or Canada*, Chapter 3 for greater detail.

62. AO, RG–11, 1–0—3, Emigration Papers, Hawke Letterbooks, Hawke to J.E. Campbell, Civil Secretary, 3 June 1847; Hawke to McElderry, 21 Apr. 1847; Hawke to McElderry, 14 May 1847.
63. *Elgin Grey Correspondence*, vol. IV, Despatch No. 162, 27 January 1848, containing Stephen De Vere to Lord Elgin, 30 Nov. 1847, p. 1347.
64. Ibid.
65. *The Berean* (Quebec), 1 Nov. 1847.
66. *Whig*, 6 Nov. 1847.
67. *Elgin Grey Correspondence*, vol. IV, Despatch No. 162, 27 Jan. 1848, containing Stephen De Vere to Lord Elgin, 30 Nov. 1847, p. 1347, postscript.
68. AO, RG11, 1–0–3, Emigration Papers, Hawke Letterbooks, Hawke to R.B. Sullivan, 9 Nov. 1847.
69. AO, RG 11 1–03, Emigration Papers, R.B. Sullivan to George Gurnett, 2 May 1848; Terrence O'Neil and Samuel G. Lynn to Samuel B. Harrison, Surrogate Court of York, 27 Nov. 1851; *British Colonist*, 11 Nov. 1851.
70. AO, RG 11 1–0–3, Emigration Papers, Hawke to Campbell, 9 Nov. 1847.
71. My own calculation based on Hawke's assumption.
72. AO, RG11, 1–0–3, Emigration Papers, Hawke Letterbooks, Hawke to R.B. Sullivan, 9 Nov. 1847.
73. *Report of the Managing Committee of the Widow and Orphans Asylum* (Toronto: Bowsell and Thompson, 1848), p. 18.
74. *Elgin Grey Correspondence*, Elgin to Grey, 13 Aug. 1847.
75. Now part of the trendy downtown neighbourhood of York.
76. *Globe*, 28 July 1847; André Charbonneau and Doris Drolet-Dubé, *A Register of Deceased Persons at Sea and on Grosse Île, 1847* (Ottawa: Canadian Heritage, Parks Canada, 1997), pp 60, 99.
77. *Mirror*, 5 Aug. 1847.
78. Ibid., 2 July 1847.

CHAPTER EIGHT

STEPHEN DE VERE (1812–1904) AND KAHKEWAQUONABY'S 'EXTENDED SYMPATHIES'

A Case Study of Famine Irish Emigration and Canadian First Nations

Jason King

On 23 June 1848, Stephen De Vere visited the Anishinaabe (Ojibwa) Methodist preacher and chief Peter Jones (1802–1856), or Kahkewaquonaby (Sacred Feathers), in 'Munsee Town Indian village' in southwestern Ontario, then Canada West. He recorded in his unpublished journal having 'dined with Revd. Peter Jones, Indian Chief, & Wesleyan missionary married to an English manufacturer's daughter, who fell in love with him in London & followed him to America'.[1] As chief of the Mississaugas of the Credit River, Kahkewaquonaby had contributed £12.10*s* 'to the Irish and Scotch Relief Fund' on behalf of the 'Indian Tribes, Canada West' the previous year.[2] Although De Vere is best known for his harrowing eyewitness account of travelling steerage in a coffin ship during the Irish Famine migration of 1847, he also kept extensive unpublished journals, which have now been digitized, as he sought to resettle with former tenants from his estate in Curragh Chase, County Limerick, near London, Ontario.[3] He was uniquely positioned amongst Famine Irish emigrants not only in risking his life to document the suffering of steerage passengers, but also in bearing witness to the heroic and 'exemplary conduct of Catholic Clergy'[4] at the quarantine station on Grosse Île, Quebec, to 'that noble army of martyrs, the nuns'[5] in Montreal's fever sheds, and to 'poor McElderry's death of fever at Toronto'.[6] The first part of this chapter tracks De Vere's voyage across the Atlantic and his eyewitness impressions of emigrant suffering as well as the heroic self-sacrifice of their Canadian caregivers. The second part examines his encounter with Kahkewaquonaby, who was not only an indigenous contributor to Irish Famine relief but also implicated in, and then repudiated, the foundation of Canada's residential schools. Ultimately, De Vere attested to heroic acts of salving migrant misery while beholding the origins of an enduring Canadian tragedy.

There can be little doubt that Stephen De Vere was a heroic figure in his own right. Although he was born into an aristocratic Anglo-Irish Protestant family in Curragh Chase, he felt closest to the Irish Catholic tenants on his estate, many of whom he sought to help escape from Ireland when it was stricken by the Great Hunger. According to his younger brother, the Victorian poet, Aubrey De Vere:

> he took passage for Canada with a considerable number of those who had been employed ... under his supervision, and conducted them to Quebec, sharing with them all the sufferings and perils which then belonged to a crowded steerage passage. Those who escaped fever on their sea-passage frequently caught it on landing, the dormant seeds of disease becoming rapidly developed by the stimulus of better air and food, and by infection. It was so on this occasion. They reached Quebec in June of 1847, and in a short time nearly all of those whom he had taken with him and lodged in a large, healthy house were stricken down in succession, during a period covering about eight months, and received from him personally all the ministrations which they could have had from a hospital nurse ... His letter describing the sufferings of emigrants was read aloud in the House of Lords by Earl Grey, then Secretary for the Colonies, and the 'Passengers Act' was amended, due accommodations of all sorts being provided in the emigrant vessels. Most of those emigrants who on reaching Quebec went into the crowded and infected hospitals died there. It is impossible to guess how many thousands of emigrants may have been saved by this enterprise.[7]

In his classic study *A Pattern of Government Growth* (1961), Oliver MacDonagh concurs that De Vere's testimony 'made a profound impression on the commissioners. It is scarcely too much to regard it as the basis of most of their future legislation for ship life'.[8]

De Vere bore witness to the harrowing conditions of the transatlantic crossing in print and in his unpublished journals and letters. His testimonial to T.F. Elliot, on 30 November 1847, remains the most widely cited description of the Famine voyage. 'Before the emigrant has been a week at sea', wrote De Vere:

> ... he is an altered man. How can it be otherwise? Hundreds of poor people, men, women, and children of all ages, from the drivelling idiot of ninety to the babe just born, huddled together without light, without air, wallowing in filth, and breathing a fetid atmosphere.[9]

Yet the privations De Vere and his household labourers endured in the steerage of the *Birman* were mild compared to other vessels as they suffered no fatalities at sea. It was not until he reached the quarantine station at Grosse Île on 16 June 1847, that De Vere experienced the full horrors of the Famine voyage. As he recorded in his journal:

> Arrived at Grosse isle quarantine about 7 am. Detained waiting for dr till evening, when he inspected & gave us clean bill of health – abt. 40 ships detained there – villages of white tents on shore for the sick. Daily mortality about 150. One ship, Sisters of Liverpool, in with all passengers & crew in fever of this ship, all but the Cap'n and one girl died.
>
> Laid alongside of 'Jessy' in which many ill. Water covered with beds, cooking utensils refuse of the dead. Ghastly appearance of boats full of sick going ashore never to return. Several died between ship and shore. Wives separated from husbands, children from parents. Ascertained by subsequent enquiry that funds in agents hands altogether insufficient for care. Medical attendance bad. Exemplary conduct of Catholic Clergy.[10]

De Vere was profoundly moved by the harrowing spectacle of 'wives separated from husbands, children from parents' on 'ghastly boats full of sick going ashore never to return'. But it was the heroic conduct of the clergy that defined his impression of Grosse Île.

After leaving the island, De Vere travelled to Quebec City and Montreal, where, on 24 June, he observed in his journal 'frightful mortality. Emigrant Sheds hospitals & generally throughout the town'.[11] He elaborated in an entry written in crosshatching that there was 'Great mortality amongst Catholic clergy. Impossible to find nurses. Grey Nuns undertake it all not knowing how many dead! 48 now ill. Blessed nuns able to leave convent to take charge of sick orphans of Quebec and Montreal steamers ill of fever'.[12] As at Grosse Île, De Vere was struck by these scenes of compassion, courage, and self-sacrifice amongst the clergy and 'that noble army of martyrs, the nuns'.[13] He was one of the only witnesses to record what transpired both on Grosse Île and in Montreal's fever sheds where up to six thousand Irish emigrants perished in each location, the largest Famine Irish mass graves outside of Ireland.[14]

Stephen De Vere continued to register his fellow migrants' misery as he travelled upriver to Kingston and across Lake Ontario to Toronto.[15] In fact, he had delayed his departure from Montreal for over a week when his household labourer J. Hanly fell ill of ships' fever on 4 July.[16] 'Send off my party to Toronto remaining myself to take care of patient', De Vere wrote in his journal on 6 July.[17] He finally embarked on 12 July: 'Steamer going down the rapids. Cornwall canal by night ... – cannot bear heat of the fur cloak, sleeping on deck', he recorded.[18] The next day, De Vere noted their arrival:

> at Kingston change steamers. New fortifications. Kingston in a great scale for the protection of harbour. Immense crowd of German and Irish Emigrants on board of the worst description. Great apparent disease.[19]

He regarded the overcrowding of emigrants of the 'worst description' on the Canadian steamers to be no less dangerous than in the steerage below deck on transatlantic vessels. From his journal entries, he wrote a more elaborate description of the dire 'steam transmission up the country' to T.F Elliot on 30 November. In his own words:

> I have seen small, incommodious and ill-ventilated steamers arriving at the quay in Toronto, after a forty-eight hours passage from Montreal, freighted with fetid cargoes of 1,100 and 1,200 Government emigrants of all ages and sexes. The healthy who had just arrived from Europe, mixed with the half-recovered convalescents of the hospitals, unable, during that time, to lie down, almost to sit. In almost every boat were clearly marked cases of actual fever—in some were deaths—the dead and the living huddled together. Sometimes the crowds were stowed in open barges, and towed after the steamer, standing like pigs upon the deck of a Cork and Bristol packet. A poor woman died in the hospital here, in consequence of having been trodden down when weak and fainting in one of those barges. I have, myself, when accompanying the emigrant agent [Edward McElderry] on his visit to inspect the steamer on her arrival, seen him stagger back like one struck, when first meeting the current of fetid infection, exhaled from between her decks.[20]

In a letter dated 20 April 1848 to his sister Ellen, De Vere reiterated that 'the principal cause of disease [is] the miserable system of internal transmission of emigrants within the colony'. He further insisted in a letter dated 8 June 1848, that these Canadian steamers:

> ... were 'small, ill-ventilated, & incommodious' if considered with reference to the numbers & condition of those whom they carried, those squalid masses of filth and disease whom they disgorged daily. The effect of ill ventilation & infected air upon those in health was distinctly visible. I saw one poor fellow beginning to droop, took a cabin passage for him at once, put him into a clean, airy berth, & had the pleasure of seeing him land at Toronto in perfect health.[21]

De Vere exposed the horrific conditions on Canadian steamers in which 'the dead and the living huddled together' and became 'squalid masses of filth and disease' as they had in the holds of transatlantic vessels.

Stephen De Vere arrived in Toronto on 14 July 1847, found his household labourers, and set off with them to establish a household near London, Ontario. During his first few months in Canada West, he travelled extensively and recorded several scenes and stories of emigrant suffering and the care and compassion they received. On 24 August 1847, he had returned to Toronto and recorded that 'clergy all sick but the Bishop who has to attend the Hospital and emigrant sheds. 10 deaths in hospital yesterday'. He was in the city once again on 29 September, with 'Bishop Power very ill of typhus fever'. De Vere eulogized him in his journal on 1 October:

> Rev. Michael Power DD. Catholic bishop of Toronto died this morning. He was a man of great generosity and nobleness, most kindly and charitable in a true and most extended kindly sense, an humble Christian. By his example, his justice, his unfailing attention to the duties of his high station, & the strictness of his discipline, he brought into perfect order a diocese which he found almost in anarchy. His death is attributable, under providence, to the noble and devoted zeal with which, since the illness of so many of his clergy, he has visited the beds of every sick and dying emigrant. He did not spare himself, but God has spared him a longer sojourn on earth.
>
> He was a man of no political party, of no religious bigotry. He was too strong-minded to be a bigot, & too wise to be a partisan. He was therefore respected and beloved by men of all creeds and parties. May Almighty God have Mercy on his soul.[22]

De Vere was inspired by Bishop Michael Power's 'noble and devoted zeal'. He set a heroic example in giving his life, like many of the clergy on Grosse Île and the Grey Nuns in Montreal's fever sheds, to visit 'the beds of every sick and dying emigrant'.[23]

De Vere similarly paid tribute a few weeks later to the city's Emigration Agent, Edward McElderry, who died on the 29 October 1847. He noted in his journal on 6 November that, 'I regret to hear of poor McElderry's death of fever at Toronto'.[24] As noted, De Vere had often accompanied McElderry to inspect steamers arriving at Toronto's Dr Rees's Wharf and had seen him 'stagger back like one struck, when first meeting the current of fetid infection, exhaled from between her decks'. 'In Toronto [De Vere] closely and frequently inspected the Hospital sheds, crowded as they were with contagious fever, and accompanied the Emigrant Agent [McElderry] in his visits to Steamers as they arrived with their loads of passengers, and to the Emigrants Sheds', reported the *Toronto Patriot* on 23 May 1848.[25] The *British Canadian* similarly recorded that:

> In Toronto, this philanthropic gentleman [De Vere] attended in the emigrant office, and rendered much assistance to the lamented and indefatigable agent, Mr. McElderry, boarding with him every steamer filled with the wretched cargoes, and transmitting to the 'proper authorities' the result of his laborious experience.[26]

Mark G. McGowan notes in his chapter in this volume that De Vere unsuccessfully petitioned the Governor General, Lord Elgin, for a pension to support McElderry's destitute pregnant widow, Rose Anne Lawlor, and their seven children. In paying tribute to the compassion of Bishop Michael Power and Emigrant Agent Edward McElderry, De Vere did not mention having had similarly risked his own life.

Stephen De Vere also documented the plight of ordinary Irish emigrants as he travelled extensively in the hinterland of Canada West. On 20 November,1847, he was in London, Ontario, and recounted in his journal:

> A family from Mayo came out this year apparently in the most abject poverty. They consisted of a father mother uncle a little boy about 12 years old. They were transmitted to Toronto at the govt. expense. The mother was there taken into hospital suffering from a rapid cancer in the breast. She soon died. The father, uncle, little boy took a poor lodging close to me. I frequently met them and the father complaining to me of dysentery. I recommended him to send for a doctor, but he said he was too poor. He at last went into hospital, and died, from want of care in the early stage of the disease, leaving his little son in possession of 300 sovereigns tied up in an old rag, which had, during the voyage, been tied under the mother's breast and had produced the cancer of which she died.[27]

On 9 January 1848, De Vere recorded a similar story in Port Stanley which he elaborated upon in a letter to his mother on 20 January.[28] He wrote:

> One of the few Irish emigrants who landed last year at Port Stanley was an elderly man with his wife and their grown up daughters. They were not very poor, and having moved a little inland, procured a house. Shortly after, a lumber waggon was seen in a lonely part of the forest, moving towards a burial ground. It bore three coffins. An old man drove the oxen and a weak old sickly woman toiled alongside. The coffins were those of the three young women who had all died together of fever. So great was the fear of infection that none of their neighbours (there were no Irish there) would attend the funeral.
>
> The old man with difficulty borrowed a team of oxen, and waggon, and with the assistance of his poor wife, dug his daughters' graves and buried them. In a few days the wife died and the old man now survived the last of his family.[29]

These heart-breaking scenes were commonplace in the towns and villages of Canada West beyond Toronto. While De Vere expressed compassion for these dying emigrants, he felt little 'fear of infection' himself.

De Vere's resolve to bear witness to their suffering was inspired by his religious beliefs. On 11 February 1848, he wrote to his elder brother, Sir Vere Edmond, with 'an important disclosure upon the reception of which depends my future fate in life'.[30] 'My Dear Brother', he confessed:

> In my letters home I have left one thing unsaid, which is for you alone. You know what had been for a considerable time (8 or 9 years) the tendency of my religious

opinions. I could no longer, when thrown independently upon the world, reconcile it to my conscience to conceal them & I have, since I reached America, conformed to the ordinances of the Catholic Church. Whether this has got wind at home, or not, I do not know. My principal reason for leaving my own country was to save my mother the pain which I feared the avowal of my convictions would have caused to her, nor will I ever reside in Ireland if that avowal gives her more pain than my presence would give pleasure ... I leave the matter wholly in your hands to disclose or conceal as you think best for my mother. Should your reply be unfavourable, I am determined, at any cost, to remain an exile for conscience sake. If favourable, being 'functus officio' here, & having probably laid the foundation of much benefit to my native land, I am ready to return and share the fortunes of my family & home; but I will never live again at home concealing my faith, a faith from which I have derived strength to bear every hardship & consolation under every misfortune & privation.[31]

De Vere's confession reveals that he was 'ready to return' to Ireland in February 1848. He had become 'an exile for conscience sake' in shepherding emigrants across the ocean. He often displayed the 'strength to bear every hardship & consolation under every misfortune & privation' in British North America. His religious conversion was a primary motivation for his departure.

Yet De Vere's confession also provided retrospective justification for returning to Ireland after the failure of his resettlement plan.[32] His declaration to be 'functus officio' seems at odds with his original intention to relocate his former household labourers to Canada West. On the other hand, his letter to T.F. Elliot, on 30 November 1847, had indeed laid 'the foundation of much benefit' in exposing the harrowing conditions on emigrant ships. On 26 February 1848, De Vere noted that he had received:

... a letter from uncle [Lord Monteagle]. He mentions that Lord Grey [the Colonial Secretary] requested leave to forward my letter to [Governor General] Lord Elgin & also lay it before Parliament. May it do good! I surely seek neither gain nor fame for myself.[33]

Despite his self-deprecation, there is a form of slippage in De Vere's letter between his 'principal reason for leaving' his country from his 'sense of duty' to guide migrants abroad, and then saving his 'mother the pain' occasioned by his religious conversion. Moreover, his desire for reassurance that he would be welcomed back in Curragh Chase to 'share the fortunes of my family & home' was not readily forthcoming. He was dismayed to have received no reply to his confession. De Vere wrote on 14 March 1848:

I cannot but surmise that the continued silence may result from my communications on the subject of my change of religion. God grant that if any evil tidings be

> the course, they may be of a nature affecting myself alone. I would be unworthy of the blessing of the faith I hold, if I did not consider it a glorious privilege to suffer for it.[34]

His self-consolation was short lived. On 3 May, he received a letter from Vere Edmond mentioning 'that he has not yet made the disclosure of my religious change to my mother ... I write to Vere urging him to inform her at once'.[35] In his letter, De Vere insisted: 'Let her know the truth, and may God grant that I'll be spared the misery of giving more than a moment of pain to a mother, and such a mother'.[36] He was not spared such misery. Indeed, in De Vere's final letter, written on the eve of his departure from New York on 16 July 1848, he implored his younger brother Aubrey for news of his disclosure. 'My journey from Canada has been slow but most interesting', he wrote:

> I waited a long time in London hoping to receive an answer to my last letter to Vere, but it had not arrived nor has it been forwarded to me here as I expected. You may imagine how intensely anxious I am to have a line to tell me how my mother has taken the information my letter to Vere conveyed, so pray write to meet me in Liverpool.[37]

There is no record of any reply, or of whether he found the courage to tell her himself.

Stephen De Vere's final encounter in Canada West was with the Anishinaabe Methodist preacher and chief Peter Jones, or Kahkewaquonaby, whom he visited in 'Munsee Town Indian village' on 23 June 1848.[38] The aforementioned last pages of his journal record how he 'dined with Revd. Peter Jones, Indian Chief, & Wesleyan missionary married to an English manufacturer's daughter, who fell in love with him in London & followed him to America'.[39] Kahkewaquonaby was born in Burlington Heights (Hamilton, Ontario) in 1802, the son of a retired American surveyor, Augustus Jones, and Tuhbenaheequay, the daughter of a Mississauga chief. In his youth, 'he learned how to hunt, fish, and canoe, and gained the reputation of being an excellent hunter', while he was also educated 'to speak, read and write in English'. He converted to Methodism in 1823 and helped establish the Credit River mission in what is now Mississauga, a suburb of Toronto, where he was elected a chief in 1829. In 1832–1833, he travelled to England to fund raise, deliver sermons 'in his Indian costume', and petition the Colonial Office. It was on this 'English tour the celebrated Indian met Eliza Field, a pious Englishwoman who came to North America in 1833 to become his wife and lifelong companion in the mission field'.[40] They had five sons. In 1837, Kahkewaquonaby returned to England and, 'exotically dressed in fringed and beaded buckskin and wearing moccasins ornamented with porcupine quills', he successfully petitioned Queen Victoria at Windsor Castle to grant title deeds to their land. As his biographer notes: 'Peter rejoiced. Unlike their American brethren, the Canadian Indians would not be removed'.[41] He condemned President Andrew Jackson's Indian removal policy which led to the Cherokee and Choctaw Trail of Tears for reducing Native Americans to 'a most deplorable state of poverty and degradation'.[42] By the time De Vere met Kahkewaquonaby in 1848, he was an internationally renowned indigenous leader of his people.

The previous year, Kahkewaquonaby had contributed on behalf of his people to the United Irish and Scotch Relief Fund. The United Relief Fund had been established following a public meeting at Daley's Hotel in Montreal in early February 1847, where Stephen De Vere later stayed when he arrived in the city on 24 June.[43] Its purpose was to relieve 'the present distress in Ireland and the Highlands of Scotland', and to respond to 'the cry of their deep and dreadful agony [that] has been sent across the broad Atlantic'.[44] Detailed subscription lists were published in the weeks and months that followed, beginning with the Governor General, Lord Elgin's, contribution of £70. Montreal's Mayor John Easton Mills, who perished on 22 November after tending to Irish emigrants in the city's fever sheds, donated £100, as did 'the Gentlemen of the Seminary' who also served in the sheds. A more modest contribution of £7 5*s* was received from 'the Irish servants of Orr's Hotel'[45] and £6 5*s* 'from the domestics of Feller's Hotel'.[46] Subscriptions from indigenous communities in Canada West were particularly newsworthy. The *Montreal Transcript* reported donations on 24 April 1847, 'from Indian Tribes, in Canada West, to the Irish and Scotch Relief Fund, handed in by Major Campbell, Superintendent General of Indian Affairs'.[47] Kahkewaquonaby's 'Mississaugas of the Credit River' contribution of £12 10*s*, as well as that of other Mississauga bands, was acknowledged in *The Gazette* on 25 April.[48] 'We today publish a most interesting fact'—the paper contended—'the contributions of the Indian tribes in Canada West, to the relief of Irish and Scotch distress. Nothing could more forcibly indicate the extended sympathies which follow the extension of civilization and knowledge'.[49] Their 'extended sympathies' were comparable in scope to the generosity of the much better known Choctaw and Cherokee donations for Irish Famine relief in the spring of 1847.[50] Lord Elgin paid tribute on 18 May to these 'Indian tribes' that 'expressed a desire to share in relieving the wants of their suffering white brethren'.[51] 'From the Iroquois Indians of Caughnawaga [Kahnawá:ke], and the Huron and Delaware of western Canada, and from her colored citizens, came contributions in money or in food', lauded John Mercier McMullen –himself a Kilkenny Famine emigrant who resettled in Brockville, Ontario, in 1848—in *The History of Canada: From its First Discovery to the Present Time* (1855).[52]

The 'extended sympathies' of Canadian indigenous peoples was not reciprocated by their 'white brethren' in 1847. That same year, Kahkewaquonaby's 'Mississaugas of the Credit River' lost access to their land, despite Queen Victoria's pledge. They were not forcibly removed, but still deprived of title to their territory. 'After the full Iroquois [Haudenosaunee] council invited them to their reserve, the Credit band accepted ... [and the] "New Credit" was founded on a fertile tract in the southwestern corner of the Six Nations reserve,' one hundred kilometres west near Brantford, Ontario.[53] Kahkewaquonaby and Eliza moved 160 kilometres further west to the mission station at Munceytown, where he had been invited to establish a new school and where he met De Vere.

Stephen De Vere was fascinated by Kahkewaquonaby. He made no prior reference to indigenous peoples in his detailed journals and letters, but described their encounter at length. He was impressed by Kahkewaquonaby's ceremonial garb and 'magnificent Indian chief's dress. Tomahawk presented to him [by] A[ugustus] d'Este', Queen Victoria's first cousin.[54] 'He is a tall, large man with marks of intelligent countenance', De Vere added: 'Highly educated. Has written volumes of hymns in Indian and English which he gave me.' De Vere noted that 'some tribes still pagan', but acknowledged Kahkewaquonaby's repudiation of colonial stereotypes: '—no cannibalism—no polygamy. [No] murder of aged people'.[55] Smith describes the mission house in Munceytown where Kahkewaquonaby, Eliza, and their family resided 'by the meandering Thames River, in the centre of the settlement of over a thousand Indians, roughly half being Ojibwas and Munsees and the remainder Oneidas, members of the Six Nations Confederacy newly arrived from New York State'.[56] De Vere noted these different indigenous peoples who lived in Munceytown as well as their poverty in his journal:

> Visit Oneida, a tribe much superior in husbandry & civilization who migrated from the states & bought land here. Visit their chief. Good house but dirty capital settlement. Language of Oneida altogether different from Chippewayas [Ojibwa]. Jones must speak and preach through interpreters. Indian tribes decreasing. Oneida stationary—much sorrow & consumption from hardship of life. Large families born.[57]

De Vere attested to the diversity of indigenous peoples in Munceytown and Kahkewaquonaby's Methodist congregation.

De Vere also inadvertently beheld the foundation and Kahkewaquonaby's disavowal of Canada's residential school system. Between 1867 and 1996, the Canadian government separated over 150,000 indigenous children from their parents and sent them to distant residential schools in order to assimilate, 'civilize', and often convert them to Christianity. According to *The Final Report of the Truth and Reconciliation Commission of Canada*: 'The establishment and operation of residential schools ... can best be described as "cultural genocide"'.[58] One of the first of these schools to be established was the Methodist Mount Elgin in Munceytown, which opened in 1851. Stephen De Vere met its superintendent, Kahkewaquonaby, or Peter Jones, who had 'moved to Munceytown to oversee'[59] its construction in 1847. 'When in England lately', De Vere recorded in his journal:

> he obtained subscriptions over £1000 for building a school for general and agricultural education of Indians. The Munsee & Chippewaya, have allocated 200 acres for the school, of which they have conveyed by deed the necessary enough for the building. The Indian tribes have assigned one 4th of their government annuities for this endorsement.[60]

Kahkewaquonaby had played an important role in the early development of the residential school system.[61] Indeed, 'the impetus for residential schooling was not part of a coordinated program by other missionary groups in cooperation with the government, but rather direct adoption of plans proposed by Peter Jones and other Methodists'.[62]

Yet Kahkewaquonaby's vision was for residential schools that would 'come under the Christian Indians' control'.[63] Stephen De Vere met him just as he was becoming disillusioned with the institution that he helped establish. By the time De Vere visited Munceytown in June 1848, the school's 200 acres had been surveyed, but Kahkewaquonaby was in failing health and resigned as superintendent 'just before the opening ceremony' the following year. De Vere's portrayal of Kahkewaquonaby is especially important because it reveals his increasing disenchantment at a time when his own manuscript records and diary entries had fallen silent. Kahkewaquonaby 'apparently thought very little of the institution he had worked so hard to establish. Not one of his sons attended', notes Smith.[64] Indeed, De Vere's final journal entry records that 'Jones disapproves of the Govt. system of providing for Indians—makes them improvident and indolent'.[65] Ultimately, De Vere registered Kahkewaquonaby's repudiation of the residential school system that he had helped to found. He provided an early warning not to develop educational institutions for indigenous peoples outside of their control. That it went unheeded is part of the residential schools' legacy of betrayal of indigenous children, institutional sexual abuse, and national shame.

In conclusion, Stephen De Vere returned to Ireland shortly after his encounter with Kahkewaquonaby in June of 1848. Before his departure, he was lauded in the Canadian press as 'a zealous and devoted man'. Although he was 'a gentleman of fortune, and the proprietor of some estates in the south of Ireland', reported the

British Canadian, 'landlord and tenants fared alike' on the transatlantic voyage, 'the former taking careful notes of the events of the passage'.[66] Stephen De Vere was then inspired by the Canadian caregivers of the Famine Irish, such as the clergy on Grosse Île, the Grey Nuns in Montreal's fever sheds, Bishop Michael Power and Emigration Agent Edward McElderry in Toronto. He witnessed their compassion in caring for stricken migrants and attested to their sacrifice. Despite his apprehension, De Vere was welcomed back to Curragh Chase in 1848 and lived openly as a Roman Catholic for the rest of his life. He later became an MP for Limerick (1854–1859), then High Sheriff of the County, and inherited the estate in 1880 after the death of his elder brother, Sir Vere Edmond. In his later years, De Vere eschewed the life of a landlord and retired to a labourer's cottage on Foynes Island, Monare, in the Shannon Estuary; he helped establish a Gothic Catholic church in Foynes, where he is buried. He also suffered from terrible nightmares and 'lamentable howls' in his sleep.[67] No doubt Stephen De Vere recalled the terrible scenes of 1847 in British North America. His legacy was defined by the sympathies that he extended to emigrants and their caregivers alike.

The 'extended sympathies' of Kahkewaquonaby's 'Mississaugas of the Credit River' in contributing to Irish Famine relief was also registered in the Canadian press, but not that they lost their homeland shortly thereafter. By the time Stephen De Vere returned home in the summer 1848, they had been deprived of their own. In his final encounter in Canada with Kahkewaquonaby, De Vere met an indigenous leader of international stature. He recorded Kahkewaquonaby's sense of disillusionment as superintendent of Mount Elgin residential school that opened after his resignation. It was one of the first of many such institutions over which indigenous peoples would have no control. More broadly, De Vere inadvertently beheld the establishment of the residential school system that would engulf indigenous children for generations to come. The discovery of the remains of 215 children in unmarked graves with ground-penetrating radar on 27 May 2021, at the former Kamloops Residential School in British Columbia, prompted widespread revulsion and a sweeping re-evaluation of the role of Canadian historical figures in the creation of these institutions. On 30 June 1847, Eliza Jones had given birth to her and Kahkewaquonaby's fifth son, Wuhyahsakung, who was baptized by 'Egerton Ryerson, Peter's closest white friend'.[68] Ryerson is renowned as 'the most influential figure in education in West Canada', but he also 'recommended the establishment of residential schools for Aboriginal children'.[69] Ryerson's statue was toppled on 6 June 2021, in front of the Toronto university that bears his name, its head removed and mounted on a pike on the Six Nations of the Grand River reserve near where Kahkewaquonaby's 'Mississaugas of the Credit

River' resettled in 1847. Stephen De Vere could have no inkling of the unfolding tragedy of residential schools when he met Kahkewaquonaby in Munceytown in 1848. Yet his journal makes clear that it was not in his name.

NOTES

1. Stephen De Vere, unpublished journal, Trinity College Dublin Manuscripts [hereafter TCD], MS 5062, p. 55.
2. *Montreal Transcript*, 24 Apr. 1847.
3. Stephen De Vere's unpublished diaries and letters written between April 1847 and June 1848 while he was in Canada are housed in the Manuscripts and Archives Research Library, Trinity College Dublin. His unpublished Canadian famine diaries MS 5061 and MS 5062 have been digitized and made publicly accessible on Canada Ireland Foundation's 'Irish Famine Migrant Stories in Ontario' virtual exhibit, funded by Digital Museums Canada, Canadian Museum of History: https://irishfaminestories.ca/en/bearing_witness (Jason King, 2021): https://irishfaminestories.ca/. Also see Jason King, *Irish Famine Migration Narratives: Eyewitness Testimonies. The History of the Irish Famine*, vol. 2. Eds. Christine Kinealy, Jason King, Gerard Moran (New York: Routledge, 2019), pp 43–70; Jason King, 'The Famine Irish Migration to Canada in 1847–8: Assisted Emigration, Colonisation, and the Unpublished Famine Diaries of Stephen De Vere', in Patrick Fitzgerald and Anthony Russell (eds), *John Mitchel, Ulster, and the Great Irish Famine* (Newbridge, Co. Kildare: Irish Academic Press, 2017), pp 30–45.
4. TCD MS 5061, p. 3.
5. TCD MS 5075a/2, p. 174.
6. TCD MS 5061, p. 49. See Mark G. McGowan's chapter for more on Emigration Agent, Edward McElderry.
7. Aubrey De Vere, *Recollections of Aubrey De Vere* (London: Edward Arnold, 1897), p. 253.
8. Oliver MacDonagh, *A Pattern of Government Growth: Passenger Acts and their Enforcement, 1800–1860* (London: MacGibbon & Gee, 1961), p. 195.
9. Stephen De Vere, *Minutes of Evidence before Select Committee on Colonization from Ireland, letter to the Select Committee* (30 Nov. 1847) in *British Parliamentary Papers, Emigration*, vol. 5 (Shannon: Irish University Press, 1968), pp 45–48.
10. TCD MS 5061, p. 3.
11. Ibid., p. 7. Also see, See Jason King, 'Mortuary Spectacles: The Genealogy of the Images of the Coffin Ships and Fever Sheds,' in Marguérite Corporaal, Oonagh Frawley, Emily Mark-FitzGerald (eds.), *The Great Irish Famine: Visual and Material Cultures* (Liverpool University Press, 2018), pp 68–85, 81–85.
12. Ibid., p. 12.
13. TCD MS 5075a/2, p. 174. The Sisters of Charity or Grey Nuns' eyewitness accounts of caring for Famine Irish emigrants in Montreal's fever sheds in 1847 have been digitized

and can be found at Jason King (2015) Irish Famine Archive, http://faminearchive.nuigalway.ie. Also see Jason King, 'Montreal's Grey Nuns, the Great Hunger Migration, and the Miracle of Rose's Marble', in Christine Kinealy, Jason King, and Gerard Moran (eds), *Heroes of Ireland's Great Hunger* (Hamden, CT: Quinnipiac University Press/ Cork University Press, 2021), pp 205–220; Jason King, 'Remembering and Forgetting the Famine Irish in Quebec: Genuine and False Memoirs, Communal Memory and Migration', *Irish Review* 44 (2012), pp 20–41, pp 30–34; Jason King, 'The Famine Irish, the Grey Nuns, and the fever sheds of Montreal: Prostitution and female religious institution building,' in Christine Kinealy, Jason King, and Ciarán Reilly (eds), *Women and the Great Hunger* (Hamden, CT: Quinnipiac University Press/Cork University Press, 2016), pp 95–108; Jason King, 'The Remembrance of Irish Famine Migrants in the Fever Sheds of Montreal', in Marguérite Corporaal, Chris Cusack, Lindsay Janssen, and Ruud van den Beuken (eds), *Global Legacies of the Great Irish Famine: Transnational and Interdisciplinary Perspectives* (Brussels: Peter Lang, 2014), pp 245–266.

14. Rev. Bernard O'Reilly also served on both Grosse Île and Montreal's fever sheds during the summer of 1847. See Jason King, *Irish Famine Migration Narratives*, pp 27–33, 227–241.
15. See King, 'The Famine Irish Migration to Canada', pp 34–36, for a more detailed discussion of De Vere's journey upriver.
16. TCD MS 5061, p. 11.
17. Ibid.
18. Ibid., p. 13.
19. Ibid., p. 15.
20. Stephen De Vere, *Minutes of Evidence*, p. 47.
21. TCD MS 5075a/2, pp 140, 177.
22. TCD, MS 5061, pp 29, 40–41.
23. Also see Mark G. McGowan, 'Bishop Michael Power of Toronto (1804–1847): A Reluctant Hero,' in Kinealy, King & Moran (eds), *Heroes*, pp 191–204; Mark G. McGowan, *Michael Power: The Struggle to Build the Catholic Church on the Canadian Frontier* (Montreal & Kingston: McGill-Queen's University Press, 2005).
24. TCD MS 5061, p. 49.
25. *Toronto Patriot*, 23 May 1848.
26. *British Canadian,* 20 May 1848.
27. TCD, MS 5061, p. 54.
28. TCD, MS 5062, p. 8.
29. TCD, MS 5075a/2, pp 63–64.
30. TCD MS 5062, p. 16.
31. TCD, MS 5075a/2, pp 81–82.
32. See Jason King, '"The Atrocious Avarice of the Irish Landlords": Canadian Public Sentiment and the Irish Famine Migration of 1847', in Marguérite Corporaal and Peter Gray (eds), *The Great Irish Famine and Social Class: Conflicts, Responsibilities, and Representations* (Oxford: Peter Lang, 2019), pp 237–256; Jason King, 'Stephen De Vere's "Political Lesson": A Case Study of Famine Irish Emigration, Settlement, and Political

and Social Unrest', in William Jenkins (ed.), *Canada and the Great Irish Famine* (Montreal & Kingston: McGill-Queen's University Press, forthcoming).

33. TCD MS 5062, p. 19.
34. Ibid., p. 23.
35. Ibid., p. 37.
36. TCD MS 5075a/2, p. 147.
37. Limerick City Archive, Aubrey De Vere Letters: P22/397.
38. TCD MS 5062, p. 55.
39. Ibid.
40. Donald B. Smith, 'Jones, Peter', *Dictionary of Canadian Biography*, vol. 8, University of Toronto/Université Laval, 2003— www.biographi.ca/en/bio/jones_peter_8E.html
41. Donald B. Smith, *Sacred Feathers: The Reverend Peter Jones (Kahkewaquonaby) and the Mississauga Indians.* Second Edition (Toronto: University of Toronto Press, 2013), pp xxxiii, 165.
42. Peter Jones [Kahkewaquonaby], *History of the Ojebway Indians: With Especial Reference to their Conversion to Christianity* (London: A.W. Bennett, 1861), p. 238. Also see Smith, *Sacred Feathers*, pp 174–175.
43. *The Gazette*, 10 Feb.1847; Stephen De Vere, TCD MS 5061, p. 7.
44. *The Gazette,* 16 Feb. 1847. Also see Harvey Strum, 'Aid to Ireland during the Great Hunger from Ontario and Quebec', 'National Social Science Association Virtual Proceedings, National Technology and Social Science Conference', 74 (12–14 Oct. 2020), pp 1–14.
45. *The Pilot and Journal of Commerce*, 23 Feb. 1847.
46. *Montreal Transcript*, 22 Feb. 1847.
47. Ibid., 23 Apr. 1847.
48. On 5 June, 1847, the *Pilot and Journal of Commerce* reported more fully that 'The Indian Tribes in Canada West have transmitted the following sums, through their Superintendents, for the relief of the destitute Scotch and Irish :-By Capt. Anderson, Superintendent at Toronto – Mississaugas of the Credit, £12 10; Mississaugas of Alnwick, £10; Mississaugas, Rice and Mud Lakes, £27 10 1; Chippewas, Lakes Huron and Simcoe, £25; Chippewas, Saugeen and Owens' Sound, £15; Mohawks, Bay of Quinte, £12 10s. By Lieut. Col. Clements, Superintendent at London – Six Nations; Grand River, £25; Wyandotts, of Anderdon, £5; Chippewas up the Thames, £7 10s; Chippewas, Chenail, Ecarte's, and St. Clair, £20; Merovians up the Thames, £5— Total, £175.'
49. *The Gazette*, 25 Apr. 1847.
50. See LeAnne Howe and Padraig Kirwan, *Famine Pots: The Choctaw–Irish Gift Exchange, 1847–Present* (East Lansing, MI: Michigan State University Press, 2020); Christine Kinealy, *Charity and the Great Hunger in Ireland: The Kindness of Strangers* (London: Bloomsbury, 2013), pp 104–105.
51. Earl of Elgin to Earl Grey, 28 May 1847, 'Copies of despatches addressed to the Secretary of State from the Governor of Her Majesty's colonial possessions relative to money voted and subscriptions raised for the Relief of the destitute Poor in Ireland and Scotland', in *Papers Relative to the Relief of the Destitute Poor in Ireland and Scotland 1847* (Copies of despatches), 1847, vol. 53, p. 7.

52. John Mercier McMullen, *The History of Canada: From its First Discovery to the Present Time* (Brockville, C[anada] W[est]: J. M'Mullen, Publisher, 1855), p. 485. John Mercier McMullen's genealogy can be found at https://gw.geneanet.org/belfast8?lang=en&n=mcmullen&oc=0&p=john+mercier
53. Smith, *Sacred Feathers*, p. 212. As a result, 'no Ojibwa territory would be established in Upper Canada. No fertile tract remained in Ojibwa hands by the late 1840s. There could be no self-supporting Anishinabe homeland', Smith adds.
54. TCD MS 5062, p. 55. Smith reproduces a calotype of Kahkewaquonaby in Edinburgh with the tomahawk dated 4 Aug. 1845, which 'has been identified as the oldest surviving portrait of a native North American', *Sacred Feathers*, p. 227.
55. TCD MS 5062, pp 56–57. Also see Smith, *Sacred Feathers*, pp 185–187.
56. Smith, *Sacred Feathers*, p. 192.
57. TCD MS 5062, p. 57.
58. Truth and Reconciliation Commission, *Canada's Residential Schools: The History, Part 1 – Origins to 1939. The Final Report of the Truth and Reconciliation Commission of Canada. Volume I* (Montreal & Kingston: McGill-Queens University Press, 2015), p. 3. https://publications.gc.ca/collections/collection_2015/trc/IR4-9-1-1-2015-eng.pdf
59. Ibid., pp 63, 78.
60. MS 5062, p. 56. Also see Smith, *Sacred Feathers*, p. 193.
61. See Truth and Reconciliation Commission, pp 73–76.
62. Hope Maclean, 'Ojibwa Participation in Methodist Residential Schools in Upper Canada, 1828–1860', *Canadian Journal of Native Studies* 25 (2005): pp 93–137, p. 111.
63. Smith, *Sacred Feathers*, p. 214.
64. Ibid., pp 213, 188, 214.
65. TCD MS 5062, p. 57a.
66. *The Church*, c. 23 May 1848; *British Canadian*, 20 May 1848.
67. Joan Gwynn Jones, *The Abiding Enchantment of Curragh Chase: The Big House Remembered* (Cork: Clo Duanaire, 1983), p. 28.
68. Smith, *Sacred Feathers*, p. 213.
69. Daniel Murphy, *A History of Irish Emigrant and Missionary Education* (Dublin: Four Courts, 2000), p. 291; Truth and Reconciliation Commission, p. 154. The Commission notes that 'early in his career, Jones developed a close relationship with Egerton Ryerson, the future Ontario superintendent of education. The two men worked together to establish both a church and a school at Credit River, where Jones had assumed the position of chief', p. 73.

CHAPTER NINE

PATRICK DONAHOE (1811–1901), THE *PILOT* AND IRISH FAMINE RELIEF, 1845 TO 1882

Catherine B. Shannon

The international relief response to Ireland's famine crisis of the 1840s has been an important feature of recent famine historiography. Christine Kinealy's *The Kindness of Strangers* (2013) documented aid that came from throughout the globe, while Stephen Puleo's recent *A Voyage of Mercy* (2020) focused on the USS *Jamestown*'s role in a broad American effort that brought approximately $3 million worth of aid to Ireland during the tragic year of Black '47.[1] Captain Robert Bennet Forbes of Boston has been hailed for his inspired leadership in the *Jamestown* effort, but, as Forbes insisted at a Cobh banquet in his honour, the real heroes of Irish relief were those individuals back in Boston and New England who organized and contributed to Irish relief funds. One of the most important individuals in this regional New England effort was Patrick Donahoe, editor of Boston's Catholic newspaper, the *Boston Pilot.* This chapter will document Donahoe's consistent and effective role in raising funds for Irish relief, not only during *An Gorta Mór,* but also in Ireland's other less well-known famines of 1862–1863 and 1879–1882.

Patrick Donahoe was born in Munnery, Kilmore parish in County Cavan on 17 March 1811, the only son of Terence and Jane (née Christy) Donahoe. His mother died when he was 2-years-old, and his father remarried shortly after. In addition to working a small four-acre farm, Terence was a linen weaver whose skills became increasingly less remunerative owing to the industrialization of British textile production during the first two decades of the nineteenth century. The family's fortunes were further compromised by bad weather in the winter and spring of 1821 which damaged not only grain production, but also the potato harvest that was so crucial to the diet of families like the Donahoes.[2] Faced with these hard times, Terence and his son Patrick emigrated to Boston in 1821 to find employment that would support his second wife and two daughters back in Cavan. Although Terence may have intended to return to Ireland, that did not happen and young Patrick never saw his homeland again.

When Patrick and his father arrived in Boston, Irish Catholic immigrants were few in number and faced considerable hostility and discrimination from the city's Protestant community. At that time, Boston had one priest to serve about 3,000 Catholics, most of whom were unskilled labourers living in crowded and unhealthy conditions near the Boston waterfront. Having attended a hedge school in County Cavan, Patrick was enrolled in the Adams school where his religion and ethnicity led to him being beaten and bullied by his Protestant classmates. Thus, Patrick left school at age 14 for a position at the *Columbian Sentinel* newspaper. His tasks were menial: sweeping the floor, folding newspapers and hauling the water needed for the production process for an annual wage of $40. This experience instilled in young Patrick a determination to gain the skills required for a career in the newspaper business. His next position was at the *Boston Transcript* which was the organ of the city's Protestant elite and where he encountered more anti-Catholic bigotry. At one point, he was threatened with dismissal when he did not come to work on Christmas Day. Yet as an apprentice there, Patrick learned typesetting and eventually became a skilled compositor, and simultaneously advanced his own general education. Thus, at a young age, he came to appreciate the power of the press for good or evil.[3]

In 1833 Donahoe was hired by Bishop Benedict J. Fenwick as editor of the three-year-old *The Jesuit*, a weekly paper whose mission was to explain the essentials of Catholic belief to the region's Catholics and defend them against anti-Catholic attacks by various Protestant leaders like Revs. Lyman Beecher, Henry Ward Beecher and Samuel Morse. The 1830s were marked by increasing hostility by the native working class to the Irish Catholic immigrant community as shown by the burning of the Ursuline Convent in Charlestown in 1834, the Broad Street Riot of June 1837, and the dissolution of the mostly Irish Catholic Montgomery Guards in 1838.[4] These events undoubtedly increased young Donahoe's determination to defend his faith and fellow Irishmen through journalism. Bishop Fenwick sold the paper to Donahoe and Henry L. Devereaux in 1834 and its name was changed initially to *The Literary and Catholic Sentinel,* and eventually to the *Boston Pilot* in 1836, the latter title inspired by a Dublin newspaper that promoted the Irish national cause. With Devereaux's departure in 1839, Donahoe became the sole owner of the paper.

Donahoe's goals for the *Pilot* were two-fold. First, to continue *The Jesuit* mission to provide regional Catholics with news and information about their church and to represent them as loyal, well-informed and productive American citizens. He also aimed to give his readers exposure to uplifting and entertaining Irish and Irish American literary works through serialized novels and poetry. Donahoe urged his fellow Irish immigrants to apply for citizenship as soon as possible, just as he had done in 1832 at age 21. Second, Donahoe wanted the *Pilot* to serve as a bonding link between Irish immigrants and their homeland and to foster pride in their ethnic heritage as well as support for Daniel O'Connell's campaign for Repeal of the Act of Union. O'Connell's public and parliamentary speeches were fully reported in the *Pilot* as were the meetings and speeches of Boston's Repeal leaders. Donahoe's belief in the compatibility of Irish ethnic pride with loyalty to the United States was symbolized in two mastheads he used for the *Pilot*. The initial one featured the American Eagle with shamrocks and an Irish harp, while the second had female figures representing Ireland and America along with a republican Lady Liberty with an eagle and a harp in the background. In the second image, America was offering support to a despairing Ireland, reflecting not only American philanthropic assistance during the famine crises of the 1840s and later, but also American support for Ireland's liberation from British rule. The motto that adorned the masthead was 'Be Just, Fear Not, Let all the ends thou aimest at be thy God's, thy Country's, and Truth's'. It was faithfully followed during Donahoe's career as *Pilot* owner and sometime editor.[5]

Donahoe had a winning formula in this combination of Catholic and Irish news coverage as shown by the increase in the *Pilot* subscriptions from 600 in 1838 to 7,000 by 1844, and to 10,500 by 1848. He traveled widely through New England and the mid-Atlantic area to recruit subscribers and used agents to canvass more distant regions. Donahoe acknowledged the increasing support for Repeal among the diaspora in the early 1840s as a significant factor in gaining new subscribers.[6] There were 1,248 members in the five branches of the Boston Repeal Association by 1843.[7] The *Pilot* subscriptions were not confined to New England, but spread across the country to areas of the mid-west such as Cincinnati, St Louis, Chicago, and even San Francisco where the *Pilot* was enthusiastically received by Catholic nuns anxious for news from Boston.[8] As well as keeping Irish immigrants throughout America informed about the local and national news from the homeland, it was crucial in alerting them about the devastating details of hunger, disease, starvation and death during *An Gorta Mór*, as well as the flaws and failures of the British government's response. Most importantly, the *Pilot* network facilitated the raising of significant relief funding from these areas in Black '47 and, subsequently, in 1862–1863 and during the 'Forgotten Famine' of 1879–1881. The huge influx of Irish immigrants in the two decades after 1847 boosted the *Pilot's* subscriptions to about 103,000 by 1872 and they never fell below 70,000 for the next 20 years, so that the paper was known widely as 'The Irishman's Bible'.[9] In short, the *Pilot* played the role that CNN and Go Fund Me play in our contemporary society to inform citizens of various humanitarian crises, and enabling people to respond quickly to provide aid to their fellow humans.

By the mid–1840s Donahoe was an influential and respected figure in Boston's Irish community as seen by his involvement in the Charitable Irish Society of Boston, the local Repeal Association, and the Young Catholic Friends Society. His business interests had expanded into a publishing company, a store that sold books on Catholic and Irish topics, a passenger and money exchange bureau and, eventually, an emporium for church furniture and accessories.[10] On the eve of the Irish famine, Donahoe and Andrew Carney, a fellow Cavan man, were the richest Irishmen in Boston and both would take leading roles in organizing relief for Ireland during her hour of greatest need.

The *Pilot's* coverage of Irish news in the 1840s and 1850s relied on Irish and English newspapers that arrived in Boston, via British mail packets, about twice a month. As the trans-Atlantic crossing took approximately 14 days, Irish news was often two to six weeks old when *Pilot* readers saw it. It was only after the laying of the trans-Atlantic cable in 1866 that the news-cycle between Ireland and Boston was reduced to two to three days. Although there were reports in the *Pilot* of excessively wet weather that might damage the Irish wheat and potato crops in the early autumn of 1845, on 8 November the *Pilot* reprinted the *Cork Examiner* report of significant potato crop losses as follows: 'Accounts continue to reach us of the deplorable state of the potato crop.[11] The malady is increasing and the district which was free yesterday is today visited with pestilence'.[12] The Cork paper called on the government to open the ports to facilitate foreign grain imports, as well as to ban exports of grain to provide an alternative food source for those usually dependent on the potato. The arrival of the HMS *Britannia* in Boston on 20 November brought confirmation that approximately one-third of the potato crop was lost.[13] The *Pilot's* 22 and 29 November issues reported the late October efforts of a Dublin Corporation delegation of leading citizens, which included Daniel O'Connell MP, Lord Cloncurry and the Duke of Leinster, to press the Viceroy, Lord Heytesbury, to open ports to food imports, ban oat exports, authorize public works and raise a million-pound loan to avert an impending famine. These pleas fell on deaf ears as the Viceroy responded on 3 November that the matter was one for the Cabinet in London to decide upon.

These grim reports of potato crop losses and a seemingly indifferent British government served as a catalyst for Boston's Irish community to respond. On 25 November, the President of Boston's Irish Repeal Association, John W. James, urged his eight ward captains to solicit funds for their 'suffering brethren'. Before this meeting adjourned, $90 had been collected for Irish relief.[14] Meanwhile, the popular pastor of St Mary's in Salem, Rev. Thomas J. O'Flaherty, used the *Pilot* to announce a meeting on 2 December at the Stackpole Tavern in order to design an effective Boston relief effort. A native of County Kerry and a doctor prior to becoming a priest, O'Flaherty graphically described the dire consequences that a potato crop failure held for the rural poor, and especially for children. He enlisted 60 wardens to solicit contributions in the city's 11 wards and made plans for a major solicitation event at the Odeon Theatre, one of the city's largest venues, to launch the Irish Charitable Society. Among those who made generous pledges of $10 that evening were *Pilot* editor, Patrick Donahoe, Rev. O'Flaherty, his clerical friend Father O'Reilly, noted Irish historian Thomas Mooney, while Daniel Crowley and his family pledged a total of $45. Bishop Fitzpatrick pledged $5, while his father, Bernard Fitzpatrick, pledged $3 and volunteered his services as a warden in East Boston. The names of the wardens were published in the *Pilot* so that readers knew whom to contact to give their donations.[15] The Odeon meeting on 8 December attracted 3,000 people who responded to Father O'Flaherty's powerful appeal by contributing a total of $750 to the Irish Charitable Fund. Another meeting, attended by 1,500 people, took place at the Odeon a week later, raising $350 dollars, including a donation of $25 from Thomas Colley Grattan, the British Consul in Boston.[16] The working-class members of St Nicholas parish in East Boston, along with some of their Protestant neighbours, contributed $264 to the relief fund. Daniel Crowley of East Boston, a successful contractor, served as the fund treasurer and raised $1,100 from his employees and his associates.[17] By the end of 1845, Boston had sent at least $19,000 in relief to Ireland.

During the fall of 1845 through the spring of 1846, *Pilot* readers learned of the British government's slow response to the unfolding crisis from reprints of the Reports of the Commission on the Potato Disease established by Prime Minister Robert Peel, excerpts from parliamentary debates, and from pleas of the Mansion House Committee, as well as efforts by Dublin Corporation to secure effective government intervention.[18] Front page coverage was given to the Mansion House Committee's 18 November letter to Prime Minister Peel in which its chair, Lord Cloncurry, warned 'While you hesitate—if hesitate you shall—the people of Ireland are about to perish in countless numbers ... Famine and pestilence are at our door and can be averted only by the most extensive and active precautions'. The committee's recommendations included: opening the ports to grain, banning exports of grain as well as its use in distilling spirits, providing employment via public works, and raising a one-million-pound loan to pay for these measures.[19] Two weeks later, the *Pilot* printed letters received by the committee from Catholic and Protestant clergy and local gentry describing the serious peril facing their people unless government aid was forthcoming. The same issue contained the committee's resolutions strongly condemning the government inaction, which they sent to Queen Victoria in the hope that she would direct her ministers to act.[20]

Organised relief efforts and *Pilot* coverage declined in the first half of 1846 as no one anticipated a second potato crop failure. Peel's purchase of a substantial supply of American Indian corn, his public works program and temporary provision of outdoor relief in the most distressed areas, seemed adequate. Boston's Repeal leader, John W. James, prioritised donations to O'Connell's organisation in Dublin, arguing private charity could never solve the fundamental problems of Ireland's economic ills and human misery.[21] An important factor in this development was a letter sent from Dublin and published in the *Pilot* in late January in which Thomas D'Arcy McGee endorsed the priority of Repeal, falsely claiming that this was the preferred policy of the Dublin leadership.[22] Although McGee's letter met with a strong rebuke from Father O'Flaherty and the *Pilot* urged its readers to support both causes, the unexpected death of Father O'Flaherty on 29 March 1846 ended the Irish Charitable Fund.[23] Money sent from Boston to Ireland for the remainder of 1846 consisted primarily of private donations of Boston Irish residents to their relatives in Ireland.

The complacent assumption that Peel's measures had contained the Irish crisis were dashed when reports of a second and almost total potato crop failure and mounting distress filled the *Pilot* columns during the autumn.[24] On 5 December 1846, the *Pilot* reported that $10,000 in donations had been sent from Boston via the *Arcadia* and urged its readers to send whatever they could spare to their parents and relations in Ireland. A *Pilot* editorial a month later noted that Boston was the first place to organize a relief effort in 1845 and lamented that it had dissipated in early 1846. Donahoe urged his Boston readers to act quickly to match New York, Philadelphia and Baltimore whose combined relief donations in 1846 were $1,001,650.[25]

The arrival of HMS *Hibernia* in Boston on 20 January 1847 confirmed earlier reports of escalating starvation, disease and death as well as plans to close the public works programme, which had employed 750,00 people at its' height. Public works had been the central relief provision of the Whig administration of Lord

John Russell whose government was dominated by laissez-faire ideology. Details of horrific conditions of starvation and disease from Skibbereen and many other localities printed in Irish newspapers filled the *Pilot's* next three issues.[26] These grim reports led Donahoe and other influential local leaders, such as Andrew Carney and Bishop John Fitzpatrick, to launch a new and broader effort to secure relief aid to mitigate the Irish calamity. On 7 February, the newly installed Bishop Fitzpatrick issued a powerful and compelling pastoral appeal to his entire diocese emphasizing, with many scriptural quotations, their Christian duty to feed the hungry and provide for the sick and dying as the most urgent priority and obligation. The impact of the Bishop's sermon was so great that the Relief Association for Ireland was established and received pledges of $3,000 by nightfall. Patrick Donahoe not only published the full text of the bishop's passionate pastoral in the *Pilot*, but also served as an association secretary and a collector for his Broad Street and South Cove neighbourhood. Andrew Carney served as Secretary for the fund. Donahoe published the names and parish affiliations of 67 collectors in the city and set a goal of $20,000 for donations from the New England region to be sent to Ireland by 1 March.[27] The largest donations toward this goal came from Andrew Carney at $1000, Patrick Donahoe and Bishop Fitzpatrick at $100, Thomas Mooney at $200, and James Ryan, owner of the Stackpole House where Rev. O'Flaherty had launched his fund, at $50. Most donations, ranging from 25 cents to $5.00, were from ordinary parishioners, many of them women.[28] These small donations entailed much personal sacrifice as Fitzpatrick noted in describing the donors to Archbishop Crolly: 'Their numbers are not great, their means are still less for nearly all are poor. But there are those and many too who are unwilling to think about tomorrow for themselves because they wish to do something for the relief of Ireland today'.[29] The goal that Donahoe set was more than achieved when the *Cambria* departed Boston on 1 March 1847 with $19,652 from Bishop Fitzpatrick's fund along with $3,000 from the Hartford Diocese where the *Pilot* had some subscribers. The ship carried another $167,000 in drafts from individuals which brought total aid for that voyage to $220,000.[30] Within a few weeks, an additional $4,000 was sent to Archbishop Crolly from Bishop Fitzpatrick's fund.

Donahoe gave publicity and lent support to various Boston events that were organised for Irish relief, including a 20 March concert at the Melodeon Theatre and two lectures by Rev. Henry Giles of Tremont Temple, an Irish born Protestant with Repeal sympathies, who spoke both in Boston and in Brooklyn in New York.[31] As early as 6 February, Donahoe endorsed a proposal that Faneuil Hall be used for a large fund raiser, one that became a reality later that month when Boston Brahmin leaders set up the New England Committee for the Relief of Ireland and Scotland and which, in turn, led to the historic voyage of the USS *Jamestown* to Cork seven weeks later.[32] Captain Robert Bennet Forbes, a highly experienced businessman and sea captain, oversaw the *Jamestown's* refitting, crew selection and loading of 800 tons of provisions collected from throughout New England for the starving Irish. Donahoe served on the New England Committee and his paper gave full coverage to the ship's departure from Boston, praising Captain Forbes and noting that the ship's burgee flag of shamrocks flying with the stars and stripes was a fitting symbol that showed Ireland that:

> ... their countrymen in America are not alone mindful of their cause, but that the Americans themselves are ready to fly to the rescue. The Stars and the Shamrock are sisters in the cause of freedom and humanity, and as ready to battle for Irish independence as to be engaged in the great work of charity.[33]

The *Jamestown* carried 800 tons of provisions, valued at $35,868, arriving in a record time of 14 days.[34] The enthusiastic welcome that the citizens of Cork gave to the *Jamestown* was described in the *Pilot* including this poem that was written to pay tribute to American generosity:

On the Arrival of the Jamestown
Three cheers for the bark,
And three cheers for her seamen
Yes, cheer them, for mark!
They are all of them freemen,
Cheer her 'star-spangled banner'
Bright emblem of freedom
Cheer the heroes who man her,
Thus come when we need 'em.
From the far-west she bounds.
She's already at anchor
While she's staunching our wounds,
Let us cease not to thank her.
Left vilely to perish,
By Saxon enslaver,
Let Erin's heart cherish
The hand stretched to save her—
Then hurrah! for that bark
And hurrah for her seamen
Yes, cheer them, for mark!
They are all of them, freemen.[35]

In an accompanying editorial Donahoe hoped that future historians would fully describe the: 'daily bleaching with the bones of starving humanity ... that future generations may be horror struck at the cruelty of a government, which starves out its subjects merely for the purpose of carrying out a system of the most iniquitous laws that ever disgraced the annals of legislation ... If future generations shall have reason to burn with indignation at the past conduct of the British government, their indignation will melt into joy and gratitude when contemplating the noble conduct of America'. He added that Captain Forbes' initiative, courage and efficiency in completing the *Jamestown* mission had earned him the affection of every Irishman and a ranking 'as one of the most illustrious of American citizens'.[36]

Donahoe knew that Ireland would require continuing assistance from America and the *Pilot* continued to publish letters of appeal from Ireland, such as one sent from John McGowan from Ballyshannon in County Donegal on 24 March. This lengthy letter graphically described starving children, begging mothers, roadside deaths of the elderly, crowded workhouses with deaths averaging ten per day, and the abandonment of the usual funeral rites. McGowan warned that the upcoming closing of the public works would leave 141,000 labourers completely destitute. Since Boston was now the home of so many from this area, McGowan hoped his letter to the *Pilot* would stimulate former Donegal residents to send additional aid.[37] McGowan's dire account of rising starvation in Donegal was confirmed by Derry's Bishop Maginn's 9 April letter that was published in the *Pilot* on 5 June. A week later, Donahoe published an open letter that Archbishop John MacHale wrote to Prime Minister John Russell attacking the inadequacy of British relief policy, as well as one from Lord Cloncurry to William Smith O'Brien that attributed Ireland's current travails to four decades of misguided British economic policy. Donahoe's outrage over such reports was reflected in the accompanying editorial:

> There is something awful in the contemplation of the deep terrible distress of Ireland, when read alongside of the account of the rich *exports* which are made monthly from the chief ports of the country. There is wrong—deep and damning wrong—in a state of society which shall demand of men to observe law, obey the behests, and cry Peace, and die of starvation with the last rattle in their throats, utterly feeble and faint—*peaceful agitation* ...
>
> English law and English legislation, and the absence of legislation, has produced this profoundly terrible state of Ireland. To its sins of commission and omission, lie the death of nearly a million in Ireland, within the present two years.[38]

Donahoe believed that had Ireland possessed its own legislature, a famine would not have happened and he speculated that should these conditions continue, a violent uprising was likely.[39]

As thousands of Irish famine refugees poured into Boston in the spring and early summer of 1847, the *Pilot* protested at the ill-treatment that so many encountered, including the diversion of the *Brig Mary* to Halifax, when its captain could not pay the recently imposed bonds for his 46 Irish passengers. He urged the Boston authorities to devise a plan to deal with destitute and ill immigrants rather than sending them to Canada or back to Ireland.[40] The city officials eventually used Deer Island in Boston Harbor as a refuge for arriving immigrants who displayed symptoms of disease and illness.[41] The summer of 1847 witnessed considerable media hostility against the arriving famine refugees as well as intimidating parades of nativists through Irish sections of the city.[42] As early as 1845 Donahoe had urged the arriving immigrants to seek employment and better housing in towns like Quincy, Lynn, Fall River, Canton, Worcester and beyond rather than stay in the crowded and disease infested neighbourhoods near the Boston waterfront.[43] Similar advice to move beyond Boston came in 1847 when the *Pilot* published historian Thomas Mooney's letter urging immigrants to go west or to Canada where land and employment opportunities were greater.[44]

Given the challenges that newly arrived emigrants faced, Donahoe repeatedly urged the creation of an Emigrant Society in Boston to provide them timely assistance with housing, employment or even helping them to move west.[45] Donahoe was crucially involved in establishing the Boston Emigrant Society in April 1850 and served as its President through 1855. Membership was one dollar with quarterly dues set at 25 cents, thus insuring wide support even among those with limited resources. Within three weeks of its establishment, an office was opened on Congress Street to enroll new members and, eventually, to provide advice and help to recently arrived immigrants. The *Pilot* publicised and reported on lectures and concerts whose proceeds went to the new organization. Archbishop Fitzpatrick and many clergy endorsed this effort and urged their flocks to contribute to it. As he had done in 1847, Rev. Henry Giles gave two lectures to raise funds for the society. The effort proved so popular that branches of the society were set up in Milford, Massachusetts and in East Boston.[46] Edward Ryan served as the society's agent, collecting memberships and dues, meeting arriving ships to provide food and shelter to destitute immigrants who arrived from Ireland as well as from the Canadian provinces. Only three months after its founding, the society was providing emergency food, clothing, accommodation and transportation to their final destinations to 107 destitute Irish immigrants who survived the shipwreck of the *Seraphine*, which had left Newry on 5 April bound for New York but was wrecked near Halifax, Nova Scotia. Collections by the society and by Boston's Catholic churches ordered by the Bishop Fitzpatrick raised $320 to meet these costs.[47] In its first 20 months, the agency secured employment for 425 males and 478 females and wrote more than 1,000 letters to help immigrants contact relatives and friends already in America. Fifteen hundred persons used the agency to purchase cheaper railway tickets to western states and thus avoided being scammed by the numerous railway runners and unscrupulous agents who preyed on newly arrived immigrants.[48] These services continued up through 1857. As President of the venerable Charitable Irish Society from 1851 to 1854, Donahoe arranged an annual $300 contribution to this agency over the next seven years.[49] Donahoe frequently published notices regarding fund raising efforts by the House of the Guardian Angel, the Home for Destitute Catholic Children and St Vincent's Orphan Asylum, institutions that served large numbers of poor and orphaned Irish children in the city. He and his wife made regular contributions to these institutions.[50]

In the spring of 1851 when the exodus from Ireland remained extra-ordinarily high, Donahoe published in serial form the *Irish Emigrant's Guide for the United States* by Rev. John O'Hanlon of St Louis. It was featured on the *Pilot's* front page from 12 April to 14 June and consisted of 18 chapters, giving highly detailed information to prospective emigrants on everything—from planning their departure from Ireland, what to expect on the voyage, how to find housing and employment upon arrival as well as what areas of America provided the best opportunities for securing jobs and land. Donahoe also arranged to sell a complete edition of this useful volume through his office. The *Pilot* also ran a series on the process of naturalization by John Tighe to encourage new arrivals to apply as soon as possible.[51]

Although tenant farmers in Leinster and Munster experienced an improvement in their economic status in the 1850s, residents of counties Galway, Mayo, Sligo and Donegal advanced little and were hurled back into famine-like conditions in 1862 as a result of the combination of three seasons of bad weather, depressed agricultural prices, and the re-emergence of potato blight.[52] Once again, the *Pilot* and Patrick Donahoe played a critical role in making Irish Americans aware of the crisis and sending financial aid to the Central Relief Committee, to various Irish bishops, and to individual parish priests whose appeals on behalf of their impoverished flocks were published in the *Pilot*. The presence of 307,691 Irish born residents in New England and over a million and a half nationally, many of whom had personal memories of the trauma of the 1840s, was an important factor in generating over £300,000 in aid from the United States during this crisis.[53] This was a huge amount considering the financial challenges that Irish American families faced from the U.S. Civil War and a depressed economy. The war situation, as well as increased nativist hostility to the Irish, tended to limit contributions from the wealthier classes who had provided aid in 1847. Yet, in 1862–1863, the Dublin Central Committee received £2,000 from Boston and New England, including £70 transferred to it by Donahoe.

As in the 1840s, the *Pilot* alerted its readers early to the looming threat of famine in early 1862 by publishing not only Irish newspaper reports, but also reprinting the open letters that Archbishop John MacHale of Tuam sent to Lord Palmerston, the British Prime Minister, calling on the government to take action to meet the emerging crisis. The appeals that a delegation from Dublin Corporation made to the Lord Lieutenant were also published.[54] One especially disturbing article from the *Cork Examiner* reported that three-quarters of the potato crop was diseased and that it was the worst wheat crop in 20 years. The parish priest of Berehaven stated that 200 families in his parish were starving and that there was no prospect of any assistance from landlords or the government. It recommended that the *Pilot* use its columns to organize a nation-wide subscription in every church in the United States so that every family who had sympathy for their famished countrymen might contribute even a small amount before it was too late.[55] The 15 and 22 February issues of the *Pilot* carried very emotive appeals from Rev. Jeremiah Vaughan of Clare and Rev. Patrick Lavelle of Partry, Co. Mayo, both of whom had witnessed the horrors of 1847 and were renowned for their strong nationalist sympathies. The impact of these reports on *Pilot* readers was immediate as evident in the organization of a 'Father Vaughan Committee' in Boston the day after his appeal was published. By 1 March the Vaughan committee had 34 members representing men from Boston, Charlestown, Roxbury, Medford and Dorchester. Thomas Healy, a local attorney, served as Treasurer and Donahoe offered his exchange bureau services to send the donations to Ireland. By 20 March, the committee had sent $930 to Father Vaughan and more donations followed in the next few months reaching a total of $1,283 by 5 July 1862.[56] Donahoe not only served on this committee but he also provided a discounted exchange rate in making the transfers from Treasurer Healy to Father Vaughan.[57] The reach of the *Pilot's* influence was reflected in donations that came from Vermont, New Hampshire, Kentucky, Wisconsin and Canada West.[58] In the spring of 1863 Father Vaughan called on Donahoe and the *Pilot* to publicise the need for continuing aid for his impoverished flock and express his conviction that Britain was using its land law and commercial organisation to extirpate the Irish.[59] The appeal of Rev. Patrick McManus from Clifden in Galway describing the extreme distress in his district and the British government's indifference was published in the *Pilot* in early April with the result that by August he had received donations through Donahoe totaling $309.[60] Rev. Patrick Lavelle was another frequent correspondent with Donahoe and the *Pilot*. As an outspoken critic of the British connection and of the proselytizing of the Plunkett family in his district, Lavelle was a familiar figure among Irish-born immigrants and thus his calls for donations to finance his schools as well as famine relief came from many quarters in the United States, especially from those associated with the recently established Fenian branches.[61] Boston Fenians set up a committee to help Lavelle in March 1862 and recruited 50 men pledged to help. James Donnelly, a close friend of Donahoe's, served as chair, overseeing a committee of 18 collectors, three of whom were women.[62] Between April and October 1862, approximately $1,180 in donations were sent to Father Lavelle through the Donahoe's exchange office, the highest amounts coming from Boston, Springfield, and Lowell, while smaller ones came from Indiana, Missouri, and Michigan.[63] Contributions to Lavelle from soldiers serving in the Union army were often transferred through Donohoe's offices, especially after he announced that he would drop the exchange fees for soldiers sending their donations to the *Pilot* office. Among such contributions were $10 from the Irish Brigade in Virginia, $45 from F Company 10th Regiment and $31 dollars from the 28th Massachusetts Volunteers.[64] The officers and the crew of the USS *Somerset,* then stationed in the Gulf, sent $298 for Irish relief to the *Pilot* for transfer to Ireland in October 1863.[65] Lavelle's frequent letters to the *Pilot* provided an on-going commentary on the suffering of his parishioners, details of local evictions, and the evils of British government policy over the centuries, undoubtedly helped to stimulate this generous response. The following editorial endorsement of Father Lavelle by Donahoe also helped to generate contributions:

> Father Lavelle is an unspoiled priest, of noble talents, of noble nature. His country owes him a perpetual debt. His 'Fund' is yet in this office. Let all who can contribute to it. Distress, hunger, persecution are yet in Partry, and the holy shepherd watching the Book, deserve to have his cries responded to. In with the responses.[66]

The *Pilot* regularly published Archbishop MacHale's public letters to British officials and speeches complaining of the government's refusal to provide adequate relief funds or public works to meet the on-going distress in the west of Ireland.[67] As with Fathers Vaughan and Lavelle, Donahoe offered his services to send donations directly to the Archbishop. Between May and late August 1862, donations from places as diverse as Crawfordsville, Indiana, Watertown, Wisconsin, Bangor, Maine, Greenland, Michigan, Providence, Ohio and Lawrence, Massachusetts, amounting to $2,734 in relief money, was sent to MacHale through Donahoe's exchange bureau.[68]

In early 1863, the *Pilot* published numerous reports that conditions in Ireland were even worse than in 1862. Archbishop MacHale's letter to the Prime Minister, as well as appeals by Dr McEvilly of Galway and Father Curley of Louisburg, Co. Mayo, all described the acute distress that was spreading geographically and moving further up the social scale to include shopkeepers and farmers, noting also that landlords were hurt by the inability to collect rents. Father Curley had two hundred totally destitute families in his parish and had to redeem 62 pawn tickets to ensure some families had clothing. The report of the re-established Central Committee for the Relief of Distress in Ireland confirmed these horrendous conditions, adding that it expected there would be 90,000 people dependent on relief by March, and that there were as many pawn tickets out as in 1846 when the population was two million more.[69]

Donahoe reacted quickly to these reports, calling for a national campaign that would collect one dollar from everyone attending Catholic churches on St Patrick's Day since it was doubtful the British government would do anything to alleviate mounting Irish distress. He suggested that the Archbishop of New York should initiate such an effort, which would be seconded by every clergyman in the country.[70] In his 21 and 28 March editorials, Donahoe scolded the Boston Irish for falling behind New York City and Philadelphia in setting up an Irish relief campaign, and urged Boston's Irish societies to act, asking: 'Are the suffering people to be remembered only in sentiment, parades and speeches?' Donahoe's scolding words proved effective as meetings of the city's Irish leaders were held at Young's Hotel on 26 and 31 March leading to the organization of a Boston Irish Relief Committee. Donahoe was elected as President and Treasurer, and together with a committee of six, a formal public appeal was drawn up and published in the *Pilot* and other journals. The committee also lobbied the Board of Trade to secure donations from the city's merchant class. The published appeal drew a stark picture of the hunger and suffering in Ireland and quoted Archbishop MacHale, the local Irish press, and a few sympathetic English papers to drive home the urgency of the situation.[71] At the same time, Archbishop John J. Williams announced a diocesan-wide collection for Irish relief to be held on 26 April. Donahoe published the Bishop's pastoral letter in which he emphasised the special obligation that Catholics in New England had to provide aid given the great benefits that they enjoyed, in comparison to their friends and relatives in Ireland. Donahoe urged everyone attending Mass on 26 April to donate one dollar to this fund, noting that some would contribute more. The pastoral and Donahoe's advice were highly effective: ultimately, the proceeds of this collection provided $41,870 for Irish relief.[72] Bishop McFarland in the neighboring diocese of Hartford sent £2,000 to Ireland from his flock. Among the significant contributions that flowed from the Boston Relief Committee appeal was $700 from George Upton and $1,000 from Gerrit Smith of Peterborough, New Hampshire.[73] Lectures and concerts were held for Irish relief over the next few months. The Robert Emmet Association lecture, given by Judge Daley on 29 April, netted $314 dollars. The Montgomery Union concert brought in $1,000 or £149, which was sent to the

Central Relief Committee in Dublin.[74] Patrick S. Gilmore, the famous bandleader, did a complimentary concert at the Boston Theatre on 16 May. A play performed by the Sodalists Literary Society provided sufficient funds to send £51 to Rev. Daniel O'Donnell to help his impoverished parishioners at Templecrone, Co. Donegal.[75] Company F, 20th Regiment of the Massachusetts Volunteers in Falmouth, Virginia sent $192 to Donahoe for Irish relief.[76] The *Pilot* continued to publish appeals by clergy and nuns in the spring and summer of 1863 and offered to forward receipts to Ireland.[77] By 27 June, Donahoe had sent drafts worth $2,528 to Ireland.[78] A contribution of $229 from the officers and crew of the SS *Huron* was sent to Archbishop MacHale by Donahoe in June 1863.[79] It is not possible to calculate accurately the total amount of relief funds that were raised by the Boston organization and sent through Donahoe's exchange bureau, but the above examples show the enthusiasm and generosity that Donahoe and the *Pilot* generated in Boston and the New England region. Meanwhile, Donahoe's frustration, if not rage, at the failure of the British government to provide relief and introduce land law reform was reflected in his strong editorial of 28 June, which argued that these repeated crises were not the work of Providence, but a result of England's 'always bloody and rapacious' policies. He proclaimed: 'We are no revolutionaries where there is a legitimate and humane government. But there is neither legitimacy nor humanity in the rule of England over Ireland'. He suggested that it would be patriotism if the Irish clergy joined with the people in a rebellion against English rule. He told his readers that it was both mercy and patriotism to contribute relief aid, finishing with the exhortation 'In-in-in with contributions for the dear and never-to-be-forgotten Ireland where most of us were born'.[80]

When Ireland was threatened with famine again in 1879, Patrick Donahoe was no longer owner of the *Pilot* as he had been forced by financial reverses to sell the newspaper to Archbishop Williams and John Boyle O'Reilly in 1876. Donohoe's fortune had vanished as a result of a combination of the Great Fire of 1872 that had destroyed his printing presses, the headquarters of his exchange bureau, and a depression that wiped out his banking assets. Yet when word reached Boston in the autumn of 1879 that the west of Ireland was faced with yet another famine crisis, Patrick Donahoe joined with John Boyle O'Reilly, now the *Pilot* editor, to rally their fellow Irish Americans to come to the assistance of their ancestral land. Donahoe was part of the Boston committee that organized Charles Stewart Parnell's visit to the city in January 1880, during which time considerable funds were raised for relief as well as for the recently formed Irish Land League. The *Pilot* and its editor, O'Reilly, along with Patrick Collins and Thomas Flatley, continued to rally Irish Americans to the cause of

Irish self-government, insisting that this was the only solution that would effectively end the curse of poverty and frequent famines in their beloved homeland.[81]

Patrick Donahoe's life and career provide an extraordinary example of the vital and living links between Ireland and the United States that were established in the nineteenth century, links that proved beneficial to both societies. Arriving as a poor young immigrant in 1821, he went on to build a highly successful career as a journalist, businessman and noted philanthropist. His commitment to American values of fair play, equality, democracy and active citizenship was deep and enduring, and he longed for his homeland to enjoy the same advantages that gave him success in America. Yet Donahoe never forgot his native land and used his talents as a journalist and businessman to save the lives of hundreds of Irish men, women and children from the ravages of famine, disease and British government neglect during three serious famines. He knew firsthand the challenges that newly arrived immigrants faced and did all he could to provide them with the shelter, information and advice that would enable them to build successful and secure lives in the United States. The exemplary life Donahoe lived, especially in his philanthropic work, led to his receiving the Laetare Gold Medal from Notre Dame University in 1893 and to a large civic testimonial in Boston the following year. These were fitting tributes to a man who said at the height of his wealth, 'I have enough now ... my earnings henceforth will go to the poor'.[82] Patrick Donahoe, founder and owner of the *Pilot*, deserves recognition as one of the most significant and effective heroes of Irish famines.

NOTES

1. See Chapter on William Rathbone and his role in the voyage of the *Jamestown*.
2. 'Scarcity of Provisions in Ireland', *Hansard,* House of Commons debates, 29 Apr. 1822, vol. 7, cc. 146–150.
3. *Pilot,* Mar. 1901, Patrick Donahoe Obituary; See also Mary A. Frawley, *Patrick Donahoe* (Washington, Catholic University Press, 1946), pp 3–33 for details of Donahoe's early life.
4. For an account of Protestant nativist-Irish conflict in the 1830s and 1840s, see Robert H. Lord, et. al, *History of the Archdiocese of Boston* (New York, 1944), vol. 2, pp 205–265.
5. This mast head illustration was launched in January 1848 and lasted through 1852.
6. 'Reminiscences of an Old-Time Journalist: the Late Patrick Donahoe of Boston,' *Records of the American Catholic Historical Society of Philadelphia* (Sept. 1904), vol. 15, no. 3, p. 315.
7. Oscar Handlin, *Boston's Immigrants, 1790 to 1880, 50th Anniversary Edition* (Cambridge, 1991), p. 247.
8. Frawley, *Patrick Donohoe*, p. 34.
9. Ibid., p. 31.

10. Ibid, p. 295.
11. *Pilot,* 13 Sept., 25 Oct. 1845.
12. Ibid., 8 Nov. 1845.
13. Ibid., 22, 29 Nov. 1845.
14. Ibid.
15. Ibid., 6 Dec. 1845.
16. Ibid., 13, 20 Dec. 1845.
17. *Pilot,* 6, 13, 20 Dec. 1845; A. Crosby Forbes and Henry Lee, *Massachusetts Help to Ireland During the Great Famine* (Milton: Forbes House, 1967), pp 1–3.
18. *Pilot,* 22 Nov., 6, 13, 27 Dec. 1845.
19. Ibid., 13 Dec. 1845.
20. Ibid., 27 Dec. 1845.
21. Ibid., 13 Dec. 1845, 10 Jan. 1846.
22. Forbes and Lee, pp 3–4; *Pilot,* 31 Jan. 1846. For McGee's views on Repeal and famine relief, see David A. Wilson, *Thomas D'Arcy McGee* (Montreal: McGill Queen's University Press, 2008), pp 118–121. The once cordial relations between McGee and Donahoe soured when the latter discovered that McGee's letter was sent without approval by the Repeal leaders in Dublin. Donahoe had been McGee's mentor during his Boston residence between 1843 and 1845.
23. A beloved figure among the Boston Irish, Rev. O'Flaherty's funeral service and procession drew 10,000 people to pay their respects. *Pilot,* 4 Apr. 1846.
24. Ibid., 5, 12, 19, 26 Oct. 1845.
25. Ibid., 9 Jan. 1847.
26. Ibid., 23, 30 Jan. 1847, 6 Feb. 1847.
27. Ibid., 13 Feb. 1847.
28. *Sydney Chronicle*, 1 Mar. 1847.
29. Fitzpatrick to Crolly, 27 Feb. 1847, Fitzpatrick Correspondence, Boston Archdiocese Archives.
30. *Pilot,* 6 Mar. 1847. This edition has Carney's listing of contributions received from Boston parishes as well as from others in Massachusetts, New Hampshire, Maine and Vermont.
31. *Pilot*, 6 Mar. 1847. Giles' Brooklyn lecture raised $600 for Irish relief.
32. Catherine B. Shannon, 'Captain Robert Bennet Forbes and his 1847 Voyage of Mercy to Cork,' *Heroes of Ireland's Great Hunger,* Christine Kinealy, Jason King, Gerard Moran (eds) (Hamden; Quinnipiac and Cork University Press, 2021); also see Forbes and Lee. A full account of the American national effort for Irish relief in 1847 is in Stephen Puleo, *Voyage of Mercy* (New York: St Martin's Press, 2020)
33. *Pilot,* 3 Apr. 1847, 8, 15 May 1847; A number of other men who had been involved in Bishop Fitzpatrick's collection also helped with the New England Relief committee effort. At least 24 were associated with the Charitable Irish Society of Boston. *The Atlas*, 19 Feb. 1847; Catherine B. Shannon, *With Good Will Doing Service: The Charitable Irish Society of Boston, 1737–1857* (Boston, Charitable Irish Society, 2015) n. 72.
34. The New England Committee raised a total of $150,000 during its campaign and used the USS *Macedonian* and private ships to transport the rest of the provisions donated or

purchased. For details of the *Jamestown* effort see, Shannon, *Captain Robert Bennet Forbes,* pp 39–52.

35. *Pilot*, 15 May 1847, reprinted from *Dublin Freeman*.
36. Ibid., 15 May 1847.
37. Ibid., 8 May 1847.
38. Ibid., 12 June 1847.
39. Ibid., 12 June 1847.
40. Ibid., 5 June 1847.
41. John McColgan details the history of Deer Island and its dedicated medical staff in an accompanying chapter.
42. *Boston Evening Transcrip*t, 10, 26 June 1847.
43. *Pilot*, 5, 12, 19 June 1847, 19 Oct. 1845.
44. Ibid., 4, 25 Sept., 20 Nov. 1847.
45. Ibid., 19, 26 June 1847.
46. Ibid., 13, 20, 27 Apr., 11, 25 May, 15 June 1850, 22 Mar. 1851.
47. Ibid., 1 June 1850.
48. Ibid., 4 Jan., 27 Dec. 1851, 24 Apr. 1852 for details of the agency's income, expenses and number of persons assisted.
49. Shannon, 'With Good Will Doing Service', p. 22; Charitable Irish Society Records, vol. 3, Minutes, 29 Mar. 1852, Massachusetts Historical Society.
50. *Pilot,* 4, 18, 25 Oct. 1851.
51. Ibid., 5 Apr. 1851, and 12 Apr to 14 June 1851.
52. James S. Donnelly, 'The Irish Agricultural Depression of 1859–1864', *Irish Economic and Social History Journal,* ii (1976).
53. 8th Census of the United States, 1860, pp xxi-xxxii; Summary of report of the Dublin Central Relief Committee, *Pilot,* 29 Aug. 1863.
54. *Pilot,* 18, 25 Jan., 1, 15, 22 Feb. 1862.
55. Ibid., Letter from Daniel Sullivan, 22 Feb. 1862.
56. Ibid., 12 Apr., 10 May, 21 June, 5 July 1862.
57. Ibid., 12 Apr. 1862.
58. Ibid., 20 Mar., 12 Apr. 10, 24 May, 21 June, 2 Aug. 1862.
59. Ibid., 9 May 1863.
60. Ibid., 5 Apr., l7 May, 5 July and 2 Aug. 1862.
61. For a full biography of Father Lavelle, see Gerard Moran, *A Radical Priest in Mayo: Fr Patrick Lavelle, The Rise and Fall of an Irish Nationalist, 1825–86* (Dublin: Four Courts Press, 1994).
62. *Pilot*, 8 Mar., 10 May 1862.
63. Ibid., 12 Apr., 30, 31 May, 7 July, 21 Aug., 25 Oct. 1862.
64. Ibid., 30 Apr., 2 Aug. 1862, 9 May 1863.
65. Ibid., 8 Nov. 1863.
66. Ibid., 2 Aug. 1862.
67. Ibid., 15 Mar, 17 May, 28 June 1862, 16, 30 May 1863.

68. Ibid., 2, 10 May, 7, 28 June, 9, 30 Aug. 1862.
69. Ibid., 21, 28 Feb. 1863.
70. Ibid., 21 Feb. 1863.
71. Ibid., 4, 11 Apr. 1863.
72. Ibid., 11, 18 Apr., 13 June 1863.
73. Ibid., 18 Apr. 1863; Central Relief Committee Report, Appendix C (Dublin, 1864).
74. Ibid., 23 May 1863.
75. Ibid., 1 Aug. 1863.
76. Ibid., 2 May 1863.
77. Ibid., 9, 16 May 1863 for appeals from Sisters of Mercy at Cork and Swinford, and 16 May and 13 June for appeals from Rev. Curley, Father Murray and Peter Ward.
78. Ibid., 25 Apr., 9, 16 May, 2 June 1863.
79. Ibid., 28 June 1863.
80. Ibid.
81. See Catherine B. Shannon, 'Boston and the Forgotten Famine of 1879–1882' in *Irish Famines before and after the Great Hunger,* Christine Kinealy and Gerard Moran (eds) (Quinnipiac University Press, Hampden, 2019) pp 195–212 for an account of Boston's response to the 'Forgotten Famine'.
82. *Pilot*, 8 March 1930.

CHAPTER TEN

BOSTON IN THE FAMINE

City Government and the Emigrant Crisis

John McColgan

In June 1847, Captain Robert Bennet Forbes gazed out at the spectacular view of the city harbour from his home on Milton Hill near Boston as he wrote to his friend, the noted Irish author, Maria Edgeworth. In his letter, Captain Forbes described the disturbing scene he beheld:

> Within sight of my window, I can count more than twenty ships and vessels, containing several thousand immigrants undergoing quarantine, some of whom are suffering from ship fever. It is appalling to contemplate the amount of suffering at this moment on the Atlantic, & I dare not anticipate the recital of scenes of unparalleled mortality probably now in progress on the ocean.[1]

One of his prominent collaborators in Ireland, Edgeworth worked with Forbes in the Boston Brahmin initiative that would deliver several shipments of relief to famine-stricken communities in Ireland, Scotland, and even Liverpool. Forbes had famously captained the sloop of war *Jamestown*, borrowed from the government of the United States, on the first and most renowned of these voyages, dramatically speeding 800 tons of foodstuffs and supplies to Cork in April 1847. Reports of the Famine's horrors reaching Boston had aroused a deluge of humanitarian sympathy for the suffering, and an outpouring of generosity supporting a singular relief effort organized in February by Boston elites at a mass meeting in Faneuil Hall. Yet, while Bostonians could feel self-satisfied with their alleviation of suffering an ocean away, many soon came to experience emotions other than compassion when thousands of refugees fleeing that catastrophe showed up in the harbour. Shock, anger and outrage prevailed among many native inhabitants, as they watched the pauperized victims of that tragedy stream into the city, menace public health with famine-induced disease, degrade the old neighbourhoods of the 'Athens of America' in noxious ghettos and waterfront tenements, undercut the wages of the native working class, and burden the public treasury with increasing costs of poor relief.

All along the Atlantic seaboard, the flight of refugees descended upon one city after another as 'Black '47' ravaged Ireland with hunger, pestilence, and obscene levels of mortality exterminating within a few years over a million people. In the explosive emigration of 1847, the notorious 'coffin ships' carried tens of thousands of people on nightmarish transatlantic journeys, people fleeing the catastrophe that Captain Forbes and well-meaning New Englanders hoped to allay by their charitable shipments of food and provisions. Though extricated from desolation in Ireland, famine refugees were now subject to deplorable conditions aboard vessels designed for hauling cargo, not human beings. On ships, steamers, barques, schooners and brigs, people crammed into holds that soon acquired the ambient quality of cesspools. Ship masters frequently flouted Britain's already loose regulations governing the passenger trade. Food was mean in volume and poor in quality. Hygiene was abominable. Water was inadequately provided and other basic amenities were minimal, if present at all.

Such horrid conditions caused tremendous suffering during awful, misery-laden voyages. Typhus, an appalling and frightful lice-borne disease, which had raged through Ireland's famine-stricken rural areas, went on to attack the poor quarters of Irish, English and North American cities whence migrants fled, earning the moniker 'ship fever' as it rampaged a flotilla of emigrant vessels on the Atlantic. Typhus took the lives of untold thousands on the voyage from Ireland to North America in 1847—on the vessels lined up on the river waiting to discharge passengers; in the hopelessly inadequate medical facilities at the Grosse Île immigration depot; and on the journey inland where thousands of infected immigrants suffered, died and spread the virus further afield. At the end of 1847, the Boston *Pilot* estimated that the voyage to Canada and the catastrophic emigrant dispersal at Quebec had taken 20,000 lives.[2]

While Boston would be spared such extremes of death and chaos, the city, as a famine refugee destination, could expect serious impact. The spring of 1847 would, in fact, bring an influx of impoverished and sick emigrants that Boston had never before seen, and create an emergency that would test the mettle of city government. Much is written of the cold welcome given to the Irish by native Bostonians in the nineteenth century, the religious and racial prejudice, employment discrimination, and the sometimes-violent confrontations. Yet, a closer look at historical sources reveals that the host community, and city government in particular, was not altogether without compassion, and was ready and able to accept the challenge of caring for thousands of sick and impoverished strangers, while protecting the city from a virulent and dangerous epidemic. In June 1847, at the height of the famine refugee influx, the President of the Common Council reminded the people of Boston of the virtue of caring for those in need regardless of who they were. 'Remember', said the Brahmin, George Hillard:

> That if these poor people had not thus taxed our benevolence they must have died. You will not, I am sure, be weary in well-doing, or refuse to feed from the crumbs of our abundance the starving poor, even though they be aliens to the soil. They are our brethren still. They have the claims of a common humanity, besides those of urgent need. We are men before we are Americans or Englishmen. They are as near to us as the faint and bleeding Jew was to the good Samaritan. The starving man is our neighbour and he that is in distress is a brother.[3]

Hillard gave this address only days after the opening of Deer Island Hospital, where city physicians were treating hundreds of newly arrived famine refugees suffering from the scourge of typhus. The initiative of city leaders, and the work and sacrifices of city doctors and staff at Deer Island, suggest it was in this spirit they endeavored to save the lives of Irish Famine victims in Black '47 and beyond.

By April and May, hundreds of diseased and destitute famine refugees were flocking to city institutions in South Boston and overwhelming their resources. At the House of Industry, temporary wooden structures were filled with sick and impoverished aliens as fast as they could be built. The ship fever brought ashore from emigrant vessels was spreading to the staff of city institutions and the native inmates. And in the neighbourhoods, public ire was rising with the revelation that city authorities were conveying diseased alien paupers straight from arriving vessels to public asylums without levying statute-mandated bonds to cover the cost of their care. The extraordinary emigrant influx, and the public alarm it created, galvanized City Hall into action. On 18 May, the City Council formed an eleven-member 'Special Joint Committee on Alien Passengers' that would lead Boston through its Irish Famine emigrant crisis over the next 18 months.[4] At its first meeting, a representative from the city's House of Industry informed the committee that the institution had admitted 355 recently-landed alien paupers, comprising nearly half of all the institution's inmates. They were 'in a most deplorable condition', he stressed, 'many of them being entirely prostrate with the 'Ship' or 'typhus' fever in its worst form, and all of them being exceedingly filthy and entirely unfit to mingle with the ordinary inmates'. The fever, he asserted, had 'assumed the character of an epidemic at the South Boston institutions and that some cases have appeared in the city proper'.[5]

The Committee straight away decided to construct an emergency medical facility to relieve municipal institutions, and to situate it on one of the harbour islands in an effort to isolate the disease from the city. After touring the harbour on the following day, they decided against the traditional quarantine site on Rainsford Island in favour of Deer Island, which offered more spacious accommodation and was more favourably situated for anchorage, lying at the harbour entrance. Subcommittees were assigned to arrange for boats and conveyances, construct buildings, hire medical and support staff for setting up and running a hospital, procure supplies, employ police to ensure security, and to oversee finance. As owner of the island, the city canceled a lease on its resort facilities, and immediately began erecting new buildings and additions to existing structures in the north of the island to serve as hospitals. New, stricter quarantine regulations were issued. The island's southern tip, about a half-mile from the hospitals, was designated for quarantine anchorage and passenger landing. Here, the port physician would evaluate the health of passengers aboard vessels or sheltered in tents on the quarantine ground, transferring the sick to the hospital up-island, while the Alien Passengers Inspector would collect alien entry fees from shipmasters and ensure the bonding of paupers. The hospital opened for business on Saturday, 29 May 1847. Members of the Alien Passengers Committee assembled on the island to oversee the launch of their plan for managing the emigrant influx, which they expected would continue to grow.[6] There, they witnessed a system start-up conducted by the principal officials responsible for bringing that strategy to fruition.

A County Kerry surname was rare among the higher echelons of Yankee society in the Bay State. However, the family history of this branch of the Moriartys demonstrates the possibilities in life for enterprising Irish families in the eighteenth century who turned Protestant. At the outbreak of the American Revolution, Dr Moriarty's merchant great-grandfather brought the name from Ireland to Salem, where he established himself in that port's flourishing privateering industry in the cause of American independence. It was an apt occupation for one whose ancient Gaelic family name, O Muircheartagh, translates to 'Sea Chief'. His descendants carried on the tradition in their own chosen paths. His son and a grandson, both named Thomas, were master mariners who served the United States on the seas in the Revolution and in the War of 1812 respectively, and who married into the families of Salem's merchant, mariner and Revolutionary War hero elite. Another grandson, John, married the daughter of a prominent Salem sea captain, became an eminent Salem banker, and 'was very active in the formation of some of the earliest corporations of the Commonwealth'. Dr Joseph Moriarty was the son of this banker. Joseph and his older brother John Mosely Moriarty, also a physician, would themselves maintain the family tradition of establishing elite family ties. The two brothers married two sisters, granddaughters of Ebenezer Hancock, bursar of the Continental Army and grandnieces of the Hon. John Hancock, Governor of Massachusetts, President of the Continental Congress, and the first signer of the United States Declaration of Independence. The Moriarty brothers would also carry on the family association with the sea, albeit in a rather different calling from their merchant and mariner forebears: their destiny, as medical doctors, would be to stand at Boston Harbour's island gateway and battle the maladies afflicting refugees the ocean had brought in from catastrophe in their ancestral land.[7] On 25 May, the Committee unanimously elected Joseph Moriarty to be Superintendent and Resident Physician for Deer Island Hospital with an annual salary of $1,000 along with housing on the island and room and board for himself and his family.[8] The doctor was 36 years old. With his spouse, Elizabeth Lowell Hancock, they were raising three young children, ages 7, 5, and 3.

Moriarty's resolve for the Deer Island project to succeed is manifest in his recruitment of a dependable and trustworthy steward to competently oversee the many logistical tasks critical to this daunting endeavour. On the day of his own appointment as head physician, Moriarty immediately approached James Turner, a trusted caretaker for Boston's Overseers of the Poor. As one of the Overseers, Moriarty was familiar with Turner's record of competence. Turner doubted his wife would ever agree 'to going to such a place', but promised to consult with her nonetheless. If she were willing to go, he would inform Moriarty the following morning. Her objections were strong indeed, and Turner did not bother to visit Moriarty who 'supposed that was the end of the matter'. Moriarty, however, was not done. On the following evening, a knock came to the door of the Turners' Charlestown home. Mrs Turner, alone in the house at the time, answered to find her husband's boss, Dr Joseph Moriarty, and another overseer. Moriarty pleaded with Mrs Turner for her consent so that the new hospital would have the benefit of her husband's experience and skills. He promised that her duties would not include having to go among the sick, and that he, in fact, did not want her to do so. She agreed, 'after considerable persuasion', to go if her husband so wished.[9] The next day, Thursday, 27 May, found Turner on the island preparing facilities for the large intake of patients shortly to follow. On opening day, the 29 May, the committee unanimously affirmed Turner as permanent Steward at a salary of $600 with board for himself and his family. They also made a decision that would dictate where Turner would spend a great deal of time performing his most poignant duty on the island: 'By unanimous consent of the Committee a Burial Ground was located near the north west corner of the most northerly hill on the island'.[10] Turner and his crew would soon be busy there.

To transport 'sick and pauper emigrants' in the city to the island hospital, the committee purchased a sloop, the *Betsy Ransom*, and procured for it a berth at Long Wharf.[11] Patient population grew dramatically in the coming weeks, as the *Betsy Ransom* daily transferred typhus victims from Long Wharf, and vessels from Europe and the Maritimes, anchored in quarantine, multiplied off the southern tip of Deer Island. In late June, the *Boston Advertiser* reported 24 vessels in anchorage awaiting medical evaluation of 2,000 emigrant passengers on the island's quarantine ground.[12] In mid-July, with the hospital inmate population exploding, the committee raised Moriarty's salary to $1,200 and appointed Dr Thomas Welsh, fresh out of medical school, to serve as Assistant Physician for $600 plus room and board.[13]

As Superintendent of Alien Passengers for the port of Boston for the previous ten years, Calvin Bailey was charged with administering the law for registering and regulating the arrival of immigrants in the harbour. State legislation in 1837 had created the position to manage a revenue stream from emigrant vessels to cover the city's costs for the care of foreign paupers, and to ensure that the most abjectly indigent aboard were bonded against public liability. Appointed soon after the law was passed, Bailey would spend the next decade processing tens of thousands of immigrants arriving on thousands of vessels, charging the shipmaster a two dollar 'head money' commutation fee for each passenger landed. What he never did until 1847 was slap a $1,000 bond on shipowners for every pauper they brought into port, as provided in the statute, covering charges for their public support over ten years.

In 1837, however, city government had seen fit to forgo bonding requirements in favour of using head money to subsidize foreign pauper relocation to other jurisdictions where there were friends, relatives or employment, or even back to their country of origin—thus obviating Boston's potential liability for their support as paupers. The environment of 1847 bore scant appreciation for such creatively economical humanitarianism. The major political embarrassment it instead engendered for city government resulted in his eventual firing, and henceforth in the strict enforcement of the law's bonding provision, at least in the most obvious cases of passenger indigence. Now, with new quarantine procedures at Deer Island, the committee specifically instructed Bailey to 'notify all pilots to bring every emigrant ship to an anchorage on the south side of Deer Island, the said vessels to remain there until duly examined by the Port Physician and the sick are removed, and furthermore [in a pointed allusion to the bonding requirement] to see that all other provisions of the alien passengers law are enforced'.[14] Simultaneously, to inform the shipping industry of the change in policy and practice, the Board of Aldermen ordered the Mayor to print 100 copies of the law, and to forward them 'to the American Consuls at Liverpool and other

English and Irish ports to be by them placed in the hands of ship owners and masters for their information and guidance'.[15] Bailey began to levy pauper bonds on vessels that had arrived in April and May, but through July, when forced to resign, continued underwriting the transmigration of the foreign poor.[16]

Dr Jerome Von Crowninshield Smith, Boston's long-time Port Physician, was known publicly by the initials of his given name, 'J.V.C. Smith'. An outspoken vaccine advocate in past smallpox outbreaks, wags delighted in rechristening him 'Just Vaccinate the Children' Smith. An active man of diverse talent, Smith was an accomplished author, medical journal editor, travel journalist and amateur sculptor. In the 'Know-Nothing' electoral sweep of 1854, Boston voters would elect him Mayor on the 'American', or Know-Nothing ticket. His long experience as Port Physician likely kindled his opposition to allowing paupers into the country but, unlike many Know-Nothings, he apparently harboured inappreciable religious bigotry, seeing that he sculpted a bust of Bishop Fitzpatrick.[17] Transferring from his long-time post on Rainsford Island, he would now oversee the new quarantine station on the southern tip of Deer Island. As Port Physician, his task was to examine all vessels entering the harbour for any 'malignant' diseases found among passengers and order their removal to the hospital. Following three days' anchorage in quarantine free of further outbreaks, the ship could then enter the port with its apparently healthy passengers (although many of these would soon display symptoms and be returned to the island).[18]

Apart from Moriarty's first report on 6 June, his surviving documentation in June and July is scarce. The large patient population in the hospital's first two months and the medical attention they demanded may explain the absence of reports from Moriarty in this period. On 13 August, the Committee instructed Moriarty 'to make a weekly return of the condition of the sick in the hospitals at Deer Island, and that the said returns be made to the secretary every Thursday Morning'.[19] On 18 August, Moriarty duly reported that since 29 May there had been 1,373 admitted, 731 discharged, 122 deaths, 13 brought ashore dead, and one person 'absconded'.[20] With the exception of a stillborn child and one case of diarrhea, all the deaths were ascribed to typhus.[21]

In early August 1847, the ship *Iowa* arrived at Deer Island after a month's journey from Liverpool. Aboard were the McCarthy family from Sligo: Patrick and Alice, in their forties, with seven sons ranging from 13 years to six months. Five-year-old Patrick later in life wrote of his family's harrowing and tragic experience emigrating to Boston. On the eve of their departure, someone broke a hole in the thatch roof of their cottage and ran off with a large side of bacon meant to sustain the family on their journey to America. Presumably, saving himself from starvation, the thief deprived the family of the sustenance that may have averted the deaths that robbed the boy of his parents and two siblings on Deer Island. Through the eyes of his five-year-old self, Patrick recalled the much-traveled route of the Famine emigrant: the cattle boat to Liverpool—a cruel and galling symbol, played many thousands of times, of people and food exported from Ireland on the same boat. Following the stay at Liverpool and the Atlantic journey, the family landed at Deer Island, where a large tent on the quarantine ground failed to shelter them from the rain. City death records reveal his 3-year-old brother Philip dying of typhus on the island on 9 August, and the infant, Peter, of diarrhea, on 2 September. On the 7th of the month, Patrick and his brother John were walking about the grounds when their father opened a window, crying, and calling to them that their mother was dead. 'A few days after this happened', Patrick wrote, 'I noticed a large striped plaid dress of my mother's, hanging on a line out of doors, and stood looking at it for a long while. A woman came to take it away and I made a vigorous outcry of protest and was hustled off somewhere'.[22] Six months later, his father died at the hospital of a fever relapse. After release from the island the orphans, sheltered and fed by relatives and Catholic charities, survived the streets of Boston, except younger brother James, taken by cholera at the Fort Hill Hospital in 1849. Up against such a childhood, Patrick McCarthy would nonetheless one day obtain a law degree from Harvard and be elected Mayor of Providence, Rhode Island.[23]

On the day the McCarthy family disembarked from the *Iowa* at Deer Island, the city took from the vessel's captain a $1,000 bond on each of its 23 passengers, including Patrick's mother and two younger brothers. The requirement for ship-owners to bond indigent passengers had been on the statute books for ten years, but not until the Famine influx of 1847 was it enforced. In April 1847, as legions of desperately poor and frequently sick foreign emigrants suddenly appeared on Boston's streets and at the doors of public institutions, petitions poured into the State House and to City Hall demanding measures to stem the admission of foreign paupers to the Commonwealth, including enforcement of the bonding mandate. Called to testify before a State Senate committee, Calvin Bailey admitted that he had never levied pauper bonds in more than six instances since 1837: 'My only plea is humanity', he responded when asked why he permitted such evasion of the law, 'and if you were to see them dying and suffering, as I do, on their arrival, I doubt whether you could deny them the privilege of landing'.[24]

However, city records reveal that at the very beginning, the municipal government had authorized his alternative to pauper bonds. Instead of bonding, Bailey used a portion of head money revenue to underwrite journeys of the foreign poor to other towns and states, or back to Ireland and Canada to be with friends and families. This, the City Fathers found a more palatable solution than forcing people to remain in Boston's waterfront slums where opportunity was limited, and where emigrants were more likely to become a public charge.[25] The benefit of this nuanced approach to pauper management was understandably invisible to 1847 taxpayers. Bailey's manner of dispensing human kindness to unsupported foreign paupers at public expense generated increasing public indignation, and not just among radical nativists. It had an unnerving impact among relatively more tolerant middle-class taxpayers who were otherwise 'not unmindful of their obligations as Christians to suffering humanity'. Freely admitting indigents to the House of Industry without the support of a ship-master's bond was:

> not only taxing our citizens for their maintenance, but spreading disease, pestilence and death amongst our own virtuous but unfortunate poor at [the city's institutions in] South Boston [and] endangering the health and lives of the keepers of those institutions and the whole community.[26]

The widespread perception of the egregiousness of his practice won influence for the radical nativists, whose petitions for Bailey's dismissal ultimately forced the city to replace him.[27] Under duress from state and city lawmakers in April and May, and his job at stake, Calvin Bailey was at last compelled to take passenger bonds from the masters or owners of emigrant vessels. On 20 May, he began by tracking down the owners of the *Thomas W. Sears* (whose arrival with sick and dying passengers on 2 April was made notorious by press coverage) and retroactively procuring bonds on ten of its passengers.[28] From April through July, when his tenure came to an end, his reports show $27,178 taken in head money from 13,627 passengers, 637 bonds taken from vessels on paupers they brought in, $2,378.43 expended on the journeys of about 700 people out of Boston, and $22,696.09 paid into the City Treasury.[29]

Ship owners or captains nearly always complied with the city's demands to bond indigent passengers. There were exceptions, which on occasion could lead to angry, even physical confrontations. On 17 May, presumably for the first time ever, an emigrant vessel, the brig *Mary* from Cork with 46 steerage passengers, was refused landing in Boston Harbor for failure to post bonds on paupers. Learning they were to be diverted to Halifax, passengers seized control of the windlass and handspikes, and attempted to take over the brig before the anchor could be weighed. A crew commanded by Captain Sturgis from the Federal revenue cutter *Hamilton*, armed with cutlasses, quickly put down the insurrection, and by evening, the *Mary*, with its disappointed passengers, was on its way to Nova Scotia. The *Boston Advertiser* sympathized with 'the unfortunate passengers': their resistance was 'not to be wondered at, when it is considered that they were not landed at the termination of the voyage, but forced to go in an entirely different direction from what they contemplated'. Yet, rules had to be followed and laws enforced, the paper declared, 'however painful the duty may be' to Captain Sturgis and his officers.[30]

Outraged by 'such a shameful, villainous transaction', the editors of the *Pilot* castigated city government for a heartless act of inhumanity, starkly contrasting it with the compassionate benevolence that launched the *Jamestown's* mission of mercy to the starving of Cork only weeks before. They hoped 'that the worthy Captain can reconcile the performance of this obligation to his conscience and sense of brotherly love and charity. After all, 'no man is obliged to draw a cutlass upon starving strangers'. The *Pilot* acknowledged the city's obligation to take measures protecting the health and welfare of its citizens, 'but in the name of humanity, let them not repel the supplications of the perishing; let them not cast off fellow-beings, merely because they are destitute and hungry; let not poverty be a crime deserving the scorn and retribution of the City Government'. They would 'trust that another instance of this extremely nice and scrupulous sense of duty will not again be recorded in this city'.[31]

Thereafter, an occasional emigrant vessel would be turned away, though not at the point of a cutlass. In June, passengers on the brig *Seraph* prevented the harbour pilot from boarding, when told they were being sent to Saint John, New Brunswick. After weeks anchored in the harbour, with many aboard 'very sick' and provisions low, acting British Consul William Elliott boarded the vessel and arranged for relief supplies. Mollified by the Captain's promise they would be given tickets back to Boston from Saint John, the insurgent passengers allowed the pilot to board and get the vessel under way.[32] On 2 July, the barque *Scotland* arrived with 190 souls 'in a most destitute and wretched condition', 17 of them sick and the ship's steward 'very sick'.[33] Initially refused landing, the vessel was allowed entry on 6 July only after the captain obtained financing to make bond on 40 passengers.[34]

On 14 June, the Alien Passengers Committee employed 36-year-old North End resident Jotham Bradley Munroe to assist Calvin Bailey in the arduous task of processing increasingly large numbers of incoming alien passengers. In July, he succeeded Bailey as Superintendent when Bailey was forced to resign. From his date of hire to the end of the year, Monroe would board over 300 arriving vessels, collect head money on more than 12,000 passengers, and take bonds from ship captains for the support of over 900 paupers.[35] Enforcement of pauper bonding regulations may have discouraged emigrant shipping to Boston from Liverpool and Irish ports. October and November witnessed a steep decline in the arrival of these vessels. From 29 September to 29 November, Munroe registered a total of 104 vessels from all ports, and processed 4,717 emigrants aboard. Only 11 of these vessels came from Liverpool and none from Ireland. Those from Liverpool brought in a mere 914 passengers, nearly 600 of whom were aboard five large ships.

Well over half the emigrants to Boston in this period arrived from Eastport, Maine on a single steamship, the *Admiral*. Eastport thus manifestly outpaced Liverpool as an alien passenger port of origin in these two months, as the steamer's eight trips brought 2,653 passengers, triple the total number from Liverpool.[36] Eastport bordered New Brunswick where many thousands of Irish emigrants arrived from Ireland and Liverpool with plans for a second leg of their journey to Boston. For the previous three years Captain Rogers had dominated this market with the Steamer *Portland*, owned by prominent Boston merchant, James Cunningham. By 1847 demand was such that Cunningham replaced the *Portland* with the *Admiral* and its far more ample passenger capacity.

Of the 76 passengers bonded in the period, 75 arrived aboard two Liverpool ships packed with Irish emigrants in miserable circumstances. Both arrived on 22 October: the *Sarah & Louisa*, with 237 passengers, 65 bonded; and the *Mary Ann* with 154 passengers, ten bonded.[37] All the bonded passengers were sick, mostly with typhus, and admitted to Deer Island Hospital. Unlike the ships of Liverpool, the *Admiral* refused to bond indigent passengers. Denying entrance to 80 paupers, Munroe compelled the healthy among them to remain aboard the steamer, while the sick were conveyed to the hospital for medical attention. All were eventually returned back northward aboard the *Admiral*.[38] Cunningham likely calculated it would be more economical to return paupers as ballast to Eastport than to fund their public support in Massachusetts.

While the overall numbers of typhus cases began to lessen after the summer's horrific crest, the scourge was not leaving any time soon. The disease remained prevalent among the hundreds interned in the hospital and persisted as the major cause of death. Joining Moriarty's medical team in August was 27-year-old physician Dr. J.B. (Jabez Baxter) Upham, already a seasoned typhus fighter after months battling the disease in the House of Industry since early spring. In February 1848, *The Boston Medical and Surgical Journal* would publish his accounts of a sampling of the hundreds of cases he had treated at both South Boston and Deer Island. At the time, little was known about the cause of the malady. He hoped his descriptions of patient symptoms and postmortem analyses would 'serve to elucidate the pathology, the habits and treatment of this disease'. Graphically detailing the symptoms and treatment of select patients, he describes their ordeal, demonstrating how the illness could be fatal even in 'an instance of direct contagion occurring in a subject of vigorous health, of fearless disposition and well-tested powers of endurance'. Typical among the multiple agonies of the disease were 'increasing prostration'; 'constant and harassing pain in the head, back and limbs'; 'hot skin, restlessness, considerable nausea and unease in the stomach'; 'dizziness'; 'little sleep except with larger doses of morphine'; 'much apathy and stupor'; 'tongue uniformly covered with a foul yellowish-brown coat'; eruption of 'maculae' on the body; 'delirious at intervals, manifested by low muttering'; 'face of leaden hue, dull and stupid'; 'no appetite [but] much thirst'; 'much restlessness and jactitation'; and 'urine and faeces passed involuntarily'. After a fortnight of such agonies, a patient might feel better after a quiet night and appear to improve. However, while patients did recover, a premature return to a regular diet during a promising convalescence frequently resulted in a horrendous gastric relapse and death.[39] Such was the suffering of hundreds at Deer Island Hospital in these months, and such was the challenge for its doctors and nurses in the care of these sufferers.

Wherever there were famine fever hospitals, doctors and staff themselves were at risk of its contagion, and mortality among them was inevitable. In 1847 and much of 1848, having swept through Ireland's famine-stricken areas, typhus chased refugees to wherever they fled: workhouses, the docks and slums of Dublin, Belfast, Glasgow, Liverpool, the eastern seaboard of the United States and, most horrifically, Quebec's quarantine station on the St Lawrence River island of Grosse Île. In all these places medical personnel contracted the disease, and many died. More than an academic exercise, Upham composed his essays to help prepare fellow physicians now called upon to fight this repugnant ailment. 'The whole subject demands the attention of the medical community', he asserted. Typhus, he observed, 'has proved particularly fatal in this country whenever it has assailed the ranks of our profession'.[40] This, he had just personally experienced first-hand when typhus attacked both Dr Moriarty and Dr Welsh in early December 1847. Welsh recovered, but Joseph Moriarty, a highly regarded physician and public servant and much beloved of his staff, passed away on 4 December amongst his young family at the Hancock Mansion on Beacon Hill.

The Committee responded swiftly to the hospital's loss, sending out the city's head Consulting Physician, Dr. Henry Grafton Clark, pending a new Superintendent. Convalescents, Clark reported, were now separated from the sick, men from women and children, beds and ward arrangements were better organized, buildings were cleaned and ventilated, and empty beds were made ready for new patients. Stoves were provided to alleviate the cold and help stem typhus and 'fever lungs' appearing in the sheds at Deer Island's southern point, where passengers waited for their ships to clear quarantine. Clark made a number of recommendations including little tables be placed next to patients' beds to enhance overall neatness, more cows to make the island self-sufficient for milk, curbing the Alien Passengers Superintendent's attempts to preempt duties beyond his jurisdiction, investigating 'the improper use of intoxicating liquor' which had resulted in 'several accidents' involving the *Betsy Ransom*, and limiting visiting clergy access 'only to those really in peril of death, & only under the direction & by the express permission of the Physician', or otherwise 'the committee will find it necessary for various reasons to prohibit them altogether'. He extolled the institution's success. Deaths had 'been less by more than 50 per cent than at other Emigrant Hospitals in the country'. Its location had been an act of 'prudent and intelligent foresight' with its 'favoring gales from the sea' facilitating fresh air and ventilation. He praised Dr Moriarty: 'To fill so difficult a post to the satisfaction of all parties and to obtain the confidence of all, as he did, is abundant proof of his faithfulness and ability'. He commended the Alien Passengers Committee: 'No one can calculate the amount of disease and misery which the city had been saved by the erection and wise conduct of the Hospitals under the charge of this committee'.[41]

The Committee appointed Joseph's brother John, a tall, stout man of 300 pounds, to succeed him. Some sources say John Moriarty was 'extremely generous, a thorough gentleman, marked for his geniality', and that the Irish admired Moriarty for his commitment to caring for immigrants.[42] The new Dr Moriarty was, however, not so popular among his late brother's senior staff. The steward, James Turner, resigned early on, unhappy with his new terms of service, which assumed his wife would become hospital matron, and at not being paid for burying 365 bodies.[43] Intense personality conflict with the new Superintendent led Dr Welsh to resign later in the year. Job descriptions developed by Moriarty, however, suggest a humane disposition toward his immigrant charges. They bound the head physician to 'give all requisite personal attention to their medical, moral and physical treatment, and to their regimen and diet'; to protect the money of the patients while they were on the island; to keep proper medical records on each patient; to ensure 'neatness, economy and order' in the facilities; and manage the hospital's finances. The Steward and the Matron were responsible for supervising the attendants and for administering to the non-medical needs of the male and female patients respectively. They were to 'receive ... patients when brought to the Island, and see that they are properly prepared ... that they are kindly treated, and their food is properly served and distributed, that their apartments are kept clean and in good order and properly warmed and ventilated'.[44]

In February 1848, a drop in inmate population prompted a 50 per cent staff cut.[45] Typhus persisted, but its decline as a virulent epidemic may be traced through falling numbers in the monthly hospital reports. During that year, the population never reached 300 except for two weeks in early January 1848 when 91 passengers were admitted from a single ship, the *St Petersburg*. By summer, patient numbers were down in the 100s. By autumn, the typhus epidemic abated significantly. In November, the patient population was down to three.[46] In late December 1848, with the threat of typhus epidemic from abroad now apparently contained, the City Council dissolved the Alien Passengers Committee and transferred administration of the island facility to the directors of the overcrowded and outworn House of Industry.[47] Since June 1847, Deer Island had admitted 2,820 patients, of whom 500 had died.[48] Typhus claimed 324 victims, over two-thirds of the deaths. Sixty died of diarrhea (12 per cent), 50 of dysentery (10 per cent), and 54 of a wide array of other maladies (11 per cent).[49]

The House of Industry in South Boston meanwhile bulged with more than 600 people crammed into its aging, dingy, ill-ventilated wards. Its directors pleaded with the City Council to address unprecedented overcrowding that was aggravating disease. Applicant numbers were at an all-time high. The directors predicted that appalling conditions in immigrant neighbourhoods would drive even more to the workhouse in the coming winter and oblige the city 'to provide for a greater number than ever before of wholly dependent paupers'. The place simply could not take any more inmates safely.[50] The city finally decided to transfer municipal institutions in South Boston to Deer Island and construct a permanent building to house them, a propitious development for South Boston residents, who for years wanted their neighbourhood rid of these places.

Within four years construction was completed on the new House of Industry, an architecturally significant structure designed by world renowned architect Gridley J. F. Bryant in consultation with Louis Dwight of the Prison Discipline Society.[51] For decades, medical services continued on the island for an evolving complex of institutions serving the indigent, the disabled, the orphaned, the truant, the delinquent and others in need of such special attention. John Moriarty remained head doctor on the island assuming additional duties of Port Physician in 1850, and Superintendent of the House of Industry in 1854.[52] By 1892, the city had disbursed these services elsewhere, handing island facilities over to the House of Correction, the last city institution on the island, lasting another 100 years.[53] The large Gridley J. F. Bryant building continued in use until all institutional structures were razed in 1991 to make way for a giant, court-mandated sewage treatment plant, with its widely visible cluster of enormous, egg-shaped sewage digesters, which politician and convivial latter-day Brahmin John Winthrop Sears sardonically critiqued as Boston harbour's 'Statue of Liberty'.

Boston's 'famine heroes' were the municipal government and its officials and workers. They served their community protecting public health against horrific, epidemic-threatening illness. They instituted effective and economical policies and procedures for the administrative and financial management of so sudden and severe an emergency. In procuring a harbour island hospital and affording 'all the necessary measures for the support of foreign paupers', the city was running up against policy trends of the state, which over time was trying to reduce its remuneration to towns for the care of foreign paupers. Increasingly, the state was linking poverty with immigration and through a series of enactments gradually centralizing responsibility for alien passengers under its control.[54] In May 1848, the State legislature repealed the 1837 Alien Passengers Act, replacing it with legislation requiring head money to be paid into the State Treasury instead of the City Treasury. This put the city in a quandary. Repeal of the 1837 law meant the termination of the Alien Passengers Committee's powers and duties. Without head money revenue collected under that statute, how would the city manage the 'constant influx of foreigners ... who are infected with a disease dangerous to the public health who must be provided for?'[55] To the rescue came the City Solicitor with the ingenious solution that the committee reconstitute itself under a separate law that required local boards of health to remove infectiously ill foreigners 'to a separate house or otherwise, and by providing nurses and other assistance and necessaries'. If the indigent person or their family could not pay for the services and lacked 'settlement' in a Massachusetts municipality, then the Commonwealth would have to foot the bill. In a moment, the City Council Joint Committee on Alien Passengers was voted out of, and back into, existence; John Moriarty was re-hired as Resident Physician and Superintendent of Deer Island Hospital; and J.B. Munroe, though now a state employee, continued his duties as Superintendent of Alien Passengers for the Port of Boston.[56]

Testament to the work of the city came from none other than the mouthpiece of Boston's Irish community. The Boston *Pilot*, the widely read voice of Boston's Irish, applauded the city government for its emigrant hospital on Deer Island, especially when regarded in the light of the catastrophic emigrant landing in Canada. On 4 December 1847, coincidentally the day Joseph Moriarty died, the *Pilot* praised:

> ...[T]he timely precaution taken by our City Authorities to procure a hospital for the sick immediately on their arrival. And we say it with pride and pleasure, that in no part of the country are the poor creatures attended with more care than at the hospital on Deer Island. Had the Canadian Authorities taken the same precautionary means that were taken in New York and Boston, hundreds of lives might have been saved.[57]

Courageous and self-sacrificing individuals heroically garrisoned the front lines of the crisis at the risk and sometimes loss of their lives. Joseph Moriarty lost his, caring for his emigrant patients. Captain Ellis and his crewman James Knell aboard the sloop *Betsy Ransom* lost theirs bringing the sick from Long Wharf to hospital care on the island.[58] Captain Daniel Chandler, famously converting to Catholicism on his deathbed, lost his, managing the typhus-ravaged House of Industry. The families of these heroes in the vanguard lost their loved ones.

Calvin Bailey, Boston's Superintendent of Alien Passengers from June 1837 to July 1847, survived the Famine years, but, unjustly, his job and professional reputation did not. Bailey had practically never taken bonds from shipmasters that would indemnify the City Treasury for expenses on foreign paupers. He instead used a portion of head money revenue to assist thousands to journey on to their desired destinations, and thereby relieve the city of expense if they remained in Boston and joined the relief rolls. Ignoring the good he had done helping people get to where they needed to go, nativists effectively scapegoated him by associating the influx of paupers with Bailey's allowance of the unbonded poor into port. By way of a mass petition drive, they impelled the city to force his resignation.[59]

While Bailey's loss of employment and reputation was unjust, though not lethal, the new Alien Passengers Superintendent would make the supreme sacrifice. Typhus, while subsiding as an epidemic by late 1848, continued to lurk among emigrant vessels, and in 1853 killed Bailey's successor, J.B. Munroe. Working through the remainder of the core years of the Famine, Munroe dutifully took bonds from shipowners and captains on emigrants who clearly demonstrated insolvency and dependence. But he was no nativist. He was, rather, a diligent civil servant working to ensure that money expended on foreign paupers was borne by those who profited from bringing them. And according to the *Pilot*, no city official was a better friend to the Irish immigrant. He had assisted many new arrivals in their search for lost friends and relatives. Frequently did the *Pilot's* weekly advertisements for missing persons direct informants to contact 'J.B. Munroe, Alien Commissioner' at his Long Wharf office. His esteem in the Irish community could not be more affirmatively declared than by the Irish Emigrant Society's resolutions upon Munroe's untimely death: 'That as friends of the emigrant we deeply lament the loss of one who ever discharged the duties of his office with humane and charitable feelings blending with humanity the highest public good, and winning the approbation of the most zealous friend of the lowly stranger'; and 'That in the death of Mr. Munroe, the State loses an active and efficient officer; the emigrant, a warm and tried friend; and society, an honorable man'. An extraordinarily ecumenical cortege proceeded from his funeral services at the Old North Church to the Old Granary Burial Ground. The Columbian Artillery, the militia company consisting almost exclusively of Irishmen under the command of Captain

Thomas Cass led the procession, followed by 'the Ex–15 Engine company, Veteran Fire Association, Chief Engineers of the department, members of the city government, police, and citizens'. At the Granary, the Irish company fired a volley over the grave.[60]

This chapter closes with the hope that this work expands perspectives on Boston's Irish Great Famine experience. Its burgeoning Irish population from 1847 would profoundly change the social, economic and political face of the city, and set off decades of ethnic, religious and political tensions in an abrasive coexistence with the native majority. The anger, consternation and dismay stirred by the influx of mendicant famine refugees still colour popular perception of the nineteenth century native community. Government archives and other sources show a more complex picture: a city government taking responsibility for large numbers of sick and indigent foreign refugees suddenly landed in its harbour and on its streets; providing for their medical care, food and shelter; and accepting the risks and suffering the personal sacrifices that went along with the job.

NOTES

1. Forbes to Maria Edgeworth, 28 June 1847, Robert Bennet Forbes' Jamestown Papers, Letter Books 2/65, Massachusetts Historical Society.
2. Boston College Newspapers, Boston *Pilot* (1838–1857), *https://newspapers.bc.edu/*, 4 Dec. 1847 (Hereafter cited as *Pilot*.)
3. City of Boston *City Documents 1847, no. 26*, 'Resignation of Mr. Hillard as President of the Common Council'.
4. Four 'Aldermen and Eleven Common Councilors. Records of the City Council Joint Committee on Alien Passengers, City of Boston Archives (hereafter cited as 'JCAP'), minutes, 18 May 1847.
5. JCAP minutes, 18, 20 May 1847.
6. Ibid., 29 May 1847.
7. G. Andrews Moriarty, 'The Moriarty Family of Salem, Mass.', Phillips Library, Peabody Essex Museum, *New England Historical and Genealogical Register*, vol. 101, p. 219.
8. JCAP Minutes, 25 May 1847.
9. JCAP Correspondence, James R. Turner to City Council Alien Passengers Committee, 21 Feb. 1848.
10. JCAP Minutes, 29 May 1847.
11. Ibid., 11 June 1847.
12. New York *Evening Post*, 29 June 1847: www.newspapers.com/clip/14167826/account-of-the-seraph-from-cork-being/
13. JCAP Minutes, 16 July 1847.
14. Ibid., 24 May 1847.

15. City of Boston Archives, City Council Alderman dockets, 1847.0001. J.3.
16. Calvin Bailey quarterly reports, 1847 July 03, September 14, City of Boston Archives, City Council Alderman dockets, 1847.0001.G2, 1847.0001.G.3.
17. https://johnjburnslibrary.wordpress.com/2015/07/20/jerome-van-crowninshield-smith/; Oscar Handlin, *Boston's Immigrants, 1790–1880: a Study in Acculturation* (Belknap Press of Harvard University Press, 1991), p. 202.
18. JCAP Minutes, 30 June 1847.
19. Ibid., 13 Aug. 1847.
20. Ibid., 18 Aug. 1847.
21. Edward W. Quill, City Archivist and William E. Brown Jr., Deputy Archivist, 'Deer Island Death/Burial Registry, 1847–1850' compiled at the request of Francis Costello, Irish Affairs Advisor to Mayor Raymond L. Flynn, 16 May 1990, City of Boston Archives.
22. *Autobiography of Patrick J. McCarthy ... Edited by his Daughter Mary Josephine Bannon* (Providence Visitors Press, RI, 1927). Photocopy of relevant chapters kindly forwarded to author by Dan O'Neil of the Massachusetts Water Resources Authority, 10 Jan. 2001. Patrick states his family was booked on the *Iowa. State Senate Documents, 1848, no.74* lists Alice and sons James and Philip as bonded passengers on the I*owa*, arriving 2 Aug. 1847. Death dates are found in City Archives list of Deer Island burials, 1847–1850, compiled in 1991 from city death registers by Quill, City Archivist, 1989–1993.
23. Ibid.
24. Report of [Senate] Joint Committee, Massachusetts Senate Document No. 109, 21 Apr. 1847, pp 8–9 (emphases in the original published document).
25. 'Mayor's Message—Alien Paupers', Eliot to City Council, 31 Aug. 1837, Aldermen Dockets, 1837–0001-B2. Joint Committee 'Report on [Mayor's] Message', 11 Sept. 1837, and order passed 28 Sept. 1837, Aldermen Dockets, 1837–0001-B1, City of Boston Archives.
26. CAP, Pelham Bonney and others, Memorial to the City Council, May 1847.
27. JCAP Minutes, May-June 1847.
28. 'The Ship Thomas W. Sears', Boston *Pilot*, 10 Apr. 1847. Report of Massachusetts General Court Joint Special Committee on Alien Passengers and Paupers, 'publishing the names of persons bonded, since Jan. 1847, together with the names of bondsmen', Senate – no. 74, 1848 March.
29. Calvin Bailey quarterly reports, 3 July, 14 Sept. 1847, op. cit.
30. 'General Intelligence', *Boston Daily Advertiser*, reprinted in the *Pilot*, 29 May 1847.
31. 'British Brig Mary', *Pilot*, 5 June 1847.
32. Ibid., 'Emigrants, Deaths, &c.', 3 July 1847; New York *Evening Post*, 29 June 1847: www.newspapers.com/clip/14167826/account-of-the-seraph-from-cork-being/
33. 'Emigrants, Deaths, &c.', Boston *Pilot*, 3 July 1847.
34. *State Senate Documents, 1848, No.74;* City Treasury Alien Passenger List, vol. 3, 1846 July-Aug.–1847, City of Boston Archives.
35. JCAP, Reports of the Superintendent of Alien Passengers, Sept. to Dec. 1847.
36. Ibid.
37. The ship *Milton* arriving from Liverpool on 22 November bonded one of its 220 passengers.

38. JCAP, Reports of the Superintendent of Alien Passengers, 23 Aug. 1847, 7, 28 Sept. The *Admiral* became liable to pay for each patient a two-dollar weekly hospital 'landing fee' established by the committee in August: JCAP, Minutes, 13 Aug. 1847.
39. J.B. Upham, M.D., 'Clinical Records and Post-Mortem Illustrations of Typhus or Ship Fever', *Boston Medical and Surgical Journal*, vol. xxxvii, no. 1, 2, 9 Feb. 1848 (original from Michigan State University, https://babel.hathitrust.org/cgi/pt?id=msu.31293016929485;view=1up;seq=20;size=125).
40. Ibid.
41. JCAP, Dr. Henry Clark to Committee relating to the condition of the hospital, 27 Dec. 1847. In 1849, Clark would lead the City's battle against the cholera epidemic, establishing and supervising the special cholera hospital on Fort Hill in the impoverished Irish waterfront neighbourhoods.
42. *The Science of Separation: Quarantine in a New Light*: http://portphysicians.blogspot.com/2010/08/john-m-moriarty.html.
43. JCAP, James R. Turner request for payment for burial services, 22 Feb. 1848.
44. Ibid., Description of duties of officers of Institution (draft), undated.
45. Ibid., List of help employed and list of persons discharged, 21 Feb. 1848.
46. Ibid., Deer Island Hospital weekly reports.
47. JCAP, Minutes, Dec. 1848.
48. JCAP, Deer Island Hospital weekly reports.
49. Quill, op. cit.
50. JCAP, Correspondence and sub-committee reports, Thomas Hollis, Chairman, Directors of the House of Industry, to City Council, 11 Sept. 1848.
51. Stanley Moss, David Amorena, Pauline Chase-Harrell, 'Memorandum: Historic survey of the Deer Island House of Correction and the Deer Island Pumping Station, Deer Island, Massachusetts' (Prepared for Camp Dresser & McKee, Inc., Boston, MA, by Boston Affiliates, Inc., 1 Oct. 1985).
52. *The Science of Separation: Quarantine in a New Light*, op.cit.
53. Marsha K. King and Beth P. Miller, 'Archaeological Investigations, Haul Road Trenching, and Disturbance Documentation of the Piggery Point Burials on Deer Island. Boston Massachusetts' (submitted to Massachusetts Water Resources Authority, Boston, MA, by The Public Archeological Laboratory, Inc., Pawtucket, RI, Jan. 1991, revised Mar. 1994).
54. Kunal M. Parker, 'From Poor Law to Immigration Law: Changing Visions of Territorial Community in Antebellum Massachusetts', in *Historical Geography*, vol. 28 (2000), pp612–85.
55. JCAP Minutes, 11, 17, 24 May 1848; 1, 7 June 1848.
56. Ibid.
57. Boston *Pilot*, 4 Dec. 1847.
58. JCAP, Minutes, 3 May 1848, 21 June 1848.
59. JCAP, Petitions, May-June 1847.
60. Boston *Pilot*, 19 Feb. 1853. Two years later, the Know-Nothing government on Beacon Hill would force the Columbian Artillery's disbandment. Cass, whose statue now stands in the Public Gardens, would lead the heroic 'Fighting Irish Ninth' in the Civil War's Peninsula Campaign, perishing from his wounds in the Battle of Malvern Hill.

CHAPTER ELEVEN

JEWS AND THE GREAT FAMINE

A link with humanity

Peter Murphy

> There is but one connecting link between us and the sufferers ... That link, my brethren, is humanity.
>
> Jacques Judah Lyons, Rabbi of Congregation Shearith Israel, 1847

From 1845 to 1852, Ireland was devastated by the greatest humanitarian disaster in the history of the island. The population of more than eight million declined by over two million people, with at least one million due to death from starvation, fever, and a myriad of other diseases. More than another million emigrated, primarily to North America.[1] As one historian has noted, 'this tragedy occurred at the heart of the vast, and resource-rich, British Empire. The imperial government, however, chose not to use its resources to come to the aid of the Irish poor'.[2] Relief did, however, come from many other sources, both from within the United Kingdom and across the globe. Donations came from Catholics, Protestants, Quakers, Hindus, royalty and politicians, the rich and the poor, and many more. The charitable giving came from countries, organizations and individuals throughout the entire globe and 'these donations cut across traditional divides of religion, nationality, class and gender'.[3]

On 23 May 2010, President Mary McAleese paid a visit to the Shearith Israel Congregation in New York City to give thanks for the congregation's generosity to the starving people of Ireland 163 years earlier. When introducing her, Niall Burgess, the Consul General of Ireland in New York in 2010, said that 'In some of the conventional histories, the story of the contributions of the Jewish community here has been lost to sight over the years'.[4] Yet, on 8 March 1847, Rabbi Jacques Judah Lyons, the chazan (cantor) had held a meeting at Shearith Israel to appeal for support for the 'relief of the famishing thousands of their fellow mortals in that unfortunate and destitute country, Ireland'.[5] This act of generosity by the Jews of New York and elsewhere, has been little studied by scholars. Yet they were deeply involved in giving aid, both in America as well as in England. As early as October 1847, an Irish provincial newspaper stated that 'when Ireland was in great distress, the Jews helped them', singling out Baron Rothschild for praise.[6] The generosity and compassion shown by Jewish people from both sides of the Atlantic was unusual as they had little reason to involve themselves in the Irish tragedy other than a sense of compassion and empathy. While it is understandable that Irish ex-patriots living in faraway places such as Calcutta and Boston would raise substantial sums and donate clothing and food to the relief efforts, what would motivate groups such as Jewish Congregations in New York, Charleston and elsewhere? What would lead one of Europe's most influential and powerful Jewish bankers to organize a relief committee to help a population that consisted of only a few hundred Jews?

The history of a Jewish presence in Ireland can be traced back to the *Annals of Innisfallen*, thought to have been written during the eleventh century. The first known reference to Jews arriving in Ireland is made in 1079: 'Five Jews came are later mentioned from over sea with gifts to Tairdelbach, and they were sent back again over sea'.[7] Jews resided in Ireland around the time of Richard de Clare's (nicknamed Strongbow) arrival in 1170. Henry II, king of England, 'acknowledged their presence by assigning custody of the King's Judaism in Ireland to one of his Lords in 1174' and protected 'their rights to free exercise of their religion guaranteed and their businesses as merchants and moneylenders relatively secure'.[8] By the middle of the thirteenth century, Jewish rights had been abrogated. There is a reference in the Dublin White Book of 1241 prohibiting land transfers to Jews (*vel in Judaismo ponere*).[9] In 1714, the Irish philosopher John Toland published his treatise, 'Reasons for Naturalizing the Jews in Great Britain and Ireland, On the same foot with all other Nations: Containing also A Defence of the Jews against All Vulgar Prejudices in all Countries'. Toland argued that Jews should not be regarded as enemies and his work 'directly tackles an issue which until then had remained largely neglected: that of the conditions under which toleration could be granted to non-Christians inside a Christian state'.[10] What makes Toland's assertion even more interesting is that he had converted from Catholicism to Protestantism when aged 16 and there were very Jews in Ireland in the early eighteenth century.

Daniel O'Connell, the champion of Catholic Emancipation (the right of Catholics to sit in the British parliament), also believed in Jewish Emancipation.[11] In a letter to

Sir Isaac Lyon Goldsmid, a London financier who was one of the leaders of the fight for Jewish Emancipation in England, O'Connell wrote:

> I assure you I should be most happy, if any event should induce you to visit the 'Green Isle', to show you my sense of your kindness in the best manner in my power. Ireland has claims on your ancient race, as it is the only Christian country that I know of unsullied by any one act of persecution of the Jews.

He continued:

> On the principle of freedom of conscience, and no man can admit the sacred principle without extending it equally to the Jew as to the Christian ... you will find me the constant and active friend to every measure which tends to give the Jews an equality of civil rights with all other of the King's subjects—a perfect unconditional equality.[12]

The Irish Marriage Act of 1844 legitimized Jewish marriages according to their rites.[13] Two years later, an obsolete statute, 'de Judaismo', which prescribed a special dress for Jews, was repealed.[14] Yet, despite the long history of Jews in Ireland, their numbers were miniscule relative to the island's population, numbering only a few hundred in the mid–1840s. One source notes that by 1845, Dublin's 25 Jewish families constituted the majority of the island's Jews.[15]

During the autumn of 1846, the *Cork Examiner* carried story after story of the unfolding tragedy with headlines that read, 'Death by Starvation'; 'More Deaths from Starvation!!!'; and 'Horrible Distress in the West—Another Death from Starvation'.[16] The headlines were so unrelenting that some readers and politicians simply did not believe that this could be true. Some went to see for themselves, including Nicholas Cummins, a Justice of the Peace in Cork. A significant factor in motivating Lionel de Rothschild and others to take action to help alleviate the immense suffering occurring across the Irish Sea was a letter written by Cummins in December 1846. In the letter, addressed to the Duke of Wellington and then published in the London *Times* on 24 December 1846, Cummins described, in graphic detail, what he witnessed on his visit to Skibbereen, a small town about 80 km southwest of Cork. He wrote:

> Being aware that I should have to witness scenes of frightful hunger, I provided myself with as much bread as five men could carry ... the scenes that presented themselves were such as no tongue or pen can convey the slightest idea of ... six famished and ghastly skeletons, to all appearances dead, were huddled in a corner on some filthy straw... they were in fever, four children, a woman, and what had once been a man ...Their demonic yells are still ringing in my ears and their horrible images are fixed upon my brain.[17]

News of the suffering in Ireland prompted a global philanthropic outpouring that was unprecedented in its geographic scope. The most successful of all the relief committees to be established was founded by an English Jew, with no direct connection to Ireland. The Rothschild historian, Niall Ferguson, has written, 'perhaps the most successful gesture of public-spiritedness at this time was made by the English Rothschilds in response to the catastrophic potato blight and famine in Ireland—the worst of all calamities of the 1840s'.[18] Baron Lionel Nathan de Rothschild (1808–1879), the Jewish scion of one of the wealthiest families in the world, established the 'British Association for the Relief of Distress in Ireland and the Highlands of Scotland' at the end of 1846. He was the eldest son of Nathan Mayer Rothschild and his wife, Hannah Barent-Cohen. Lionel, unlike his father who was known for making highly speculative positions in the financial markets, concentrated on preserving the immense fortune of the Rothschild that his father had accumulated. He was described by one biographer as having 'great prudence and unfailing caution'. His father had once observed that it took a 'great deal of boldness and a great deal of caution to make a great fortune, and ten times as much wit to keep it when you have got it'.[19] Lionel was also the first practicing Jew to sit as a member of the British Parliament in the House of Commons, when this became legally possible in 1858.[20]

At the time of the Famine, the Rothschild Bank was the largest in the world. The Baron held a meeting on 1 January 1847, at the Rothschild Bank in London, which was attended by several prominent members of English society.[21] Among those in attendance were several well-known financiers, including his younger brother, Mayer Rothschild; John Abel Smith and George Robert Smith, both partners in Smith, Payne and Smiths Bank; Samuel Gurney, an English banker and Quaker philanthropist from Norwich; Henry Kingscote, a well-known cricketer and philanthropist; Thomas Baring of Baring & Co.; and the Honourable Stephen Spring Rice, an Irish civil servant who served on the Board of Customs and acted as secretary to the British Relief Association. Another Irish man, James John Cummins, a Cork-born banker who had relocated to London in 1834, served on the steering committee.[22] A few days later, David Salomons, a prominent Jewish banker and later the first Jewish mayor of London, joined the committee. Salomons was a leading proponent of Jewish Emancipation and, similar to Rothschild, would be elected to the British parliament but unable to take his seat because of his religion. Yet another eminent Jewish banker and philanthropist, Moses Montefiore, joined the committee shortly thereafter. Montefiore was connected to the Rothschilds; his wife, Judith Cohen, was the sister of Hannah Cohen Rothschild, mother of Lionel de Rothschild. He was devoutly Jewish and spent a great deal of time and money doing charitable work in

Palestine and funded the first Jewish settlement outside the walled city of Jerusalem.[23] The Association's committee ultimately consisted of a total of 22 members and was ecumenical in nature, numbering among its members Anglicans, Roman Catholics, Quakers and Jews. The Association was politically well connected, primarily with the Whig Party, which had assumed power in June 1846, in the wake of Sir Robert Peel's resignation. John Abel Smith, a close confidant of Lionel de Rothschild, was a Whig MP from Chichester and an advocate for Jewish Emancipation.[24] The Association became the largest relief organization involved in famine relief.[25] They issued a brief statement outlining the reasoning behind the formation of their body. It read, in part, that:

> Information having been received of the most distressing character, and of undoubted credibility, of the rapid progress of famine and utter destitution in many remote parishes of Ireland and Scotland ... there are but few families ... who are therefore exposed to urgent and overpowering demands for the smallest supplies of the necessaries of life, by the famishing population ... it has been determined, in dependence upon God's blessing, to form a Committee in London for the purpose of aiding the efforts made to relieve the multitudes who are suffering under the present awful calamity.[26]

Within days of the formation of the Association, more than £10,000 had been donated by its members.

Baron de Rothschild and his committee got right to work on their monumental challenge. According to the Minutes of the Association, they met daily, usually at the offices of the South Sea Company in London.[27] Quite obviously, what was needed most in Ireland and the western Scottish Highlands, was food, more especially, cheap food. A sub-committee, consisting of six members, including Rothschild, was formed to 'regulate the purchase and shipment of provisions, and the formation of depots round the coast and in the interior of the country'.[28] By early 1847, there were approximately 1,000 local relief committees established in various locales throughout Ireland. The Committee decided to take advantage of the existing machinery in place in order to expedite relief.[29] A few days after their initial meeting, the Committee obtained a ship to immediately take food to Ireland. The Peninsula and Oriental Company placed the *Royal Tar* steamship at the disposal of the Association.[30] The Great Western, the North Western, and South Western Railway Companies offered to convey on their respective lines, without charge, the supplies of food, etc., which the Association sent for shipment from the various ports of Liverpool, Bristol, and Southampton.[31] An early recipient of this relief was Father John O'Sullivan, parish priest in Kenmare. Together with the local Protestant minister, O'Sullivan had travelled to London in early February 1847 to make personal appeals on behalf of their starving congregations. Unusually, they met with both the committee of the British Relief Association and with Charles Trevelyan of the Treasury.[32] O'Sullivan struck up a strong friendship with Salomons, the two men maintaining contact throughout the famine years. In addition to receiving 105 tons of food from the Association, in May 1847, Salomons personally sent an undisclosed quantity of potatoes to O'Sullivan. The priest believed that these donations saved thousands of lives in Kenmare.[33]

By February, the Association had raised £90,000 for the 'relief of Irish distress'.[34] A few days later, a Dublin newspaper gave credit to Nicholas Cummins for raising awareness and inspiring action in England, writing that it 'would be unjust to withhold from Mr. Cummins the credit of having, in no small degree, contributed to create that consciousness'. Cummins, in a letter a few days hence, acknowledged the Association Committee's generosity when he wrote: 'I have unbounded satisfaction in being able to assure you of the glorious fact, that nine names alone in London have this day subscribed the truly noble amount of £8,000!!! Surely her merchants are princes, and her traders the honourable of the earth'.[35] Among the names that were on his list were the Rothschilds and Barings, who each gave £1,000. Another English Quaker, William E. Forster, who had traveled to Connemara with his father in the winter of 1846–47, said of the Association members: 'Rothschild, Kinnaird, and some dozen other millionaire city princes meeting every day, and working hard. A far greater sacrifice to them than mere gifts of money'.[36] According to the Association's minutes, 'all grants should be in food, and not in money. That no grant should be placed at the disposal of an individual for private distribution'. And additionally, 'That the grants from the fund should be exclusively for gratuitous distribution'.[37] Their primary targets for assistance were those who were beyond the reach of government, in particular, fatherless children and widows.[38] Food, of course, was of paramount importance and, to that end, a sub-committee was appointed, which included Baron Rothschild, to regulate the purchase and shipment of provisions, and the formation of depots round the coast and in the interior of the country. The Rothschilds devoted two of their steamers to this service.[39] Other members of the Rothschild family became involved to a lesser degree. In a letter dated 11 January 1847, Hannah, Lionel's mother, wrote to his brother Mayer:

> I am exceedingly sorry to observe the continued distressing accounts from Ireland and other places. Lionel informed me of the donations given which are very munificent and I pray that the situation of the Poor may soon be ameliorated by a plentiful supply of food ... I would willingly say, add my donation from my account.[40]

Mayer occasionally sat in for his brother at Association meetings when Lionel was not available.

One of the significant obstacles that the committee had to overcome was the contempt and hostility towards Ireland expressed by a portion of the English press. The prejudice expressed towards the Irish would have been familiar to many Jews who had also been subject to prejudice and attempts to convert them.[41] A frequent accusation levelled at the Irish poor was that their susceptibility to famines was caused by their laziness and lack of enterprise. One paper wrote that 'Notwithstanding all that is done for the relief of the Irish...they will accept neither wages nor employment—they clamour for food, to consume in riotous idleness'.[42] The *Economist* declared that the distress was 'brought on by their own wickedness and folly'.[43] The most influential paper was the *Times*, which had the largest circulation by far of any newspaper in Britain. The *Times* exerted a tremendous amount of influence, being referred to as the 'leviathan of the press'.[44] The paper took the view that the approach to relief for the Irish should be 'minimalist' as they were underserving of British support.[45] An editorial of 12 October 1847 referred to 'a case of permanent and inveterate degradation'.[46] Throughout the early years of the Famine, the *Times* was relentless in its attacks on the character of the Irish people as well as the expenditures involved. One of the paper's strategies was to minimize the extent of the crisis by arguing that the Irish were indeed wealthier than they let on. It appears that the *Times'* objective was to end the Exchequer's support for the Irish. The sums that the Association raised, along with the Quakers, is even more impressive in the face of such strong prejudice against the Irish by so many in England, especially among the influential press. Perhaps the coverage of the Famine by the British press can be best expressed as being 'coloured by traditional anti-Irish prejudice and by political and practical considerations: its general tenor was that the Irish were a backward race and lived on an inferior food—the potato; they were ungrateful and disloyal; Ireland was a drain on British resources; and Britain was being flooded with Irish paupers'.[47]

Despite so much negative press, the response to the Association's appeal was immediate. The Queen contributed £2,000, quickly followed by donations from every member of the Royal Family, including from the King of Hanover. The Queen's husband, Prince Albert, gave £500.[48] Sultan Abdülmecid I of the Ottoman Empire originally offered to send £10,000 but reduced it to £1,000 when advised by his Majesty's ministers that a gift greater in size than that of the Queen's would offend her Majesty.[49] In an undated letter of thanks to the Sultan, the Committee expressed 'our deepfelt thanks and gratitude for the munificent act of benevolence and attention lately displayed by your Majesty towards the suffering and afflicted inhabitants of Ireland'.[50] While the most financially successful, the British Relief Association was one of a number of philanthropic endeavours on behalf of the Irish poor. The Society of Friends, often referred to as the Quakers, had established the Central Relief Committee of the Society of Friends in Dublin in 1846 and raised more than $200,000 while also establishing soup kitchens throughout Ireland.[51] Individual donations included one from Rabbi Nathan Adler who encouraged members of his synagogue in London to observe the Day of Fast.[52] On that day, his sermon was entitled 'An appeal to the sympathy of his brethren for the sufferers in Ireland and in the Highlands of Scotland'.[53]

The Committee decided from the outset that they would work with the British government which they hoped would expedite the relief efforts by moving the aid through local relief agencies. During the first two years of the Famine, the official response from the British government was, in the words of a Rothschild biographer, 'half-hearted'.[54] The British response was 'constrained by previously determined interpretations of the crisis and twisted by colonialist preconceptions of the social or racial 'backwardness' of the Irish people'.[55] The person in the government who was most responsible for coordinating relief was Charles Trevelyan, the Assistant Secretary to the Treasury in Lord Russell's government. By choosing to work so closely with the government, the Association 'came under Trevelyan's powerful orbit'. Members of the Committee were meeting with him almost daily and he and Sir Charles Wood, Trevelyan's superior and Chancellor of the Exchequer, effectively controlled the distribution of the Association's funds.[56] Trevelyan's belief that the Famine was a 'stroke of an all-wise and all-merciful Providence', one which had laid 'bare the deep and inveterate root of social evil', contributed to the slow response to the hunger.[57] Lord Brougham, a former member of the House of Commons, affirmed the providential view of the Famine when he said that it was 'providence who sent the potato disease meant that they should be starved'.[58] In addition to his evangelical view of the causes, Trevelyan was a firm believer in *laissez faire* economics, which essentially meant that in the 'economic sphere individuals should be allowed to pursue their own interests and asserted that the Government should interfere as little as possible'.[59] Trevelyan expressed his doubts about the effectiveness of relief efforts when he confided to Lord Russell that 'feeling in London is so strong against the Irish that I doubt much progress will be made in London in subscriptions until further horrifying accounts are received'.[60] His warnings grossly underestimated the generosity that ensued almost immediately. He was also constantly meddling in the Association's efforts and was viewed as bureaucratic and domineering, in addition to taking a moralist view of events. Almost daily, he was sending instructions or asking questions of his agents in

Ireland and receiving updates from Sir Randolph Routh, a Commissary-General in the British Army, who had been appointed to be the Chairman of the Irish Famine Relief Commission in 1845, and corresponded with Trevelyan weekly. Routh's reports included financial information, numbers of sick and dying, and who was getting fed. It took the strong leadership of Lionel de Rothschild and his wealthy and influential colleagues to get the relief effort off the ground. Ultimately, Trevelyan ordered the local relief committees to work with the Association. The magnitude of the crisis slowly dawned on Trevelyan, leading him to inform Henry Kingscote, a member of the Committee, that 'this is a real famine and thousands of people are likely to die'. But he was also determined to be cautious in giving help: 'if the Irish once find out there are any circumstances in which they can get free government grants ... we shall have a system of mendicancy such as the world never saw'.[61]

If Trevelyan was parsimonious, Rothschild's efforts to alleviate the suffering in Ireland and Scotland extended beyond the considerable energies he spent devoted to the British Relief Association. In collaboration with Thomas Baring, his longtime rival, Rothschild negotiated a loan to the English government for £8,938,547 (the equivalent of approximately £987,000,000 in 2022) at a rate of 3 per cent per annum, which was below the bank loan rate of 5 per cent, which had been set in January 1847.[62] Lionel was perhaps following his father's example from a previous famine in 1821. The senior Rothschild, upon hearing rumors of an impending famine, had:

> alerted Lord Liverpool [the British Prime Minister, 1812–1827] to the possibility of buying American and East India Rice before speculators come into the market, the price of which is at present low and the Stock large and which in case of a deficiency of the Potato Crop would supply the numerous Poor of that Country with a wholesome food during the winter.[63]

According to the Rothschild archives, no papers relating to the loan survive in their series of loan contracts and correspondence, leading to the possibility that the loan may have been more of a private transaction by Lionel de Rothschild rather than official business of the London Rothschild bank.[64] All commissions on the loan were waived. Making such a sizable loan at below-market rates provides an indication of his generosity.

By July, upwards of three million persons were being supplied daily with food and relief operations were occurring in 1,800 Electoral Divisions. In the period from 1 January to 1 October, direct grants to relief committees amounted to about £100,000; provisions to the amount of £176,000 were imported by the Association into the country; and £56,000 was paid to the government for food taken from government depots. Several letters of appreciation were forwarded to the Association from various finance committees of Poor Law unions which, in the words of the Committee, 'afford the most satisfactory evidence that this large expenditure was not unproductive of the desired result'.[65] By 1848, funds were running low, the British government had declared the Famine all but over and contributions were drying up. In a letter to the Association on 20 August, Trevelyan said: 'I recommend that you should not form any new independent machinery, which you might find difficult to manage, and which would produce the impression that the lavish charitable system of last season was intended to be renewed'.[66] When the Association shut down operations in the summer of 1848, more than 15,000 persons had made donations through their ministrations.

Tragically, the blight continued but there was little support coming from Trevelyan or the *Times*. In a June letter to Edward Twisleton, the Poor Law Commissioner, Trevelyan wrote: 'I hasten to remark that you appear to contemplate a much more extensive system of assistance to the Unions than the government has any idea of affording'.[67] The *Times* continued its unceasing attack upon the Irish. In August, the paper remarked 'that the frame of mind created by the recent attempt at insurrection was 'not a good atmosphere for compassion for Ireland'. A few weeks later, the *Times* wrote that 'in no other country have men talked treason until they are hoarse, and then gone about begging for sympathy from their oppressors'.[68]

Across the Atlantic, raising relief funds was occurring throughout much of North America. The General Relief Committee of the City of New York was organized on 10 February 1847. Myndert Van Schaick, a prominent New York philanthropist, organized the Committee and chaired it as well. At their first meeting, he announced that $20,000 had already been subscribed. The call to local clergy was met with an enthusiastic response, with 'all denominations of Christians and also from the Jewish Synagogues gave cheerful and, in some cases, very liberal gifts'.[69] The Committee voted to work through the Central Relief Committee of the Society of Friends in Dublin as their agents. Within a few days, August Belmont, a prominent Jewish financier, politician, diplomat, as well as horse breeder and racehorse owner, gave $500.[70] Through his extensive contacts and business associates, Belmont solicited hundreds of more dollars, a significant sum in the 1840s. He also volunteered to serve on the General Relief Committee. Belmont, through his company, August Belmont & Company, served as agent for the Rothschild's business interests in the United States after their previous agent went bankrupt during the panic of 1837.[71] Contributions flowed in daily, some as small as a one dollar ('from A youth, saved out of his pocket money') and from all over America.[72]

One of the first Synagogues to contribute was the Shearith Israel on Crosby Street in New York City. Congregation Shearith Israel (Hebrew: תיראש תליהק לארשי Kehilat She'arit Yisra'el 'Congregation Remnant of Israel'), the Spanish and Portuguese Synagogue in the city of New York (then known as New Amsterdam), was the first Jewish congregation to be established in North America. The trustees of the Congregation Shearith Israel met on Sunday, 21 February 1847, to vote on a resolution to announce that a meeting would take place on 8 March 'with a view of contributing towards the relief of the famishing people of Ireland'.[73] At that gathering, Rabbi Lyons stood before his congregation in a specially convened meeting to ask for donations to help the Irish as they endured yet another year of famine in Ireland. The winter of 1846/1847 had witnessed the sharpest increase in mortality in Irish history and that year is referred to as 'Black 47'.[74] Many who brought aid were unprepared for the sheer magnitude of death and despair that they witnessed. Captain Robert Forbes of the *Jamestown*, who arrived in Cork in April 1847,[75] wrote:

> I saw enough in five minutes, to horrify me—hovels crowded with the sick and dying, without floors, without furniture, and with patches of dirty straw covered with still dirtier shreds and patches of humanity.[76]

While it is unlikely that Rabbi Lyons knew of Captain Forbes' account, he was undoubtedly reading what was being reported in the local newspapers. A few weeks before Lyons spoke to his congregation, the *New York Herald* had reported that 'the present condition of the Irish people, suffering even to death for want of food, brings out the characters of the benevolent...we are glad to see that the spirit of benevolence is at length fairly aroused'.[77]

The Rabbi embodied this benevolence. During the meeting soliciting donations for Irish Famine relief, he began by offering a prayer: 'God of the feeble, God of the needy! Thou who art the joy of the afflicted and the comfort of the distressed, have pity on our famishing and suffering fellow-creatures, whose distress to alleviate we have with thy permission here assembled'.[78] After delivering the Prayer, he spoke for nearly an hour. He asked two important questions early in the address that got to the heart of what he hoped to accomplish that night:

> Wherefore are the prejudices, the divisions, the hostility of all sects forgotten, and wherefore are found on the same platform men of all denominations, earnestly and zealously engaged in co-operating for a common object? Wherefore are the contests, the bickerings, the opinions of parties thrown aside to permit their respective partisans to act in unison for a single purpose?[79]

He described Ireland as a nation in 'distress, a nation is starving. Numbers of our fellow-creatures have perished, miserably perished from hunger and starvation'. He pointed out that little relief was offered until 'we were absolutely horrified and heart-sickened by the accounts of the distress'. The Rabbi continued by applauding those who have 'come forward with promptitude and generosity; contributions have poured in from all classes, from all sects'.

Lyons challenged those present to ask themselves whether they should donate and help others in their own community who were poor and destitute. He questioned if self-preservation was a law and a principle of nature or whether it was 'excuses which the lips utter, while they are rejected by the heart'. He suggested that the fundamental reason for giving was the connectedness that bound all peoples, which overcame 'prejudice, bigotry, fanaticism with their attendant spirits, ignorance, intolerance, and persecution cannot break it ... Forged as it was, by religion, virtue and charity it is indestructible, it is all-powerful'. He added 'that link, my brethren, is HUMANITY! Its appeal to the heart surmounts every obstacle'.[80]

Rabbi Lyons did not use the bible as a source of reasoning, nor Jewish creed or traditions.[81] Nor did he appeal to the congregations' sympathies, passions or pride. For him, it came down to one simple idea: not allowing fellow humans to suffer— 'I have attempted only to express the ONE simple truth, that the sufferings of our fellow-men, wheresoever and howsoever situated, demand from us alleviation, assistance and relief'. Later, he invoked the name of one of Ireland's heroes and martyrs, Robert Emmet:[82]

> And for whom do I plead? For Ireland, unhappy Ireland! the birthplace of that Emmet, who stood unrivalled for the splendor of his talents and the brilliancy of his legal attainments; for the land of that departed martyr, who, in the last moments of existence—ay, when his grave was opening to receive him—promulgated the noblest sentiments of the human heart, in accents soul-stirring and eloquent, in language beautiful and sublime.

He then asked:

> As American citizens, are we not under great and lasting obligations, to the people of Ireland? On the bloody field of battle, during our struggles for liberty, were there no Irishmen engaged in the contest?"

Many Irish, as well as many Jews, had fought nobly in the cause for American Independence a mere 70 years previously. Lyons continued by placing a little guilt in the minds of his listeners:

> I would ask if there is one in this holy edifice so lost to feelings of humanity, so heedless of the cries of distress, as to regard with indifference the least of God's creatures? ... Can you this evening retire to your stately mansions of affluence, your homes of quiet, and of comfort, and of plenty, and there, amid the dazzling splendour which surrounds you, forget the unhappy condition of those in whose behalf I am pleading? Can you this night repose in tranquility upon your richly-curtained couches, unconscious of the intense misery of those who have no beds to lie on? The bare earth is all their resting-place, its roots their food, some cliff their habitation.[83]

Over the course of the next few days, members of Congregation Shearith Israel donated $170.[84] The Franklin Street Synagogue in New York City donated $80 shortly thereafter.[85]

Donations came from Jews residing outside of New York, including Charleston, South Carolina. The *Baltimore Sun* reported that 'On Thursday last, the Israelites residing in Charleston, S.C., laid the corner-stone of a new synagogue and when the ceremonies usual on such occasions were concluded, a collection was taken up in aid of the distressed people of Ireland'.[86] The amount of the donation was not recorded. The Philadelphia Irish Relief Committee spearheaded the raising of funds and ferrying goods on ships departing from the city. According to the report of their executive committee, an 'appeal was made in the name of common humanity, and the response was from men, women, and children of all creeds, Jews and Christians, of every variety of religious denominations'.[87] Unfortunately, the records of the amount of the donations have been lost to posterity.

Set against the limitations of government relief, private donations assumed an even greater importance in terms of saving lives. The contributions of Jewish organizations and individuals to Irish relief efforts have been written about less than other groups, such as the Quakers, yet their efforts were monumental and significant. Whether it was the tireless work led by Baron Rothschild in England or the various synagogues and individuals in America who gave what they could, it was the idea that they would be so caring and generous towards a country that contained so few of their own that is to be remembered. What motivated Jews on both sides of the Atlantic to display such compassion and empathy? Was it a shared history of oppression? We may never fully understand what drove them to help. The answer may simply lie in what Rabbi Lyons so eloquently said: 'There is but one connecting link between us and the sufferers ... That link, my brethren, is humanity'.

NOTES

1. Kerby A. Miller, *Emigrants and Exiles: Ireland and the Irish Exodus to North America* (New York: Oxford University Press, 1985), p. 291.
2. Christine Kinealy, *Saving the Irish Poor: Charity and The Great Famine*, Open Edition Journals, Dec. 2015.
3. Christine Kinealy, 'International Relief Efforts During the Famine', *Irish America*, Aug./Sept. 2009.
4. *The New York Times*, 21 May 2010.
5. *The Occident and American Jewish Advocate*, vol. V, no. 1, Apr. 1847.
6. 'Londonderry Auxiliary for Promoting Christianity among the Jews', *Londonderry Sentinel*, 23 Oct. 1847.
7. *The Annals of Innisfallen*, author unknown, translated by Sean MacAirt, 1951.
8. Don Gifford with Robert Seidman, *Ulysses Annotated Notes for James Joyce's Ulysses* (Berkeley: University of California Press, 1988), p. 40.
9. Sir John Thomas Gilbert (1829–1898), *Historic And Municipal Documents of Ireland, A. D. 1172–1320: From the Archives of the City Dublin, Etc.* (London: Longmans, Green, and co., 1870).
10. Pierre Lurbe, *John Toland and the Naturalization of the Jews. Eighteenth-Century Ireland* / Iris an Dá Chultúr 14 (1999), 37–48, at: www.jstor.org/stable/30071409.
11. Also see chapter by Laurent Colantonio on Daniel O'Connell.
12. Lionel Abrahams, 'Sir I. L. Goldsmid and the admission of the Jews of England to Parliament', *Transactions of Jewish Historical Society of England*) 4 (1899), p. 116. www.jstor.org/stable/29777606.(1829) p. 151. Also see: Leon Huhner, 'The Jews of Ireland. An Historical Sketch', in *Jewish Historical Society of England,* 5 (1902), 226–42. www.jstor.org/stable/29777636. p. 239.
13. 'An Act for Marriages in Ireland', Amendment XII (1846).
14. Huhner, 'The Jews of Ireland. An Historical Sketch,' p. 239.
15. 'Jewish Life in Ireland contradictory historian says here', *The Jewish News of Northern California*, 5 June 1998.
16. 'Death by Starvation', *Cork Examiner*, 16 Oct. 1846; Jeremiah O'Callaghan, *Cork Examiner*, 'More Deaths from Starvation', 28 Oct. 1846; *Cork Examiner*, 'Awful State…', 11 Dec. 1846.
17. *The Times*, 24 Dec. 1846.
18. Niall Ferguson, *The House of Rothschild Money's Prophets 1798–1848* (New York: Penguin Books, 1999), p. 443.
19. John Reeves, *The Rothschilds: The Financial Rulers of Nations* (Chicago: A.C. McClurg & Co., 1887), p. 206.
20. Even though he was elected several times in the 1840s and 1850s, he was not allowed to take his seat because he refused to take the oath on a Christian Bible, asking instead to use a Hebrew Bible. Finally in 1858, the *Jews Relief Act* was passed, and each member was allowed to take their seat for 'any Person professing the Jewish Religion, [to] omit the Words 'and I make this Declaration upon the true Faith of a Christian'. *Jews Relief Act 1858*, Sec. 1.

21. There appears to be some confusion as to where the initial meeting took place on 1 Jan. 1847. According to the Minute Books of the British Relief Association (NLI, MS 2022), as referenced in Christine Kinealy's *Charity and The Great Hunger in Ireland. The Kindness of Strangers* (London: Bloomsbury, 2013), p. 168, the meeting took place at Rothschild's Bank in St Swithin's Lane in London. According to the *Rothschild Family Archives*, it occurred at Lionel de Rothschild's home.
22. James John Cummins (1795–1867) was a director of the Union Bank of Australia. He was a student of Hebrew and Theology. See: www.hymntime.com/tch/bio/c/u/m/m/cummins_jj.htm
23. 'Rabbi Menachem Levine, Sir Moses Montefiore: A Brief History' (Aish.com).
24. H. T. Easton, 'The History of a Banking House: Smith, Payne, and Smiths' (London: Blades, East & Blades, 1903), p. 26. Abel Smith would later introduce Lionel De Rothschild to members of the British Parliament on 26 July 1858.
25. Kinealy, *Charity*, p. 167.
26. *British Association for the Relief of the Extreme Distress in Ireland and Scotland. Report: With Correspondence of the Agents, Tables, &c., And a List of Subscribers*. BRA Report (London: R. Clay, 1849), Appendix C., p. 171.
27. Kinealy, *Charity*, p. 169. See: f.n. Minutes of BRA, 4 Jan. 1847, p. 8.
28. *Report of BRA*, p. 16.
29. Ibid., p. 13.
30. *London Evening Standard*, 21 Jan. 1847, p. 3.
31. *Coleraine Chronicle*, 30 Jan. 1847, p. 4.
32. See chapter by Colm Kenny on John of Kenmare.
33. Colm Kenny, *Kenmare. History and Survival. Father John O'Sullivan and the Famine Poor* (Dublin: Eastwood, 2021), pp 85–105.
34. *Tuam Herald*, 13 Feb. 1847, p.4.
35. *Warder and Dublin Weekly Mail*, 9 Jan. 1847, p. 2.
36. T. Wemyss Reid, *Life of the Right Honourable William Edward Forster* (London: Chapman and Hall, 1888), p. 186.
37. *Report of BRA*, p. 14.
38. *Minutes of BRA*, 1 Jan. 1847, pp. 2–3, as referenced in Christine Kinealy's 'The British Relief Association and the Great Famine in Ireland' in *Revue Française de Civilisation Britannique, French Journal of British Studies* (XIX–2, 2014), pp 49–66.
39. *Report of BRA*, pp 16–17.
40. *Rothschild Archive* @Rothschild.org.
41. 'Londonderry Auxiliary for Promoting Christianity among the Jews', *Londonderry Sentinel*, 23 Oct. 1847.
42. *Devizes and Wiltshire Gazette*, 12 Nov. 1846.
43. *The Economist*, 10 Oct. 1846.
44. Charles Greville, *The Greville Memoirs (second Part): a Journal of the Reign of Queen Victoria, From 1837 to 1852* (London: Longmans, Green, and Co., 1885), p. 406.
45. Christophe Gillissen, 'The Times and the Great Irish Famine 1846–47', *Open Edition Journals*, Dec. 2015.

46. Ibid., 12 Oct. 1847.
47. Noel Kissane, *The Irish Famine: A Documentary History* (Syracuse University Press, 1996), p. 132.
48. *Report of BRA*, p. 10.
49. *The Albion or British, Colonial and Foreign Weekly Gazette*, 21 July 1847, vol. 8, no. 29, p. 346.
50. *Report of BRA*, Appendix D, p. 181.
51. Cecil Woodham-Smith, *The Great Hunger* (London: Hamish Hamilton, 1962), p. 157.
52. 'Londonderry Auxiliary for Promoting Christianity among the Jews', *Londonderry Sentinel*, 23 Oct. 1847.
53. M. Friedländer, 'The Late Chief Rabbi, Dr. N. M. Adler', in The Jewish Quarterly Review, vol. 2, no. 4 (July 1890), 369–385, p. 381.
54. Ferguson, p. 443.
55. Peter Gray, 'National Humiliation and the Great Hunger: Fast and Famine in 1847' in *Irish Historical Studies* 32, no. 126 (2000): 193–216, at: www.jstor.org/stable/30006996 p. 196.
56. Kinealy, *Charity*, p. 197.
57. Charles E. Trevelyan, *The Irish Crisis: Being a Narrative of the Measures for the Relief of the Distress Caused by the Great Irish Famine of 1846–7* (London: Macmillan, 1880), p. 147.
58. Gray, p. 196.
59. Woodham-Smith, *Great Hunger*, p. 54.
60. Ibid., p. 169.
61. Ibid., pp 170–1. The letters reference is to Henry Kingscote, 12 Jan. 1847 and to Sir Randolph Routh, 18 Jan. 1847.
62. Jules Ayers, *Rothschild family. A Century of Finance, 1804 to 1904: The London House of Rothschild* (London: Neely, 1905), p. 42. See also: *The Rothschild Archive*.
63. Ferguson, p. 443.
64. *Rothschild Archive*.
65. *Report of BRA*, pp 26–29.
66. Ibid., pp 29–30.
67. Trevelyan to Twisleton, 6 June 1848, quoted in Woodham-Smith, op. cit., p. 367.
68. *Times*, 6, 30 Aug. 1848, quoted in Woodham-Smith, p. 366.
69. *General Irish Relief Committee. (GRC) Aid to Ireland: Report of the General Relief Committee of the City of New York; With Schedules of Their Receipts in Money, Provisions and Clothing; the Particulars of Their Shipments and Extracts from the Correspondence and Publications* (New York: the Committee, 1848), p. 9.
70. Belmont racetrack and the Belmont Stakes, horse-racing's third leg of the Triple Crown, are named after him. He married the daughter of Commodore Perry USN, later known for opening the trading ports in Japan.
71. Irving Katz, *August Belmont A Political Biography* (New York: Columbia University Press, 1968), p. 7.
72. *General Irish Relief Committee,* 1848. p. 9.
73. https://digipres.cjh.org/delivery/DeliveryManagerServlet?dps_pid=IE92546 Center for Jewish History

74. Kinealy, *Charity*, p. 38.
75. See also chapter by Christine Kinealy on William Rathbone.
76. Robert B. Forbes, *The Voyage of The Jamestown on Her Errand of Mercy* (Boston: Eastburn's Press, 1847). p. 22.
77. *The New York Herald*, 14 Feb. 1847.
78. *The Occident and American Jewish Advocate*, vol. V, no. 1, Apr. 1847. The entire speech is contained in the April 1847 issue.
79. Ibid.
80. Ibid.
81. There is a theological root for Jewish generosity –'The Jewish concepts of *tzedakah* (charitable giving), *tzedek* (justice) and *chesed* (mercy or kindness) instruct and compel all Jews to give to charity and treat people who are less fortunate with compassion', see, *American Jews and Charitable Giving. An enduring tradition at:* https://theconversation.com/american-jews-and-charitable-giving-an-enduring-tradition-87993#:~:text=Expressed%20in%20Hebrew%2C%20the%20Jewish,are%20less%20fortunate%20with%20compassion
82. Robert Emmet's older brother, Thomas Emmet, a member of the United Irishmen, had lived in exile in New York from 1804 to 1827. His grandson of the same name donated $400 to the General Relief Committee of the City of New York. Two other Emmets made smaller donations.
83. *The Occident and American Jewish Advocate*, vol. V, no. 1, Apr. 1847.
84. GRC, p. 37. The receipt for the gift can be viewed on the Center for Jewish History website.
85. Ibid., p. 40.
86. *Baltimore Sun*, 5 Mar. 1847.
87. Harvey Strum, 'Pennsylvania and Irish Famine Relief, 1846–1847', in *Pennsylvania History: A Journal of Mid-Atlantic Studies* 81, no. 3 (2014), 277–99, p. 285.

AFTERWORD

JIM CALLERY (1934–)

A Modern Famine Hero

Caroilin Callery

In 2017, Jim Callery was awarded a prestigious European Prize for Cultural Heritage/Europa Nostra Awards. He received the prize at the European Heritage Awards Ceremony in Turku, Finland, for the 'the restoration and establishment of the world renowned Irish National Famine Museum & Archive [which] has been the largest act of private philanthropy for cultural heritage in the history of modern Ireland'. In honouring him, the Jury acknowledged that: 'Through his small business, Mr. Callery has saved a vital historic country estate for Ireland and has created an important museum and archive dealing with this pivotal moment in the country's history. He has ensured an expert restoration of the house, opened it to the Irish public and preserved the legacy of this important memorial'.[1] *That legacy is also secured by the Irish Heritage Trust of which Jim Callery's daughter, Caroilin, is a Director. In this afterword, she pays tribute to her father and tells the story of how he became a modern famine hero.*

A shot whistled through the crisp west of Ireland air on 2 November 1847, the bullet lodging itself firmly in the brain of Major Denis Mahon. He was the first landlord to be assassinated during the Great Irish Famine, and his murder brought notoriety to his estate, Strokestown Park in County Roscommon, which epitomized a wider story of agrarian conflict, dearth and starvation, and widespread emigration. Only six months earlier, Mahon had devised an assisted emigration scheme to clear some of the tenants from his estate. He sent approximately 1,490 of his 'surplus population' to Canada aboard some of the worst Famine ships of Black '47. Word of the extensive death toll on these vessels filtered back to Strokestown. This was followed by a savage and public row with the local parish priest, Father Michael McDermott, who reportedly condemned him from the altar as 'worse than Cromwell: and yet he lives', ostensibly sealing Mahon's fate.[2] In retrospect, Mahon was neither a famine hero nor the stereotypical evil landlord.[3] The real Strokestown famine hero was to surface over 130 years later, long after the Great Famine and after the events of that cold November day.

The Mahon family's 320-odd-year-reign in Strokestown was to end when Major Denis Mahon's great granddaughter, Olive Hales Pakenham Mahon, sold the remaining 300 acres of the Strokestown Park Estate at auction in early May 1979. Jim Callery placed the winning bid. He was a Strokestown garage owner in his early 40s, a shrewd businessman who had left school early without completing his final exams. This transaction not only ended the Pakenham Mahon family's three century presence in the town, but also placed the house and demesne in the hands of a man whose family had been tenants on a small farm in nearby Elphin in the nineteenth century.

Jim's intention for his new property was clear: he needed some of the demesne lands which backed onto his garage business to expand. He intended to keep the land required and sell the house and remainder of the lands—a simple business transaction. This was the culmination of his often fractious and litigious relationship with the matriarch of a fading estate in the west of Ireland. But what happened next was not what he had planned, and not the future that either of them could ever have envisaged for Strokestown Park House.

In 1976, in the run up to these events, Jim Callery, a founder of Westward Garage, had secured the Scania Truck Importer and Distributorship for Ireland. This was an unexpected achievement for a business located outside of Dublin. Westward Garage backed onto the Strokestown Park demesne lands, and Jim, realising that he would need more space, enquired—in a roundabout way—if they could purchase a small number of acres. Olive's response was a clear and unequivocal 'no'. Jim and Olive had battled often over the previous decade. She accused him of ruining 'her street'—the main street of Strokestown—with his unsightly dirty machinery. His Tannoy loudspeaker system in the new garage was a noise pollutant that could be heard all over the demesne. Legal proceedings had been issued by Pakenham Mahon family to stop Westward trucks from parking on 'their streets' and, when he defied it, Jim barely escaped prison by negotiating with Olive and purchasing a site for parking. Jim, on several occasions, had been summoned to Strokestown Park House for a dressing down about one issue or other.[4]

In early 1979, Olive summoned Jim once again. As the butler, Massey, showed him into the library, he was wondering what the 'dressing down' would be about this time, although Jim sensed something different when he was offered refreshments.[5]

Jim could not believe his ears when Olive informed him that her son, Colonel Nicholas Hales Pakenham Mahon, who had inherited the estate and was in charge of a regiment in Northern Ireland, would never return and intended to sell the property. He was even more surprised to learn that Olive thought that he should purchase it. 'I nearly fell off the chair, but said I would speak to my co-directors', Jim recalled.[6] Later, mulling it over in his head and discussing it with his co-directors, Tom Keogh and John Treacy, Jim realised they would never get their hands on the land behind the garage unless they bought the whole lot, took what they needed and resold it.

They set about raising the funds. Olive then summoned Jim to Strokestown House once again. She informed him that she did not wish to go ahead with the scheduled Savills/ Hamilton & Hamilton Auction in Dublin, but that interested parties would be invited to London to bid privately on a specified date. A couple of weeks later, Jim, along with his co-directors and their solicitor, Peter Connellan, found themselves sitting in a central London hotel competing with other bidders who were located in different hotels. The auctioneers, together with Colonel Hales Pakenham Mahon, circulated between them taking bids over several hours. At the end of the day, Jim Callery and Westward Garage had secured Strokestown Park House and its 300-acre demesne for in excess £IR 400,000, a huge sum in the 1970s.

Jim believes that one of the main reasons he won the bid was that they gave Olive and the Major the right to live on in the main house itself for as long as Westward owned it, albeit that it was crumbling around them. He felt that this proposition—which would save the Mahons' from substantial relocation costs—made their offer more favourable.[7] In Olive's own words 'The whole property has been sold to the Westward Garage. I like Mr Callery enormously, he is a terribly nice man. I am only living here on his kindness. It is his house, it isn't my house'.[8] And so Westward Garage became the new owners of Strokestown Park with the octogenarian landlady still in situ. Yet, saving a Palladian pile from decrepitude had certainly never been part of their business plan. Over the following two years, Jim and Olive became 'almost friends, developing a healthy respect for each other'.[9] They discovered a joint love of history from their very different perspectives.

In 1980, Major Hales Pakenham Mahon passed away. Interestingly, Olive decided to have him buried in the Catholic graveyard in Strokestown and not in the ruined mausoleum on the estate, which housed a family crypt where all of her ancestors had been buried since the late 1600s, including her own child. In failing health, Olive lived alone in a monolith of a mansion that cost a fortune to maintain. At the age of 86, she decided to leave her beloved home and move to a nursing home near Newbury in Berkshire, as her children were based in England. As she prepared to leave, Olive invited her children to sift through 300 years of family belongings for what was precious to their memories, what was valuable, and what was practicably portable. Nicholas's wife, along with a cousin, did the final clearing out of the house. Olive had been under pressure from her auctioneers to break up the contents of the estate in order to maximize her return. But there was to be one final plea for the saving of Strokestown House and its stories and that was to come in the form of voices from the past.

One weekend, Olive was visiting London and Jim asked if he could 'rummage' around the property. She responded: 'Of course you can Mr Callery. It is your house now', in her patrician tone of voice.[10]

That 'rummaging' was to change the fate of Strokestown Park. In the Smoking Room, under the leaking roof, Jim found stacks of boxes full of papers. He made a serendipitous discovery. One the first documents he put his hands on was the Cloonahee famine petition, dated 22 August 1846 and sent from starving tenants on the estate. Jim was deeply moved by its pleas. As the petition states:

> Our families are really and truly suffering in our presence and we cannot much longer withstand their cries for food. We have no food for them, our potatoes are rotten and we have no grain. We have been turned away from the relief works by the Board of Works supervisor ... We are not for joining in anything illegal or contrary to the laws of God or the land unless pressed to by HUNGER.[11]

This document was from the townland of Cloonahee where Jim lived and had been raised, as had generations of his family for several hundred years. The names in the list of signatures were familiar to him—Caulfield, Kelly, Dockery, McHugh, Tracey. These were his people. Memories of the famine stories that his grandmother, Ann Flynn Callery, had passed on to him came flooding back. As he explored the room further, he discovered more boxes of papers and, poignantly, thousands of similar pleas and petitions. What Jim had stumbled upon was a precious and unparalleled repository which would become the renowned Strokestown Park Archive. As he left the house that day, his head was filled with these voices that had not been heard for over 135 years. He feared that they had been silenced in a damp back room in Strokestown Park. In that instant, he felt a unique responsibility to give back their voice.

On Olive's return from London, Jim told her he would purchase the contents of the house if she would leave the archive. She agreed to an official valuation and to leave all of the estate papers that were not of a recent personal nature. A sum close to £IR100,000 was agreed, potentially a lot less than if they had been auctioned off piecemeal, one by one. The estate papers contained a unique repository of records from the period of the Great Famine. Amongst them was a signed first edition of Cecil Woodham Smith's classic study, *The Great Hunger, Ireland 1845–1849* (1962), which was dedicated to Olive.[12]

It is perhaps ironic that Jim was moved to save the contents of this crumbling manor house not because of its aristocratic lineage, but rather the voices of its starving tenants. He was adamant that he would preserve not just the story of those 'to the Manor born' but also that of the impoverished cottiers and labourers who had supported them. His first task was to convince the Board of the Westward Group to keep the house, demesne and archive in order to ensure public access. They all agreed. His second task was to find a curator. Jim's first cousin once removed, Luke Dodd, a recent graduate of Art History in Trinity College Dublin, was to become his right-hand man in this ambitious project. He moved into Strokestown Park and developed plans to reopen the house, examine the archive, and create a Famine museum. While Luke and Jim worked out what to do, part of the property was rented for a two-year period to German deer farmer. Soon afterwards, Strokestown Park became the location for the shooting of Pat Murphy's 1983 film, *Anne Devlin*.

Jim also undertook an extensive programme of conservation in order to stabilize Strokestown Park House in what he liked to call a state of 'arrested decay'.[13] Dilapidated but not beyond repair, it would become a time capsule of faded aristocratic grandeur that contrasted sharply with the destitution of most of the estate's inhabitants whose lives were to be explored in the Famine museum. At enormous cost, Jim funded the restoration of the house's main roof and kitchen wing which had become exposed to the elements. He ensured its preservation from the design of Richard Cassells in the form of Palladian Mansion House complete with galleried kitchen, vaulted Italian stables and 300 years of family memorabilia. In May 1987, Strokestown Park House was opened to the public by David Thomson (author of *Woodbrook*) as a rare and unique property with all its original features and contents fully intact. The National Famine Museum at Strokestown Park was opened by President Mary Robinson in 1994. It has since become internationally acknowledged as a leading centre of learning, critical reflection, and commemoration of the Great Hunger. Situated in the shadow of the Big House, the museum effectively juxtaposes the story of those who had most with those who had least.

The jewel in the crown of the Strokestown Park Estate was its extensive archive which Jim was especially passionate about preserving. It is a vast collection of over 55,000 documents that offer a micro-history of the Famine and its effect on the people of Strokestown, while encapsulating the story of Ireland and, indeed, that of many other nations in the Irish diaspora. In discovering the voices of the Cloonahee petition, Jim was inspired to safeguard the entire collection for future generations. Indeed, Seamus Heaney praised such endeavours to recover stories from the archive as 'characteristically original and meaningful'.

In 2015, the Famine Summer School was launched at the National Famine Museum, Strokestown Park, with an inaugural lecture by Fintan O'Toole. He paid tribute to Jim Callery for his dedication and sense of mission in preserving the legacy of the Great Hunger. In his own words:

> Jim didn't really choose to do this, you know, he accepted a responsibility. I'm not sure if Jim knew when he took over the house what he was getting into quite! But having bought that house and having found that archive he did what very, very few people would do, which was accept the responsibility for it. [He] seems to me to have done so without question. And I think he has done so out of a deeply instinctive compassion for his own community, for his own history, for his own closure, for Strokestown, for Ireland, but also just for people.[14]

It is a fitting tribute to Jim's dedication, passion and unceasing restoration of the National Famine Museum at Strokestown Park over a period of 40 years. More recently, he has continued to show leadership in further developing its legacy for future generations. Since 2019, Callery and the Westward Group had worked with Fáilte Ireland and the Irish Heritage Trust to redevelop the National Famine Museum into a €5 million-euro state-of-the-art facility that was unveiled in 2022. In 2021, at the age of 87, he walked 165km with his daughter, Caroilin, along the National Famine Way, an officially accredited walking trail from Strokestown to Dublin that follows in the footsteps of Strokestown Missing 1,490 Famine Emigrants who left the estate in 1847.[15] Their journey was filmed and broadcast over two episodes on the RTÉ programme *An tSlí.* But, perhaps, the final word should be left to Jim's solicitor (and later judge) Peter Connellan, who remarked on their return from London in 1979 after the acquisition of Strokestown Park House from the aristocratic Pakenham Mahon family that 'the wheel has turned full circle'.[16]

Jim Callery is a man whom I am proud and honoured to call my father, a modern-day Famine Hero, and advocate for learning from the past, in all its difficult complexities.

NOTES

1. www.europeanheritageawards.eu/winners/mr-jim-callery/. Jim Callery has also received a number of other prestigious awards and recognition for his endeavours at local and national level including an Honorary Master of Arts degree from the National University of Ireland Galway, an Honorary Doctorate from Maynooth University, and a National Person of the Year Award.
2. Peter Duffy, *The Killing of Major Denis Mahon: A Mystery of Old Ireland* (New York: HarperCollins, 2007) p. 169.
3. Jason King and Mark G. McGowan (eds), *Hunger and Hope: The Irish Famine Migration from Strokestown, Roscommon in 1847* (forthcoming).
4. Interview with Jim Callery, 7 Feb. 2022, Cloonahee House, Elphin, Co. Roscommon.
5. Ibid.
6. Ibid.
7. Ibid.
8. Jim Fahy, *The Isolated Ear – Voices from a vanishing world*: www.rte.ie/radio/radio1/stories/1218282-voices-from-a-vanishing-world-on-the-isolated-ear/ an edited version of Jim Fahy's full Interview with Olive Hales Packham Mahon in 1980/1981 before she left Strokestown for the final time.
9. Interview with Jim Callery, 7 Feb. 2022.
10. Ibid.
11. The Cloonahee petition can be viewed in the 'Treasures of the Strokestown Famine Archive' virtual exhibit, www.strokestownpark.ie/treasures-of-the-strokestown-famine-archive/
12. Jim has stayed close to the Pakenham Mahon family over the years. The family were also invited to and attended all official openings—of the House, Famine Museum, Gardens and North Courtyard Accommodation. Two of Olive's granddaughters returned to Strokestown Park in the summer of 2019 for their respective 80th and 70th birthday celebrations. Both had spent extensive time at Strokestown during childhood summer holidays with Olive.
13. Interview with Jim Callery, 7 Feb. 2022, Cloonahee House, Elphin, Co. Roscommon.
14. Fintan O'Toole, Launch of Inaugural Irish Famine Summer School, Percy French Hotel, Strokestown, 16 June 2015.
15. https://nationalfamineway.ie/
16. Interview with Jim Callery, 7 Feb. 2022.

ABOUT THE CONTRIBUTORS

CAROILÍN CALLERY is on the Board of the Westward Group who own Strokestown Park and the National Famine Museum. She is also on the Board of the Irish Heritage Trust. Caroilín is dedicated too and heavily involved in Outreach and Education in the Making History Visible through a multidisciplinary approach.

LAURENT COLANTONIO is Professor of British and Irish history at the Université du Québec à Montréal (UQAM). His work focuses on nineteenth century Irish national movements.

COLUM KENNY BCL, BL, is Professor Emeritus of Dublin City University and a journalist. He has been awarded the gold medal of the Irish Legal History Society. His books include *Tristram Kennedy and the Revival of Irish Legal Training, 1835–1885* (Irish Academic Press, 1996), *The Enigma of Arthur Griffith: 'Father of Us All'* (Merrion Press, 2020) and *Kenmare: History and Survival–Fr John O'Sullivan and the Famine Poor* (Eastwood, 2021).

CHRISTINE KINEALY is Director of Ireland's Great Hunger Institute at Quinnipiac University in Connecticut. She has authored and edited many publications on the Irish Famine and Irish abolition including, *Daniel O'Connell and Anti-Slavery. The saddest people the sun sees* (2011), *Charity and the Great Hunger* (2013), *Famines before and after the Great Hunger* (ed. with Gerard Moran, 2020) and *Black Abolitionists in Ireland* (2020).

JASON KING is Academic Coordinator of the Irish Heritage Trust and National Famine Museum, Strokestown Park, and a member of the Government of Ireland

National Famine Commemoration Committee. His recent publications include Irish Famine Migration Narratives: Eyewitness Testimonies, vol II, The History of the Irish Famine (4 vols with Christine Kinealy and Gerard Moran, Routledge, 2019).

JOHN McCOLGAN is Boston's City Archivist. Graduate of Boston College, he holds a Ph.D. in Modern Irish History and Diploma in Archival Studies from NUI Dublin, and is author of *British Policy and the Irish Administration, 1920–22*.

MARK G. McGOWAN is a Professor of History at the University of Toronto and Principal Emeritus at St. Michael's College at that same institution. He has written many award-winning books and essays on the development of the Catholic Church in Canada and the Irish Diaspora in British North America.

GERARD MORAN, a senior researcher at the Social Science Research Centre at NUI Galway, has lectured in the History Department at NUI Galway and at Maynooth University. He has written extensively on nineteenth-century Ireland, most recently, *Fleeing from Famine in Connemara: James Hack Tuke and his Assisted Emigration Scheme in the 1880s* (2018).

EOGHAN MORAN translated the chapter on Daniel O'Connell from French to English.

PETER MURPHY has a lifelong passion for history, obtaining an undergraduate degree in European history from the University of California, San Diego (1978) and a Master's degree in American history from Trinity College in Connecticut (2016). He is especially interested in Ireland's history, due in part to his extensive Irish ancestry.

CATHAL PÓIRTÉIR is a writer and broadcaster who has published books and articles on Irish folklore and social history. His book on landlord-tenant relations in a nineteenth century Donegal Gaeltacht is due for publication in 2022: An Tiarna George Hill agus Pobal Ghaoth Dobhair - Caidreamh agus Coimhlint.

CATHERINE B. SHANNON is Professor Emerita of History at Westfield State University whose publications include studies of the role of Arthur J. Balfour and Lord Randolph Churchill in Irish affairs. She has published on the role of women in the Northern Irish conflict and peace process. Her recent publications focus on the response of Boston's Irish American community to Irish Famines.

ACKNOWLEDGEMENTS

The editors would like to thank all the contributors, and their families, for bringing this project to fruition in a timely manner. An especially warm thanks are extended to the families of the editors.

We are grateful to our design team, Tad Sterling and Cindy Dubell of Integrated Marketing and Communications at Quinnipiac University, and Marsha Swan of Iota Books, for their professionalism and support. The cover image, by Jack B. Yeats, depicts Derrynane, the County Kerry home of Daniel O'Connell, the first hero in this volume.

Completing a project such as this, during a pandemic, when there were numerous travel restrictions, and many universities and public institutions were closed to the public, has presented a number of challenges. We are, therefore, particularly appreciative of the librarians and archivists who have lent their expertise. As usual, our colleagues at Quinnipiac have supported the publication in numerous ways. The librarians and archivists of Liverpool University have also been especially helpful in identifying previously un-used sources relating to the philanthropist, William Rathbone. Researching these documents would not have been possible without the help of Research Assistant, Nadia Callister.

Finally, we are fortunate that we have been able to continue to work with our partners in Ireland, the Irish Heritage Trust and Cork University Press.

The Editors.

INDEX